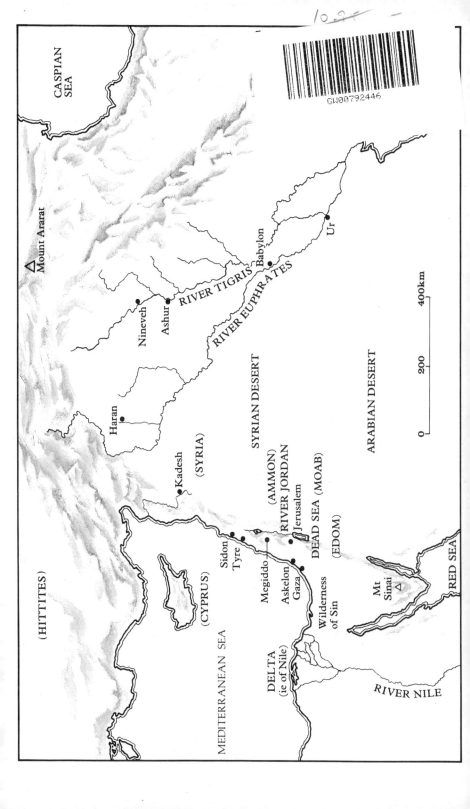

CASPIAN SEA

Mount Ararat

Nineveh

Ashur

RIVER TIGRIS

Babylon

RIVER EUPHRATES

Ur

Haran

(SYRIA)

Kadesh

SYRIAN DESERT

(AMMON)

RIVER JORDAN

Jerusalem

DEAD SEA (MOAB)

(EDOM)

ARABIAN DESERT

(HITTITES)

Sidon

Tyre

Megiddo

Askelon

Gaza

Wilderness of Sin

(CYPRUS)

MEDITERRANEAN SEA

Mt Sinai

RED SEA

DELTA (ie of Nile)

RIVER NILE

400km

200

0

KENNETH McLEISH

STORIES AND LEGENDS FROM THE BIBLE

Longman

LONGMAN GROUP UK LIMITED
Longman House
Burnt Mill, Harlow, Essex CM20 2JE, England
and Associated Companies throughout the World

First published 1988

British Library Cataloguing in Publication Data

McLeish, Kenneth, *1940–*
  Stories and legends from the Bible.
  1. Bible – Stories, anecdotes
  I. Title
  220.9'505

  ISBN 0 582 03406 X

Set in 11/13 point Garamond on Linotron 202
by CRB Typesetting Services, Ely, Cambridgeshire.

Printed and bound in Great Britain by
Biddles Ltd, Guildford and King's Lynn

In loving memory of M.E. Heath

CONTENTS

INTRODUCTION

For over one and a half billion people throughout the world, Jews, Muslims and Christians, the Bible (complete or in part) is a holy book. It tells of the relationship between God and human beings; it helps his believers to worship him. Many people believe that God himself inspired the scribes, prophets and other holy men who wrote the Bible, and that it contains all a human being needs to bring happiness, both in this and in any future life.

For some readers new to the Bible, this reputation can be terrifying. Not only that, but Bible language is not always as clear, as ordinary as the words we use in everyday life. Some of it is poetry; some is prayer; some is prophecy; all of it is two thousand or more years old. This is no problem when the Bible is used for religious purposes. There are people to study it, select from it and explain it so that all can understand. But reading it for oneself is a different matter. People call the Bible the book "most often owned, least often read" – and the reason is that it can be hard to know just where to start.

Stories and Legends from the Bible is not a religious book. It takes the main stories from the Bible and tells them in order, starting with the creation of the universe and ending with the travels and Christian teaching of Saint Paul. As in other books in this series, my aim has been to tell the stories clearly, simply and without interruption – to let them speak for themselves. (The difference between this book and the others is that many of the people in these stories are not myth-characters, but real: most Bible-stories are based on historical events.) To help understanding and increase enjoyment, I have put at the back of the book a section of additional stories, notes and alternative versions. An asterisk (*) in the main text shows where this happens. But I have given no suggestions for "follow-up reading". There is, after all, only one follow-up book to be recommended, the Bible itself. Dozens of different translations exist – in my notes I quote the Authorized Version from Shakespeare's time, because of the splendour of its English – and almost every bookshop offers a fascinating choice. I hope that *Stories from the Bible* can be read for pleasure on its own; but it is no more than a sample, a taste, of the riches the full Bible has to offer.

I should like to thank Valerie McLeish and Robert Yeatman, whose encouragement was vital as I wrote the book. My version of the creation-story (in Chapter One) appeared, in a slightly different form, in an earlier Longman book, *In the Beginning*, and I am grateful for permission to use it here.

Kenneth McLeish
Spalding, 1988

1 · IN THE BEGINNING

Creation

In the beginning, before creation, there was a water wilderness, fathomless and still. No tides stirred it; no winds ruffled it; it was neither hot nor cold. Nothing lived in it; the only thing that moved on its surface was the spirit of God.

On the first day of creation, God formed his spirit into words and said, "Let there be light." At once light appeared, shining far into the gulf of space. God separated it from darkness, and called the light Day and the darkness Night. When it was finished and he was satisfied, the first day was done.

On the second day God said, "Let there be sky," and sky appeared. It was drawn from the water-wilderness, and shared water's nature. But water was heavy with the weight of darkness, and stayed below; sky was alive with light and soared above. God called the sky Heaven, and when it was finished and he was satisfied, the second day was done.

On the third day God said, "Let there be land." He gathered together all the water under Heaven and formed it into pools. Wherever the water level sank, dry land appeared. God fixed water and land forever in their places, and called the water Sea and the dry land Earth. He covered Earth with plants. On the mountains and hillsides, where the air was cold and the soil was thin, he planted mosses, lichens and brightly-coloured alpine flowers. Lower down he planted pine-trees, firs, bracken, brambles, wild roses, nettles, honeysuckle, rhododendron and a thousand other trees and shrubs. On the plains, where the soil was thick and fertile, he planted poppies, narcissus, gladiolus, celandine, wild cherries, grasses, roots and vegetables of every kind. He made even deserts and beaches flower: wherever there was a speck of moisture cactus, thistles and dune-grass sprang up. As soon as God made each plant, he gave it seeds to recreate itself. He made Earth a fertile garden, and began its cycle of growth and seedtime, seedtime and unending growth. When he was satisfied with everything he had made, the third day was done.

On the fourth day God said, "Let there be stars." He gathered all the light he had made on the first day of creation and scattered it across the sky. Some fell in large, single drops like the Evening Star; the rest splashed across Heaven's floor in constellations and galaxies like the Milky Way. God separated the two brightest lights from all the others and called them Sun and Moon. Sun rules the day and Moon the night, and their rising and setting control all Earth's times and seasons. When the sun, moon and stars were made and God was satisfied, the fourth day was done.

On the fifth day God said, "Let there be creatures in sea and air." He stocked the sea with fish: sharks, anchovies, swordfish, octopus, herring, coelocanths, squid, codfish, conger eels. He filled the air with insects, and set birds hovering in the sky and darting from tree to tree. He made albatrosses and gulls to skim the sea, and gannets, cormorants and pelicans to plunge into it. He made plovers and swifts to sweep across the earth, and condors, falcons and eagles to soar in the air above. To live in fresh water he made ducks, herons, moorhens, swans. He made parrots, toucans, weaver-birds, parakeets and cockatoos to perch in trees, and woodpeckers, nuthatches, cranes and rooks to nest in them. As he had with the plants, he gave all these creatures the power to recreate themselves, and when he was satisfied with everything he had made, the fifth day was done.

On the sixth day God said, "Let there be land-creatures." One by one he visited all the regions of the Earth, and stocked them with the animals most suited to their climate and their plants. For the polar ice-caps in the north and south he made arctic foxes, walruses and polar bears. For deserts he made gerbils, lizards and rattlesnakes. He gave monkeys, flying foxes, boa-constrictors and ant-eaters jungle homes, and filled the plains with elephants, giraffes, rhinoceroses and buffaloes, as well as zebras, wildebeeste and the lions, hyenas and cheetahs that prey on them. He made cattle, deer, goats and sheep; he made dogs, cats, squirrels, frogs, hippos, chameleons, vipers, rabbits, pigs, wallabies, coatimundis, lynxes, dormice, pangolins, bats and snails. Last of all he made two human beings, a man and a woman. He formed the man from the dust of the ground, and breathed life into his nostrils. He formed the woman from a rib taken from the man as he lay asleep. He called the man Adam and the woman Eve, and gave them power over every other creature of land, sea or air*. When God was satisfied with all the animals he had made, and with the coming of humankind, the sixth day was done.

So in six days God created light, heaven, sea, earth, air, and everything that lives or breathes in them. On the seventh day, when everything was set in order and the world was complete, he rested.

Adam and Eve

God planted a garden in the east of the world, and called it Eden. He stocked it with every tree, shrub and plant in creation, including the tree of life (whose fruit gave immortality) and the tree of the knowledge of good and evil. He watered the garden with a slow, deep river: water flowed out of Eden in four broad streams to irrigate the world. He made Adam and Eve keepers of the garden. Adam's task was to name every fish, bird, insect and animal. By naming them he showed his authority over them, the authority of God given to the human race over every other created thing. Only the tree of knowledge and the tree of life were excepted. "Eat from any other tree or plant," God said. "But avoid the tree of knowledge. If you eat its fruit, you will surely die." Those were his words; he hid from Adam and Eve even the existence of the tree of life.

Adam and Eve lived contentedly on Eden. They were naked and innocent; without knowledge, they had no more feelings or emotions than insects, fish or animals. They were without blemish; their brains were unmarked by understanding, ambition or memory. The only creature in the garden with understanding was the Serpent. It had absorbed cunning by coiling round the trunk of the tree of knowledge. Now it slid up to Eve as she sat gazing without thought at light-patterns on the river, and said, "Why do you eat from every other plant in the garden, except the tree of knowledge?"

"Because God has told us that if we eat its fruit, we die."

"Nonsense!" said the Serpent. "If you eat its fruit, your knowledge will equal God's."

Eve's mind struggled with the first thoughts it had ever known. "If the tree is beautiful," she thought, "Why should its fruit be poisonous? What is knowledge? Why should ours not equal God's?" She picked one of the fruits, and ate it; she gave another to Adam to eat. At once, as water pours into irrigation-channels when the flood-gates are opened, knowledge filled their minds. They understood how Sky, Earth and Sea were made. They realised that they themselves had been created in God's own image, unlike any other creature. Above all, they saw that they were naked, and they were ashamed. Filled with embarassment, and terrified at the responsibility their new knowledge had given them, they pinned fig-leaves together with thorns to cover their nakedness. They heard God walking in the Garden in the cool of the day, and hid from him.

God called, "Adam, where are you?" Adam crept out of hiding, red with shame. "Who told you you were naked?" asked God. "Have you eaten the fruit of the tree I told you not to touch?"

"Eve gave me the fruit, and I ate it," said Adam.

"Eve, what have you done?" asked God.

"The Serpent tempted me, and I ate the fruit," said Eve. Instead of immediate death (the reward Adam and Eve's new knowledge had made them expect), God punished them with life. He gave Eve the pain of childbirth. Unlike other creatures, which produce their young easily and harmlessly, she would suffer agony – and so it would be for women till the end of time. God gave Adam unceasing work. The ground would no longer produce food of its own accord: to eat, Adam would have to dig, sow and reap – and so it would be for men till the end of time. As for the Serpent, God decreed that it should be the lowest of all created things, slithering on its belly, eating dust and despised by all other creatures till the end of time. God gave Adam and Eve clothes to wear. At first he let them live in the Garden of Eden as before. But then he remembered the tree of life, the tree whose fruit gives immortality. Human beings had already stolen knowledge – were they also to have everlasting life? He banished Adam and Eve from Eden, and set cherubim* to guard the gates and a fiery sword, hovering in the air, to bar the path to the tree of life.

Cain and Abel

Although Adam and Eve were foolish rather than wicked, their disobedience in the Garden of Eden tainted the human race with guilt. Their son Cain, the third human being in the world, was the first to commit real crime. Like his father Adam, he spent his days digging, sowing and harvesting, and at the year's end he made God an offering of wheat, fruit and vegetables. Cain's younger brother Abel was a shepherd. He spent his days tending a flock of shaggy sheep, and at the end of the lambing season he offered God the first-born lambs. It seemed to Cain that God was more pleased with Abel's lambs than with his own wheat, fruit, and vegetables. He brooded; he fed his soul on jealousy; in the end he killed Abel and hid his body in the ground

"Cain," said God, "Where is your brother Abel?"

"How should I know?" growled Cain. "Am I my brother's keeper?"

"Cain," said God, "Your brother's blood cries from the ground. The earth has gulped his blood, and now it cries your crime. You have poisoned the land: it will never again bear crops for you. Your punishment is to wander till the day you die. No one will welcome you. You will never rest."

God marked Cain's face with a blood-mark*, so that everyone who saw him would know his name and his crime, and would not kill him but would leave him to live out a tormented life of guilt and shame*.

Noah

After Cain and Abel, Adam and Eve had other children, beginning with Seth, their son. The children had children in their turn, until the lands around Eden were thronged with people as grass-plains teem with sheep. The more human beings there were, the greater the discontent. Their lifespan was enormous. Adam lived for nine hundred and thirty years, Seth for nine hundred and twelve, Seth's son Enos for nine hundred and five, and so on for generation after generation. The parents lived on long after their children and grandchildren had aged, and every year they produced new offspring, so that great-great-grandchildren were often far older than their own aunts and uncles, and brothers and sisters might be separated by seven or eight hundred years. The old ruled, and the country was crowded by discontented younger people, adult but powerless, waiting impatiently for their seniors to die. While they waited, the guilt inherited from their ancestor Adam soured their minds. They experimented with crimes and perversions of every kind, until in behaviour as well as numbers, humanity began to pollute the world.

God tried to regulate human beings by shortening their lives. He allowed them one hundred and twenty years from birth to death. To end their inbreeding, he encouraged them to mate with the race of giants, the earth-creatures who most resembled them, and persuaded the giants to take human wives. But none of it succeeded. Human wickedness tainted the world as weeds overrun a pasture. They polluted every other living being on earth, whether insect, bird or animal. At last, in the six hundredth year of Noah, the ninth-generation descendant of Adam and Eve and a member of the last mortal family allowed to live more than one hundred and twenty years, God decided to send a flood to cleanse to world. The water would drown every creature that walked or crawled on the earth, flew above it or burrowed into it. Creation was complete, and would not be unmade; instead, it would be cleansed and purified, as a farmer cleans his land.

God told Noah, "Build a wooden ark, the size of a house, and cover it inside and out with pitch. Make it big enough for yourself, your wife, your three sons and their wives, and one male and one female of every creature that lives on Earth. The flood will drown every other creature; only those in the ark will live."

Noah began work on the ark. It was enormous, like a three-storey, boat-shaped house. He built it on a field, far inland, and his neighbours leaned on the fence and laughed at him. "What's the point of living six hundred years," they said, "if all it does is soften the brain?" They laughed all the louder when the ark was finished, and Noah and his sons Shem, Ham and Japheth began rounding up and driving into it one male and one female of every creature that lived on Earth. It was an enormous task, stalling and feeding every animal, bird and insect; without God's help it could never have been done. But at last it was finished. Noah climbed the ramp into the ark for the last time and slammed the door. The ark stood there, marooned in its field, while the animals inside it bellowed, screeched and buzzed and the crowd outside laughed Noah and his menagerie to scorn. So many people came to mock that hucksters set up beer-stalls, and began renting vantage-points for people to watch when Noah was forced to open the ark, like the fool he was, and let all his creatures out.

Then the rains began. At first it was no more than drops on the watchers' upturned faces. Then it was a drizzle, slow but persistent. Then, as God opened the windows of heaven and released the floodgates of the sky, the drizzle turned to a downpour. It drummed on the ark's pitch-covered, wooden roof and sent the spectators scampering for cover. Puddles swelled to pools; pools became lakes; the lakes spread across the ground, filling every hollow and gurgling into every crevice. At first the people shivered in their tents. Then they moved to more solid shelters of wood and stone. Finally, they huddled with their animals on the highest ground they could find, helpless as the water rose to their ankles, their knees, their waists. Some cursed God; others lifted their arms to the sky and begged for mercy; a few threw gold and silver into the water as if it were a living thing that could be bribed to go away. Nothing succeeded. The rain lasted for forty days and forty nights, until every fold and valley on earth was filled, and there was nothing but flat, still water, lifeless as the water on the first day of creation, with Noah's ark bobbing on its surface like a walnut in a water-bowl.

For one hundred and fifty days after God closed the windows of heaven and shut the floodgates, water swamped the Earth. Then, scoured by gales, it began at last to seep away. Inside the ark, Noah waited for one hundred more days, counting them off on a tally scratched in the wooden wall. On the hundred and first day he opened a window and released a raven, to fly to and fro and look for land. The raven soon fluttered back exhausted: it had found no land to settle on. Noah waited a few days, then released a dove; it too came back exhausted. Seven days later he released it again, and this time it came back with an olive-leaf in its beak. Noah knew that land must at last be visible and that God had restocked it with living plants. Seven days later he sent out the dove again; this time it stayed away, and Noah knew that the flood waters had disappeared and that it was safe to leave the ark. He climbed out, and found the ark grounded on a steep mountain-side, green with undergrowth*. He knelt and prayed, and God said, "Noah, open the ark and let the creatures out." Noah opened the ark, and the cramped creatures flew, hopped, lumbered, ran and slithered out to restock the world. Last of all came Noah's wife, sons and daughters-in-law. They built God an altar on the mountainside, and Noah made a sacrifice from animals born during his year-long stay inside the ark. The sweet smell of sacrifice rose to heaven, and God said, "Noah, the Earth is cleaned. Human beings – you, your wife, your sons and your daughters-in-law – are still tainted with Adam's guilt. But there will be no more floods. The world's seasons, spring, summer, autumn and winter, will follow each other in unbroken sequence till the end of time. This I promise, and in token of my promise I set my bow in the sky, to reassure mortals for ever more."

God hung a rainbow in the sky from horizon to horizon. Every time rain-clouds fill the sky, and God sends the sun to scatter them, the rainbow reappears, a reminder and a guarantee of God's promise to favour the human race.

The tower of Babel

For generations after the flood, Noah's descendants stayed together in a single group, led by his sons Shem, Ham and Japheth. They were nomads, wandering from place to place, pitching their tents wherever the soil seemed fertile, growing a few crops and then moving on. As the years passed, their numbers grew; in the end, the tribe looked from heaven like an enormous herd of animals, thousands upon thousands, moving across the plains. The people came to Shinar, a stretch of land between two broad rivers, and pitched their tents. The land was flat, and so fertile that in a single year the people were able to harvest not one crop but three: one of vegetables and two of corn. At the end of the year, therefore, instead of moving on, they decided to stay where they were. In the generations that followed, they prospered. They laid out fields, one for each family, in ordered rows separated by irrigation-ditches. They lived in mud-brick houses instead of tents. They built the first boats ever seen, small replicas of Noah's ark, to ferry trade-goods along the rivers. Their barns bulged with grain. Their sheep, goats and donkeys browsed among the olive-groves, bells clonking in the heat-haze. Babies fed or slept in every house and children played in every street.

As the population grew, the people's pride grew with it. They forgot God; the great flood came to seem no more than a legend, an old wives' tale. They began to think that they had achieved everything themselves, by their own cleverness, and that the same cunning and organisation would let them do anything they chose. In the end they decided to build a tower as high as heaven, a monument to their ingenuity as if it were a god. They levelled a square of ground at the heart of the settlement, and paved it with mud bricks bonded with pitch. Above the pavement they built a second, slightly smaller square, like a solid, one-storey building, and on top of that they put a third square, smaller still. So the tower rose, storey after storey. When God and his angels came down from heaven, the tower was already enormous, like a hill made by human hands. "If the people finish it," God said, "What will they dream up next? They'll think nothing impossible. Their arrogance will outsoar the stars."

Instead of destroying the tower with lightning or an earthquake, God used the builders' own nature to stop them finishing it. Everyone in the settlement – the entire human population of the world – was one family. They were all Noah's descendants and they all spoke the same language. They bickered and argued from time to time, as all families do. But generally they lived together in peace, working together for common good. God ended their harmony forever by giving each branch of the family a different language. Brick-makers used different words from pitch-blenders; mule-drivers and carters shouted orders at each other which neither understood; the cooks who made the meals, the officials who checked the plans, the farmers beside whose fields the mud-carts lumbered, each thought that the others were talking gibberish. A babble of languages filled the sky; misunderstanding led to squabbles, squabbles to incomprehensible arguments, arguments to fights. In the end the builders threw up their arms and abandoned the tower. People gathered their belongings and their animals, took out tents unused for generations, and set off into the desert to find new homes. The human race scattered across the world, its unity destroyed. In the plain between the rivers, the tower of Babel stood half-finished and deserted, a monument not to achievement but to pride. The few families who still lived in the area forgot that the tower had been built by fellow human beings, their own relations. They clambered along its terraces, gaped at its vastness and the orderly, empty city at its feet, and decided that it must have been made by gods. They invented a whole family of supernatural beings, made statues of them in wood or stone, and worshipped them. Soon Babel, and the idols spawned there, became the source of all false religion and devil-worship in the world*.

Abraham

When the tower-builders scattered from Babel, many of them settled at Ur, a week's walk south beside the river Euphrates. There were fish in the river, the ground was fertile, and there was grazing for all their animals. Ur began as a patchwork of single farms, but soon it was a mud-brick town with paved streets, high walls and rows of domed, whitewashed houses. The people concentrated on farming and shepherding, avoiding their parents' and grandparents' pride which had so offended God.

But God was still not satisfied. The people believed that prosperity came from their own efforts or from the natural fertility of the countryside. They worshipped spirits of sun, rain, rivers, trees and fields. None had true faith in God. God decided to take one man, teach him obedience, and then let him choose whether to follow his fellow-mortals' path to idolatry or to have faith in God. The man he chose was Abraham, and the way he taught him was to uproot him from prosperity in Ur and send him, his wife Sarah, his aged father Terah, his brothers, sisters-in-law, nieces, nephews and all their animals, on a six-month journey north. They made new homes in Haran – and as soon as they were settled there God sent them wandering again, this time west and south. They struggled over mountain-passes, baked by the sun. They walked across endless, dusty plains while their animals browsed on thorn-trees. They tramped through river-valleys lush with willows. They camped at last on a hillside in a grove of trees. God walked on the hillside with Abraham, and said, "One day your descendants will fill this land."

"How can they?" said Abraham. "Sarah and I are childless. How can we have descendants?"

"One day your descendants will fill this land," repeated God.

Abraham understood nothing. He took God's words as a sign that he was to settle where he was. He built an altar on the hillside, and told his followers that their wandering was done. But before they could tether their animals or pitch their tents, God sent them on a third journey, even longer and more terrifying than before. They left fertile land and came to a wilderness of rock and sun-bleached sand. The people grumbled and cursed. Where was Abraham taking them? What lay ahead but death? Abraham gave no answer. He knew as little as they did about the future. He had nothing to guide him but trust in God. He walked ahead of his people across the sand, leaving them to turn back or struggle after him, as they chose. Soon they were several weeks' walking into the desert, with no sign of an end to it. They were exhausted, hopeless and miserable. They had nothing to drink but a few sips of water each evening, warm and foul-tasting from the goatskins it was kept in. They had long ago eaten all their food, and were reduced to slaughtering their animals. They had no idea how much more desert stretched ahead. All they knew was that there was so much behind them now that if they tried to turn back it would be certain death.

At last, after many weary weeks, God brought them out of the desert into Egypt. It was the first civilised place they had seen since Ur: settled villages, farms and towns along the green strip of land watered by the river Nile. The Egyptians welcomed them, amazed that any travellers should have escaped from the Empty Land. They gave them food, work and shelter. But even this welcome was a trap set by God to test Abraham's obedience. The reason for the Egyptians' warmth was that their ruler, the Pharaoh, had seen Abraham's wife Sarah and wanted her. He had a harem of wives and concubines, and sent word to Abraham that he wanted to give Abraham's "sister" a place in it. Abraham was terrified. He prayed to God for help. But God left him to decide for himself, to make his own choice. Abraham said to Sarah, "Tell them that you're my sister. If you say you're my wife, they'll take you and kill me. If you say that you're my sister, they'll spare us both." Obediently, Sarah said that she was Abraham's sister. The Pharaoh took her into his harem, and treated her with honour. He showered Abraham with flocks, herds, slaves, jewels and gold. Abraham became one of the richest men in Egypt. But his wealth was based on trickery, and he had chosen to put his own safety above trust in God. God sent sickness to plague the Egyptian court; the Pharaoh's wise men said that it was caused by the strangers, and that Sarah was not Abraham's sister but his wife. Furious, the Pharaoh ordered Abraham out of Egypt. He could take as much wealth as he could carry, and as many of his followers as were willing to go with him, but he was to go back into the Empty Land, to live or die as Fate decided.

Once again, Abraham set out across the desert. Sarah walked by his side, and his slaves and animals followed. But of all the people who had gone with him to Egypt, only one man, his nephew Lot, was willing to risk the desert journey a second time. He, too, took his family, his slaves and all his animals. They struggled across the desert, and north to the hillside where Abraham had long ago built God's altar. Abraham and Lot stood on the hilltop, looking down. On one side was a rocky landscape, wind-scoured and deserted; on the other was the valley of the river Jordan, a wide plain filled with fruit-groves, fields, and the white roofs of houses. "Choose, Lot," said Abraham. "If you, your family and your animals settle on the plain, we'll take the highlands. If you choose the highlands, we'll take the plain."

"We'll go east," said Lot. "We'll choose the plain."

Abraham went west and south, leading his flocks into the wilderness. After three days' walking he came to Mamre, a stretch of flat land, well watered and green with grass. He camped there, and let his sheep and goats loose to crop the grass. In the years that followed he built no settlement. He and his family lived where they were, in tents, ready to move on whenever God ordered it. In the meantime, Lot settled in Sodom, a town in the Jordan plain. At first the people were suspicious of his outlandish clothes, his foreign accent and his ignorance of their customs and their gods. But his saddlebags of Egyptian gold easily persuaded them to accept him, and he bought land and a house in Sodom and settled there.

The people of the Jordan plain were idol-worshippers. They carved gods from lumps of wood or stone and sacrificed to them day and night, leaping, shrieking and gashing themselves with knives. They were lawless and shameless; no perversion or wickedness, from rape to murder, from robbery to human sacrifice, was strange to them. The "cities of the plain" (as the people proudly called their towns), were beautiful, a second garden of Eden; but human wickedness rose from them like a stench, polluting heaven. At last God went down to Earth with two of his angels, to put an end to it. Disguised as a traveller, he came to Abraham's tent at Mamre. Abraham sent slaves to fetch water for him to wash the dust from his feet, and to spread a carpet in the shade for him to sit on while they prepared a feast. God said, "Where is your wife?"

"Sarah's inside the tent," answered Abraham.

"One day, soon," God said, "Your wife will conceive, and bear a son. Your family will grow from him, till your descendants fill this land."

Before Abraham could speak, there was the sound of laughter from inside the tent. "Why does Sarah laugh?" asked God.

"Sir," said Abraham, "I'm a hundred years old, and Sarah's ninety-nine. How can we have a child? How can our descendants ever fill this land?"*

"Believe me," said God. "One day, soon, Sarah will bear a son."

While God talked with Abraham in Mamre*, his angels went down to the Jordan plain. They too were disguised as travellers. They went to Lot's house in Sodom, and Lot gave them water to wash in and ordered his slaves to cook a meal and prepare beds for the night. But as soon as it was dark a crowd of people, armed with sticks and stones, filled the street outside. They hammered on Lot's door and shouted, "Send out those travellers. We know how to deal with them."

"What harm have they done?" asked Lot. "They're innocent."

"Listen to him!" jeered the crowd. "He's a stranger here. What makes him set himself up as judge and jury?" They hammered again on Lot's door. "Send the strangers out," they shouted. "We want to rape them."

The angels pulled Lot inside the house. They poured blindness on the mob outside, so that they groped helplessly in the dust. "Hurry," the angels said to Lot. "Take your wife and your daughters and leave Sodom, now. And whatever happens, whatever you hear behind you, don't look back."

Terrified, Lot woke his daughters and ran with them through the dark streets of the town. Lot's wife hurried behind them. Darkness pressed on them like smoke from a fire, thick and acrid. The ground heaved and churned like a dying animal. Lightning flashes split the sky; pebbles showered like rain. "Don't look back!" Lot shouted. "Watever you do, don't look back!" He and his daughters ran till their ribs ached and their legs shook under them. They fixed their eyes on the horizon, trying to ignore the earthquake-noises behind them, the the lightning flashes and the screams of terrified people. Only Lot's wife looked back. On the ridge of a hill, on the very verge of safety, she turned for a last glimpse of her former home – and at that exact moment the earth split apart, the streets and houses slid into it, and dust and fire rained from above, blanketing fields, trees and plants. When the air cleared, there was no sign of life. Where the "cities of the plain" had been there was a barren crater, surrounded by dust-hills. Where Lot's wife had stood, there was a pillar of fire-bleached stone, like a statue carved from salt. Lot and his daughters were the only survivors. Towns, fields, fruit-groves and every man, woman, child and animal had been wiped from the world as if they had never been.*

So, in Sodom, Gomorrah and the other towns, God did exactly as he promised. He carried out his word to Abraham and Sarah, too. Not long after the destruction of the cities of the plain, Sarah found herself pregnant, and in due course she bore a son. She and Abraham named him Isaac (She laughed), in memory of the time when Sarah heard God's prophecy from inside the tent, and doubted it. The little boy thrived. He was the apple of his father's and mother's eye, the beloved son of their extreme old age, their darling and their hope. They cherished him; they sat at his bedside when he was sick and danced for happiness when he was well.

But God's purpose was not yet complete. For years, Abraham had obeyed every order. He had travelled from Babel to Ur, from Ur to Egypt, from Egypt to his present home. Each time, whatever his reluctance, whatever the dangers he had had to face, he had trusted God. Now it was time to put his obedience to a last, most terrible test. He would be given free choice. On one side would be his trust in God, the trust that had never failed him. On the other would be the person he held dearest in all the world.

"Abraham," said God, "Take Isaac into the mountains, build an altar and offer him as a sacrifice."

Abraham said nothing. It was just after dawn. He sent two servants to cut wood for a sacrifice. He loaded the wood on an ass, and he, Isaac and the servants set out into the mountains. After three days they could see in the distance the place God had chosen for the sacrifice. "Wait here," Abraham said to the servants. "The boy and I will sacrifice, and come back to you."

He unloaded the wood from the ass onto Isaac's back. He took a pot of glowing embers in one hand and a knife in the other. He and Isaac left the servants and went together higher up the mountain. After a while Isaac said, "Father, we have wood, fire, and a knife. But where is the lamb for the sacrifice?"

"God will provide a lamb," Abraham said, and walked on in silence.

They came to the place God had chosen for the sacrifice, and built an altar of stones. Isaac spread the wood on the altar. Then Abraham bound his beloved son with ropes, and laid him on the wood. He lifted the knife to kill his son. But even as the blade glinted above his head, he heard a voice calling from Heaven, "Abraham, Abraham!"

Abraham bowed his head. "Here am I," he said – the humble words slaves used when their masters called their names.

"Do not harm the child. Your obedience is proved. You were willing to sacrifice even your own son, for love of God."

Abraham looked up, and saw a ram in a bush close by, caught by the horns. With joy thudding in his heart, he released Isaac, took the ram and sacrificed it in Isaac's place. Once again he heard the voice from Heaven. "Abraham, because you have made this choice, because you were willing to sacrifice your own beloved son, you will have God's blessing forever. Your descendants will be as numberless as stars in the sky or sands of the sea. They will people the world. So God promises, in response to your obedience."

In this way, just as Adam and Eve chose to disobey God in the Garden of Eden, so Abraham chose to obey him. The human race was still tainted by guilt and sin. But by his choice, obedience, he had shown that people could use free will for good as well as bad.

2 · INHERITORS

The twins

Abraham's grandsons Esau and Jacob were twins. Before they were born, God prophesied that each would grow up to be the ancestor of a great nation. The twins were the children of Isaac and his Syrian wife Rebekah*. But they inherited none of their father's gentle nature. They fought even inside their mother's womb, jostling to be first born. Esau won, and slid gasping into the light of day; his brother Jacob followed, furiously clutching Esau's heel. Esau's skin was blotched with red, and from boyhood he was hairy from head to foot, like an animal; Jacob was smooth and fair. Their mother loved Jacob best, but Isaac preferred his surly, shaggy brother, the first-born. He gave Esau a prince's education, teaching him to ride, shoot and hunt deer in the river valleys. Jacob, by contrast, learned shepherding and corn-growing, servants' jobs.

One day, when the boys were eleven or twelve, Esau galloped home at sunset, exhausted and furious. He had been hunting all day, and had caught nothing. He flung himself from his horse, shouldered the grooms aside and went to the fire where Jacob was cooking lentils.

"Give me some of those," he said shortly. "I'm starving."

"Go to your own tent," said Jacob. "The slaves will have your meal waiting."

"I said, give me some lentils," shouted Esau.

Jacob looked up at him. "The price is – your birthright," he said. "If you take these lentils, you're admitting that I'm Isaac's heir, not you."

Esau thought it was a joke. Everyone could see that he was a prince, trained to rule, and that Jacob was a servant. What words changed that? "Done!" he said.

In the years that followed, Esau went on treating his brother as a servant, exactly as before. And whenever Jacob said quietly, "Remember: I'm the heir," he shook his shaggy hair, slapped his thighs and roared with glee. Jacob spent his time sitting by the flap of Isaac's tent, listening while the old man gave his people advice and judged their grievances. Esau, by contrast, spent his days hunting and riding far from camp, as he had done since childhood. Every so often, when he came home with gazelle, he ordered the servants to make venison stew, took his father a dish of it and fed the old man as if he were a child. By this time Isaac was over a hundred years old. He was blind and frail, and his memory came and went like the sun on a cloudy day. Rebekah his wife stroked his hands and said, "Isaac, it's time to pass on your authority. Lay your hands on your son's head and bless him. Everyone will see that he is your chosen successor, and will follow him as they have followed you."

Isaac said, "Tell Esau to hunt gazelle, and bring me stew as he always does. I'll lay hands on his head, and bless him."

Rebekah told Esau this message. But as soon as Esau had snatched his hunting spears and galloped out of camp, she went to Jacob and said, "Fetch two kids from the goat-pens. I'll make stew of them. Feed it to your father, and he'll take you for Esau and give you his blessing."

"It won't work," said Jacob. "Esau's a hairy man, and I'm a smooth man. Father can tell us apart by feel."

"Fetch the kids," said Rebekah. "Leave the rest to me."

Jacob fetched the kids. She stewed the meat, and bound strips of fleecy hide round Jacob's arms and on the smooth backs of his hands. Then she dressed him in Esau's clothes, gave him a dish of stew and a skin of wine, then sent him into Isaac's tent.

"Father," said Jacob.

"Who is it?" asked Isaac, looking at him with sightless eyes.

"Your heir," said Jacob.

"Have you come so soon?" said Isaac. "Who helped you in the hunt?"

"God helped," said Jacob.

Isaac ran his hands over Esau's royal robes, and felt the fleeces on Jacob's hands and arms. "The voice is Jacob's," he said, "but these are Esau's hands." He looked sightlessly once more at Jacob. "Are you Esau, my son?" he asked.

"Yes," said Jacob.

Jacob fed Isaac from the dish of stew, and gave him wine to drink. Then he knelt in front of him. Isaac put his hands on Jacob's head and blessed him. He kissed him, and everyone in camp knew that Jacob was Isaac's heir.

That evening, Esau came back from hunting, ordered the servants to make venison stew and took it to his father as usual.

"Eat, father," he said. "Eat, and bless your son."

"Who are you?" asked Isaac in alarm.

"Esau, your first-born son. Your heir."

"Who was it, then, who brought stew before? Your brother came with subtlety, Esau, and has taken your blessing.."

"Father, bless me too," cried Esau. But Isaac made no answer, and Esau lifted his hands to heaven and wept. In the days that followed he sat muttering in his tent. His spears stuck haft-downwards in the earth, their bright blades tarnishing. His hawks moped. His horses chafed in their stalls, with no one to exercise them. His wives filled the air with wails. At last servants went to Rebekah with terror in their eyes. "Lady," they said, "Esau's plotting revenge. He's planning to murder Jacob, as soon as Isaac is dead and the days of mourning are done."

Rebekah ran to Jacob. "Escape while you can," she said. Go north to Haran. Stay with my brother Laban. When Esau's fury lessens, I'll send for you." She went to Isaac and said, "Husband, it's time Jacob, your heir, looked for a wife. Don't let him marry some wailing local woman, as Esau did. Send him to Haran, to find a Syrian wife as you found me."

Jacob knelt before Isaac, and the old man once again laid hands on him and blessed him. Then Jacob loaded a camel with food and water-skins, cloaked his face against the glare, and rode into the hills towards the rising sun.

Jacob and Laban

Jacob rode in the hills all that day, and saw no one. He was lonely and afraid. He lay down at night on the rocky ground, laid his head on a stone and slept. In the night God took pity on him and sent a dream to comfort him. In the dream Jacob saw a ladder stretched from Earth to Heaven, and angels passing up and down. God spoke in the dream and said, "Jacob, I am the God of Abraham and Isaac, and I promise this land to you and your descendants forever. Your descendants will outnumber the dust of the earth, and they will spread north, south, east and west across the world. Wherever you go and whatever you do, I shall be with you always." Jacob woke from the dream and it was morning. He made an altar of the stone he had used as a pillow, and poured an offering of oil. He called the place Bethel, "God's House", and swore to worship none but God throughout his life. Then he shouldered his pack, unhobbled his camel and went on his way. After many days' walking he came down from the hills to wide, bare plains. The land was scorched, with no food for grazing animals but dune-grass and a few scrubby thorn-trees. But then, towards evening on the second day, Jacob heard sheep crying and the sound of goat-bells, and saw in the distance an enormous gathering of flocks and herds. They milled about the plain, while the shepherds and their dogs tried to bunch them round a dozen long troughs of stone and wood, and next to them a hole in the ground stopped by a wide, flat stone. It was the only visible well in any direction, and the shepherds were gathering to water their animals before penning them for the night. "Brothers," said Jacob. "Whose men are you? Whose flocks are these?"

"We come from Haran," the shepherds answered. "Our master is Laban, son of Bethuel. These are his animals. When his daughter Rachel brings the breeding ewes with their lambs, we'll unstop the well and water the animals. Wait here till then: you'll be able to fill your water-skins and let your camel drink."

As soon as he heard the name "Laban", Jacob's heart leapt. Laban was his uncle, his mother's brother. He sat down in the shade to wait. Soon a girl came up, driving a flock of ewes with their lambs crying beside them. This was Rachel, Laban's daughter and Jacob's cousin. As soon as Jacob saw her God filled him with love for her, and he jumped up, rolled the stone from the well and began helping her to fill the water-troughs for the animals to drink. She was amazed to see tears running down his cheeks, and even more surprised to hear that he was her father's nephew, the son of Rebekah who had long ago left Haran to cross the desert and marry a man she had never seen. Rachel ran to tell her father, and Laban himself came out from Haran to welcome Jacob, embracing him like a long-lost son.

Laban feasted Jacob for a month, as custom was, before asking him his business. "I've come to ask for your daughter as my wife," said Jacob.

"What bride-price will you pay?" asked Laban.

"I'll work for you for seven years," answered Jacob.

So Jacob tended Laban's flocks and herds for seven years, and it seemed no more than seven weeks, so great was his love for Rachel. At the end of the time he said to Laban, "The price is paid. Give me my wife, as we agreed."

"Certainly," said Laban slyly. He sent out invitations to a seven-day wedding feast, and set his cooks to slaughtering animals, making yogurt and baking soft loaves and honey-cakes. On the first day of the feast, Jacob married Laban's daughter before all the people – and when she unveiled herself before him, he was furious to find that it was not Rachel but her elder sister Leah. "Give me my promised bride," he shouted at Laban.

"Not yet," said Laban. "In Haran the custom is eldest first. If you want to marry Rachel, serve another seven years."

Jacob tended Laban's flocks and herds for another seven years, and by the end of that time he was chief herdsman, with a house and servants of his own. He married Rachel, and his dearest wish was that he and she might have a son. But year after year, for six more years, Rachel remained barren, and God granted fertility to Leah, Jacob's first, unwanted wife, and to his concubines. Leah bore six sons and a daughter, and each of the concubines bore sons. Only then, when

Jacob's house was filled with squalling children, did God open Rachel's womb at last, and she bore Jacob a son and called him Joseph.

Jacob had now served Laban for over twenty years. He began to feel that unless he went home soon, he would stay in Haran till he died. But Laban, anxious not to lose his best herdsman, offered Jacob any wages he cared to ask, if only he would stay. There was only one way out of it: more trickery. Jacob said, "Let me separate out all your brown-fleeced, blotchy sheep and goats from the others, and make two herds, one for you, and one for me." Laban agreed – and as soon as the animals were separated, God made Jacob's sheep and goats thrive, while Laban's, the weaker stock, fell ill and many died. Soon Laban's sons began clamouring to their father that Jacob was stealing all their inheritance, and Jacob said to his wives, "It's time to leave." He sent his servants to round up his sheep and goats, and began driving the huge flock south into the desert. Leah and Rachel followed on donkey-back, with the concubines and all the children. It was sheep-shearing time, and Laban was so busy that it was three days before he realised that Jacob was gone, and galloped after him with his sons and a dozen armed men. It was seven more days before he found him, camped on the slopes of Mount Gilead.

It was evening. Laban camped for the night, intending to swoop on Jacob before dawn and kill him as he slept. But God visited him in a dream and said, "Laban, beware! Treat Jacob fairly; listen to what he says." Laban was terrified. He waited till the sun was high next morning, then rode into Jacob's camp with his sons beside him, and asked to talk.

"Why did you leave unannounced?" he said. "I would have held a farewell feast with songs and dancing. Why did you steal away, before I could kiss my grandchildren goodbye?"

"I was afraid," said Jacob simply. "But search the camp. If you find anything that is not rightfully ours, punish us."

Laban searched the camp, and found nothing*. At last he said, "Go in peace. I would have killed you, but God warned me in a dream to treat you fairly. Make a truce with me, and a boundary between us which our descendants will respect forever."

Jacob set a boulder upright in the hillside, and his and Laban's servants piled stones around it. Laban said, "Let this stone-pile mark our boundary forever. Swear that your people will never pass it to make war on us, and we shall swear never to pass it and invade your territory. May your God hear us, and punish whichever of us breaks our word."

Jacob sacrificed, and he and Laban swore their oaths. They spent the night in a farewell-feast, and next morning Laban kissed his grandchildren and rode away with his sons beside him, leaving Jacob, his wives, his children, his concubines, his servants and his animals to continue their journey in peace.

Jacob and Esau

The nearer Jacob came to the river Jordan, the more apprehensive he became. He had been away over twenty years, leaving Esau to rule the people in Isaac's name. Esau would now be a powerful prince, with grown-up sons and an army. Would he still be furious with Jacob for cheating him of Isaac's blessing? Would he remember his vow to kill him? God had promised to go with Jacob wherever he went – would he still stand by him now? Jacob sent messengers to tell Esau that he came in peace, and the men galloped back with news that Esau was on the way to meet them, with four hundred armed horsemen. Jacob fell on his knees and prayed, "God of Abraham, God of Isaac, you sent me home from Haran. You promised to stand by me always. Help me now!"

It was dusk, and they were making camp on the bank of the river Jabbok, a tributary of the Jordan. The shepherds were watering the animals; slaves were gathering wood for cooking-fires. Jacob divided his followers and his animals into two groups. One group, led by his most trusted servants, consisted of presents for Esau: two hundred and twenty each of sheep and goats, thirty she-camels and their colts, forty cows, ten bulls, twenty she-asses and ten foals. They were to meet Esau next day at dawn, to prepare the way for the second, main column. He himself would follow, with his wives, children, concubines and the rest of the animals. He ordered everyone to ford the Jabbok and spend the night on the other side. He alone stayed where he was, rolled himself in his cloak and lay down on the ground to sleep. He tossed and turned, groaning and muttering as he argued with God in his dreams. He felt that he was wrestling, and that he had to use every trick he knew, every twist and wriggle, to stay on his feet. At last, just as dawn was breaking, his opponent touched him in the hollow of his thigh, Jacob's leg buckled under him and he sprawled on the ground. His opponent said, "Jacob, your surname from now on, and the name of your descendants, will be Israel, (May God win). Whenever you wrestle with God, whenever you try to put your wishes before his will, remember this." Jacob crossed the ford and joined his companions who were standing in a terrified group, looking up at the hills. Esau and his four hundred armed horsemen surrounded them. Jacob shouted to Leah and Rachel to take the children. Then he walked up the slope, alone, to face his brother. He bowed seven times, humble as a slave. To his surprise, instead of attacking him Esau jumped from his horse and hugged him, tears running down his cheeks. Jacob, too, wept. The brothers, no longer amitious youths but mature men, fathers of families, put the past behind them and were friends for the first time in their lives.

"Why have you given me all these animals?" said Esau. "I've plenty of my own."

"These animals are God's blessing to me," said Jacob, "and now I share that blessing with you. Take them."

So the brothers made peace at last. Esau and his men rode back to their own country, south-east of the Salt Sea where the Cities of the Plain had once stood. Jacob bought land on Mount Gerizim, north-west of the Salt Sea not far from the town of Shechem. He built an altar to God and set up his tents. There was no more quarrelling between him and Esau. Each twin, as God had prophesised before they were born, became ruler of a great nation. When Isaac died at last in Mamre, at the age of one hundred and eighty, Jacob and Esau led the mourners at his funeral: two dignified elderly men, each surrounded by children, grandchildren and servants as numerous as the dust of the earth or the sand of the sea.

Joseph

Joseph was the eleventh of Jacob's sons, and his father's favourite. The ten older boys were the sons of concubines, or of Jacob's unwanted wife Leah; Joseph was the son of Jacob's beloved Rachel. For seventeen years, while Joseph and his brothers were growing up, Jacob treated Joseph like the first-born. Joseph's brothers wore workmen's tunics and tended sheep; Joseph wore a long-sleeved tunic of soft cloth and a striped cloak, the coat of many colours that declared him a prince. He did no work. He spent his time with his father, sacrificing, feasting visiting traders, hearing the people's grievances and settling their arguments. Joseph was a dreamer, and his dreams were all of rule. He dreamed that he and his brothers were binding sheaves in a cornfield, and his sheaf stood upright while his brothers' sheaves bowed in homage. He dreamed that he was a star in the sky, and the sun, moon and eleven other stars deferred to him. When he told Jacob these dreams, the old man laughed indulgently; when he told his brothers, they hated him and plotted to kill him. One day the brothers took Jacob's flocks to lush pastures near Dothan, a day's journey north. They planned to stay there for the whole lambing season, until the lambs were old enough to be driven home again. After some weeks, Jacob sent Joseph after them, to check that all was well. "Here comes the dreamer," the brothers muttered. "Let's deal with him." There was an underground cistern by the roadside, a cave hollowed from the rock and used for storing grain. The brothers stripped Joseph, threw him in the cistern and stoppered the entrance with a boulder. Then they waited. The road was a camel-route from Syria in the north to Egypt in the south. Traders passed continuously up and down it, their animals loaded with Syrian dates, figs and spices and Egyptian corn. The brothers waited until a group of traders camped by the roadside on their way south. Then they unstoppered the cave and sold them Joseph as a slave. The traders went on their way, and the brothers took Joseph's coat and tunic, smeared them with goat's blood, and went home to tell Jacob that lions had eaten his beloved son*.

The spice-traders took Joseph to the city of On in Egypt, and sold him in the slave-market. He was bought by Potiphar, commander of the royal guard, to be trained as a houseboy. But God, who was overseeing every step in Joseph's life, saw to it that in whatever he did, he prospered. After one year he was Potiphar's favourite houseboy; after two years he was his chief servant, after four years he was head of the household, managing Potiphar's business affairs while his master lived at court. All this time, Potiphar treated Joseph more as a trusted friend than a slave. Potiphar's wife longed for him in a different way: as a lover. She was used to making love with any male slave she chose, and one day ordered Joseph bluntly into bed. To her fury he refused. Next day, and for many days after that, she gave the same order with the same result. Finally she snatched Joseph's loincloth – all he wore about the house in the heat of the day – and ran to Potiphar, screaming that Joseph had tried to rape her. Potiphar had no choice but punishment: friend or not, Joseph was a slave and could not deny his own mistress' accusation. But instead of death (the usual slave's punishment) Potiphar sent Joseph to a prison-farm deep in the desert, where high-ranking offenders served as shepherds, cowherds and ploughmen until Egypt's ruler, the Pharaoh, decided their final fate. Once again, God saw to it that Joseph prospered. His flocks lambed twice each season; his cornfields stretched from the banks of the Nile to the distant hills; his cattle gave milk till every container overflowed. In the end the overawed prison-keeper gave Joseph charge of the entire running of the farm.

One day two high palace officials, the Pharaoh's wine-steward and his master baker, were sent to the prison-farm. They had offended their master, and were sent to the farm to await the Pharaoh's judgement. On the night before the judgement, God sent each of then a dream, and they told their dreams to Joseph. "I was standing beside a vine," said the steward, "and it suddenly grew three branches, laden with grapes. I squeezed the grapes into the Pharaoh's cup, and gave him wine to drink."

"The three branches mean three days," said Joseph. "In three days' time you'll be back in favour, and you'll serve the

Pharaoh wine as you've always done. When that happens, remember me."

"I'll remember," promised the wine-steward.

The baker said, "I dreamed that I was carrying three bread-baskets on my head. The top basket was full of pastries for the Pharaoh. But before I could deliver them, birds swooped out of the air and ate them all."

"The three baskets are three days," said Joseph. "In three days' time the Pharaoh will cut off your head, and birds will swoop from the air to pick your bones."

Three days later the Pharaoh sent for his steward and baker and announced their fate. The baker was beheaded and the steward was returned to favour, exactly as Joseph had fore-told. Birds swooped from the air and picked the baker's bones. As for the steward, he forgot Joseph entirely: joy at his freedom drove the promise from his mind.

Two years passed. Then the Pharaoh himself began dreaming dreams. He dreamed that he saw seven fat cows grazing beside the river, and seven thin cows came out of the water and ate them. Then he saw seven thin ears of corn devour seven fat ears. He told the royal magicians his dreams, and they could think of no explanation. But the wine-steward overheard and said, "Master, on the prison-farm is a man who interprets dreams. He foretold exactly what would happen to your servants, the baker you beheaded and the wine-steward you spared."

The Pharaoh sent for Joseph and told him his dreams. Joseph said, "God answers. The fat cows and corn-ears are seven years of plenty. The thin cows and corn-ears are seven years of famine. Put a wise man in charge of Egypt's food supplies while the seven good years last, or the seven years of famine will devour your people."

When the Pharaoh's magicians heard Joseph's explanation, they looked eagerly at one another. Where could the wise man he spoke of be found, except among themselves? But the Pharaoh put his own signet ring on Joseph's finger, and ordered the slaves to bring him fine linen robes and a gold chain of office. "Where you go, I go," he said. "Be second to me in Egypt. Your word is law."

In the seven prosperous years that followed, Joseph's workmen built barns all over Egypt, and crammed them with surplus grain. Then, when the years of famine began, Joseph opened the storehouses one by one and sold grain to the people. The famine spread far beyond Egypt's boundaries. From north Africa to Syria, from the Mediterranean coast to Babylon, God held back the rain. At first the people had enough to eat. But in the second and third years, when their harvests failed and their animals died, they began to trudge north, south, east and west in search of food. In his hill-camp on Mount Gerizim, Joseph's father Jacob opened his trea-sure-sacks, called his sons together and said, "They say there's corn in Egypt. Go there; buy food. But don't take Benjamin – there might be danger."

Joseph's brothers looked at each other. By now they were all in their forties and fifties, grown men, fathers of families – and still their father put them second to a younger brother, this time to Rachel's second son Benjamin who had been a baby in arms when they sold Joseph into slavery years before. But the people's need for food mattered more than family quarrelling. They harnessed camels, mules and asses and set out south to Egypt. Joseph heard of their coming and sum-moned them to his palace beside the Nile. The brothers bowed nervously to every official who came near them, in case he turned out to be the Keeper of Pharaoh's Ring. At last Joseph took his place on a golden throne, and the brothers prostrated themselves before him. They touched their fore-heads to the floor; they fixed their eyes on the ground; none dared to speak to the Ring-keeper face-to-face. Joseph was reminded of his boyhood dreams, of the brother's stars and corn-sheaves bowing in homage. He longed to embrace his brothers, to forgive them and to ask for news of his father Jacob and his brother Benjamin. But God held him back. The brothers still had to admit their guilt; they had to soften their hearts of their own free will. Accordingly, God made Joseph set his face, deepen his voice, and question the brothers not in their own language but through an interpreter. "Who are you? Why have you come? You must be spies."

"No, master," answered Reuben, the eldest brother. "We are Jacob's sons. Our brother Benjamin is at home with our father and our brother Joseph is no more. We came for corn."

"This can easily be proved," said Joseph. "Take the corn back to your father. Leave one man here as a hostage. When you come back with Benjamin, I'll believe your story and you can all go free."

"What can we do?" the brothers said to one another. "This is our punishment for selling our own brother into slavery, years ago. Now we have to persuade Jacob to trust us with the life of another beloved son. Why should he believe us? What right have we to ask?" Unknown to them all, Joseph understood every word. He longed to tell them who he was, to end their anxiety and send them rejoicing home. But once again God held him back. Joseph's servants bound Simeon, the second eldest brother, as a hostage, filled the other's corn-sacks and sent them on their way.

When Jacob heard the brothers' story, he was furious. "How many sons must I trust to you?" he shouted. "First Joseph, then Simeon, and now Benjamin. If anything happens to him, I'll die of it." The brothers tried to soothe him. Reuben offered to leave his own two children as hostages, for Jacob to kill if even a hair of Benjamin's head was harmed. Judah offered his own life in exchange for Benjamin's. But in the end it was not the brothers' arguments or promises that moved their father, but the cries of his people, dying once more of hunger as soon as the Egyptian corn ran out. "If it has to be done, then do it," he said. "Take Benjamin, as the Egyptian demands. And take the man presents: honey, spices, nuts. May God bring all of you back alive."

The brothers took the presents and the empty corn-sacks, and went back to Egypt. When Joseph saw Benjamin, it was like looking at his younger self in a mirror. He was filled with emotion, and had to hurry into another room to control himself. But he still followed God's instructions, and showed his brothers no forgiveness. He fed them in the palace hall, at tables set apart from his own Egyptian servants and his other guests. He ordered the steward to fill the brother's corn-sacks, and to bury deep in them the money each man had paid*. In Benjamin's sack the steward hid a gold-and-silver drinking-cup from Joseph's own table. Then Joseph freed Simeon, restored him to his brothers and sent them on their way. But before they were half a morning's walk out of the city, he sent soldiers galloping after them to arrest them as thieves. The soldiers dragged the brothers in front of him, spilled the coins and the corn-grains at Joseph's feet, and held up the gold-and-silver cup, rescued from Benjamin's sack.

"So you were thieves, not spies," Joseph said to the bewildered brothers. "Explain!"

"Master," said Judah, "We are not thieves. But we are guilty men, and God has chosen this way to prove it. Punish us. Enslave us, as we enslaved our own brother, years ago."

"God forbid," said Joseph. "The money means nothing. But the cup is different. I'll enslave just one of you, the man who stole the cup. The rest of you may go."

"No, master," said Judah humbly. "Our father Jacob is an old man. He had a beloved son, years ago, and we took the boy and sold him into slavery. Now this young man is his beloved – and thanks to our guilt, Jacob will lose him as well. I beg you, master, send the boy home to his father, and enslave me instead."

When God heard these words, he judged that the brothers had learned humility. He let Joseph reveal himself at last. Joseph sent everyone out of the room, servants, interpreters and guards, and told his brothers, in their own language, who he was. They shook hands, slapped each other's backs and hugged each other, and when Joseph's guards, alarmed at the shouts and cries from inside the room, ran in to protect their master, they found him and the strangers weeping tears of joy. Joseph and his brothers spent the whole night talking, and in the morning Joseph sent word to the Pharaoh that he had found his long-lost family. The Pharaoh's answer was immediate and generous. "Let your brothers fetch your father, his wives, and all their wives and children. Give them a home in Egypt, as long as the famine lasts."

Joseph gave the brothers carts to fetch his father, the women and children. He loaded ten she-asses and ten he-asses with supplies for the journey, and gave each brother Egyptian clothes, and Benjamin five suits of clothes and three hundred silver pieces. So laden, the brothers hurried home to tell Jacob that his beloved Joseph was still alive.

Even now, Jacob hardly trusted them. For two years there had been no rain; famine was everywhere; was this the time to load women and children on carts and take them from a settled home to an unknown land? Even if the brothers' tale was true and Joseph was truly alive, how would the Egyptians welcome a whole tribe of refugees? The old man prayed to God for help. God said, "Jacob, take your wives, sons, daughters-in-law and all your grandchildren, and go to Egypt. I will guide you there, and in due course I will guide your people home again. You are Israel, and your sons are the inheritors*, whose descendants will rule this land. Fear nothing; leave for Egypt; I am with you always."

Convinced at last, Jacob took his wives, his children and his grandchildren down into Egypt, and was reunited there with Joseph, his beloved son.

3 · MOSES

Young Moses

The Israelites settled in the delta of the river Nile, some of the most fertile land in Egypt. They lived there for three hundred years, until Jacob and Joseph were long dead, and the only proof that they had ever existed was Joseph's body, mummified in the Egyptian fashion and sealed in a sarcophagus. With every year that passed, the Israelites' settlement grew. Only seventy people had originally followed Jacob into Egypt, with a dozen tents and a few hundred animals. But as generation followed generation their numbers swelled to thousands. Their villages teemed with children, and their cornfields and pastures covered the delta. A new dynasty of Pharaohs had come to power. They remembered nothing of the years of plenty and years of famine, and at first took little notice of the foreigners. But the more the Israelites increased, the more the Egyptians began to feel afraid. "If we let them go on growing," the Pharaoh said to his advisers, "they'll outnumber us. When war comes, they'll side with our enemies and overwhelm us."

"Master," said the advisers, "they're easily controlled. Drain the delta. Cut up their fields with ditches and irrigation-channels. Build a city – and make them do the work."

The Pharaoh gave his orders. Soldiers galloped into the delta and read out his decree enslaving the Israelites. Their farms and flocks were confiscated. They were made state slaves, and were set to ditch-digging, road-levelling and house-building, on pain of death. The house-bricks were made of mud, mixed with chopped straw and baked in the sun. Each slave had to make a fixed number of bricks a day;

all who failed were flogged. Soon the whole delta, once a quiet area of reed-beds, cornfields and water-meadows, was transformed into a muddy building site, with the soldiers' barracks at its heart and slave-quarters where the Israelites' villages had been.

To the Pharaoh's alarm, not even this persecution stopped the Israelites from breeding. He sent for the Israelites' mid-wives, and gave them secret orders to let girl babies live, but to strangle every boy and claim it had died at birth. The midwives promised to obey, but the number of boys grew no less, and when the Pharaoh asked the reason the midwives said that the Israelite women had taken to delivering their own babies, and so knew that the boys were alive before the midwives could get to them. Furious, the Pharaoh made a new law, that every boy-child born to an Israelite from that day on was to be thrown into the Nile and drowned.

The Israelites cried and cursed, but what could they do? They were slaves; their masters owned them as surely as people owned cows or hens. Not even life or death was theirs to choose. They wept; they tore their clothes; they lifted their hands to heaven and prayed. God answered their prayers. There was a slave-woman called Jochebed, the wife of Amram. She already had two children: a son, Aaron (born before the Pharaoh's order that all boy-babies should be killed) and an eight-year-old daughter, Miriam, the personal slave of the Pharaoh's youngest daughter. When Jochebed's third child was born and she saw that it was a boy, God put it into her head to save the baby's life. She hid him for three months, feeding him in secret and lying in reed-beds with her hand over the child's mouth to hush him, every time the Pharaoh's soldiers passed. Then, when the child was too big to hide, she wove bull-rushes into a basket, smeared it with pitch to make it water-tight, and let it float down the Nile with the baby lying inside it. Miriam, the child's sister, followed it along the bank to see what happened.

The basket floated downstream until the current carried it to the bank and lodged it in a clump of reeds. There was a pool nearby, where the Pharaoh's daughter and her maids went each day to bathe. The princess heard a baby crying in the reeds and sent one of her maids to fetch the basket. "This is an Israelite child," she said. "But how can we let him drown?" She called Miriam. "Find a slave-woman who has just had a child. Give her this baby to suckle. When he's weaned, bring him back to me. If the soldiers ask the woman any questions, tell her to say that she's nursing my child, the Pharaoh's grandson."

Miriam ran with the baby to her mother Jochebed, who gladly brought up her own son as the Pharaoh's daughter's child. To the young princess, the baby was like a new toy, a living doll. She called him Moses, (Son)*, and went every day to Jochebed's house to bathe him, dress him and play with him. By the time she tired of him, everyone was used to treating him as one of the Pharaoh's official grandsons, and he was brought up and educated as an Egyptian prince. He lived in luxury in the palace; priests taught him reading, writing and the secrets of their religion, and the soldiers and slave-masters gave him immediate, unquestioning obedience.

The burning bush

Moses' comfortable life in Egypt came to a sudden end. He was walking one day in the new city. Slaves were stacking bricks, lifting them in hods or carrying them, quick as monkeys, up ladders and along the scaffolding. He heard cries of pain, and found a slave cringing on the ground in a side-alley, his arms up to protect his head, and an Egyptian savagely beating him. No one else was about. Moses dragged the Egyptian back, cracked his head on the corner of a wall, and the man fell like a stone. The slave scuttled into the shadows like a frightened spider.

Moses scrabbled in the sand, his hands unused to digging, until he had made a shallow grave. He tipped the Egyptian's body into it, covered it and hurried away. He thought that would be the end of it. But the very next day he separated two brawling slaves, and when he asked why they were quarelling one of the man spat at him and said, "Who made you our judge? D'you mean to kill me, as you killed that Egyptian yesterday?" It was the slave he'd saved from beating. Moses said nothing. If the Egyptian was missed, if the slave talked, not even his royal rank would save him. He saddled a horse and rode into the desert.

By evening Moses was beyond the frontier, and the justice, of Egypt. He dismounted to rest beside a well. Shepherds were watering their flocks, and as Moses watched seven girls came up to fill water-jars, but could find no way past the throng at the well. Moses shouldered men and animals aside, and helped the girls to fill their jars. They were the daughters of Jethro, a priest, and their father gave him food and shelter. Jethro's people were Midianites, and they pastured their flocks between the uplands of Sinai and the northern tip of the Red Sea.

To Moses, Midian meant safety. No Egyptians, not even soldiers hunting a murderer, would risk crossing Sinai. They would assume that he'd died in the hills, or been enslaved or killed by passers-by. As long as he stayed in Midian, he was safe. He offered to serve Jethro as a shepherd, and some months later married Zipporah, one of the old man's daughters, and used the sheep and goats of her dowry to begin a breeding flock of his own. By the time his sons Gershom and Eliezer were born, he had become so much a Midianite that when he told tales of his royal life in Egypt he struggled for words like a man trying to recall a dream.

While Jethro's other shepherds kept to the lowlands, in sight of the sea, Moses used to drive his sheep into the foothills of Sinai. There was a bowl of flat land, and the mountains all around kept the air cool and the pastures green even in the hottest months of the year. Moses often stayed there for weeks on end, moving from pasture to pasture across the plateau, touching the hills' very edge. He was sitting in the shade one day, in a gully on the lower slopes, when he heard the crackle of flames from further up the mountain. At first he thought nothing of it. On the dry, bare hills thorn-trees were forever bursting into flames, sprinkling the rocks with ash. But this bush was different. Although flames flared all around it, and Moses could feel the heat even from where he sat, neither branches, twigs nor leaves were so much as singed. The tree stood green and unharmed in the fire's red heart: a miracle. Moses ran to look closer, and a voice from the bush said, "Moses, come no closer! Take off your shoes; this is holy ground."

"Who are you, Lord?" asked Moses.

"I am the God of Abraham, Isaac and Jacob. I have heard my people's cries, and seen their misery. I shall lead them out of Egypt into a land flowing with milk and honey, the land I promised them. Go to the Pharaoh now, and tell him to let my people go."

"Lord," said Moses, "who am I to speak to the Pharaoh?"

"You are God's servant; you speak for me."

"But what name shall I tell the people? Who shall I say you are?"

"I am that I am*: that is the name of God."

"Lord, what if they don't believe me? What proof can I show them?"

"Throw your stick on the ground," said God. Moses dropped his shepherd's stick, and it changed into a rearing, hissing snake. "Pick it up," said God. Moses reached trembling for the snake, and as soon as he touched it, it turned back into a stick in his hands.*

"O Lord," said Moses, "How can I speak to the Pharaoh or the people? I'm no orator. How can I find words?"

"God, who opened mortals' lips and gave them speech, will teach you," answered God. Moses still hesitated, and God said, "Take Aaron your brother. Let him speak for you."

Moses would have aked more questions. But the fire faded and the flames disappeared, leaving the bush green and leafy as before. Moses rounded up his sheep and drove them down across the plain to Jethro. "Father-in-law," he said, "let me go back to Egypt, to be with my people."

Jethro answered, "Go in peace." Moses saddled an ass for Zipporah his wife and the two children, took his shepherd's stick in his hand and set off across the hills to Egypt. God sent Aaron to meet him, and Moses told him, trembling, the wonders he had seen and heard on Sinai.

At first, when Aaron took Moses back to the slave-villages in the delta, the people distrusted him: a stranger, clean-

shaven and dressed in foreign clothes. But when he threw his
stick on the ground and God turned it into a snake as he had
on Sinai, and back to a stick again, they fell on their knees and
prayed. They listened while Aaron told them of the land
flowing with milk and honey; then they elected Moses and
Aaron their leaders, and sent them to ask the Pharaoh to let
God's people go.

God and the Pharaoh

Moses and Aaron stood before the Pharaoh. The Pharaoh was
furious. "Your people have stopped working," he said.
"Explain!"

"God answers," said Moses. "Let my people go."

"Who is this God?" asked the Pharaoh. "I'm a god myself;
I've never heard of him."

"The God of Israel speaks," repeated Moses. "Let my
people go."

The Pharaoh waved a hand to dismiss them. "Get your
people back to work," he said, "or see them suffer." He called
to his slave-masters. "The Israelites have too little to do," he
said. "In future, give them no more straw. Let them cut their
own, in the stubble of the fields. But each man must make the
same number of bricks as before, or be flogged for it."*

So each day, before they could even begin the back-break-
ing work of brick-making and building, the Israelites had to
spend hours cutting straw in the fields. They rounded on
Moses. "Is this how you lead us?" they cried. "Before you
came we had nothing, and now, thanks to you, we have even
less."

"Lord," Moses said to God, "why have you hardened the
Pharaoh's heart? Why do you allow such suffering?"

"It will soon end," said God. "Soon Pharaoh will drive
them out of Egypt as eagerly as he now imprisons them. Ask
him again. He will refuse again – and each time he refuses, I
will send proofs, to him and to my people, that I am God."

Moses and Aaron went again to the Pharaoh, and Moses
asked him to let God's people go. This time Moses remembered the first proof of God's power he had seen on Sinai. He

told Aaron to throw his stick on the ground, and the stick changed to a hissing snake. The Pharaoh at once snapped his fingers for his magicians. Their sticks ringed Aaron's and turned into snakes. But Aaron's snake ate them all before Pharaoh's eyes, and turned back to a stick in Aaron's hand. "God says, Let my people go," said Moses. But the Pharaoh set his face and refused to hear.

"Tomorrow," God said to Moses, "go down to the Nile in the morning, when the Pharaoh and his courtiers go to bathe. Ask him again to let my people go, and if he refuses, tell Aaron to touch the water with his stick."

Next morning Moses and Aaron went down to the river. The Pharaoh and his courtiers were bathing, and the Pharaoh splashed like a sulky child to drown out Moses' words. Moses said to Aaron, "Dip your stick in the water." As soon as the stick touched the surface, every part of the river, its head-waters, its delta, its rapids, its pools, turned to thick, coagulating blood. Every fish, every crocodile, every river creature died and their bodies stank in the sun. Sticky and furious, the Pharaoh struggled from his bathing-pool and went back to his palace. He ordered the doors to be locked against Moses, and for seven days refused to listen to him, while the river of blood turned to dust in the sun and the people dug desperately for water in the fields and olive-groves.

At the end of seven days God said to Moses, "Tell Aaron to stretch out his stick above the river." Aaron did as he was told, and at once the blood turned back to water, flowing deep and fresh as it had always done. But with the loosening of the blood, God sent a second plague. The water grew cloudy with tadpoles, wriggling and thriving in the reeds. There were no predators: the fish were all dead, and every tadpole grew into a full-grown frog. They swam in the river, they polluted the wells, they swarmed over the fields, they slimed food on the tables and smothered babies as they slept. At last the Pharaoh sent for Moses. "If your God rids us of these frogs," he said, "we'll admit that he's the Lord, and set his people free."

Moses prayed to God, and at once every frog in Egypt died. Their bodies carpeted the streets, the fields, the houses, and the people raked them into heaps to rot in the sun. "The frogs are gone," Moses said to the Pharaoh. "Now do as God orders: let his people go."

"No," said the Pharaoh. "You claim that your god did this. But my magicians can conjure frogs out of nowhere just as easily, and kill them off again. Get your people back to work."

For the third time, Moses told Aaron to hold out his stick, this time across the land. At once lice began crawling from the dust, and flies bred in the putrid bodies of the frogs. The insects swarmed into the Egyptians' houses, polluting all they touched. At first the Pharaoh claimed that this, too, was conjuring, and ordered his magicians to create lice and flies of their own. But the magicians failed, and finally the Pharaoh said to Moses, "If your God rids us of these pests, I'll let your people go three days' journey into the desert to sacrifice. Three days: no more."

Moses prayed to God, and the lice and flies vanished as suddenly as they had come. But when Moses asked the Pharaoh to keep his promise, God hardened the Pharaoh's heart once more and he refused. God infected all the Egyptians' cattle with plague, so that they died and stank; but not a single Israelite cow was harmed. The Egyptian people were now convinced. They kept superstitiously away from the Israelites, and begged the Pharaoh to admit that God was Lord and to let his people go. But the more they begged, the more the Pharaoh behaved like a sullen child. He sat on his god-king's throne in full regalia, and his executioners beheaded anyone who failed to grovel on the ground before him. God sent ulcers to torment the Egyptians' animals, and boils to plague the people. Even the Pharaoh's magicians were covered in sores, and the Pharaoh's own body festered. But the Pharaoh would still not yield. He sat on his throne, scratching, and shut his ears to the crowds howling at the gates. God sent thunder, rain and hailstones as big as pebbles; the Egyptians' fields were flooded and their crops were flattened; only the Israelites' land remained untouched. He filled the skies with locusts, and they stripped evey leaf from the Egyptians' fields and orchards. He blanketed the land with darkness, so that for three days and nights the people huddled terrified in their houses; only the Israelites had light. After each new plague the Pharaoh promised, briefly, to let the Israelites go, and his promise lasted as long as it took each plague to disappear. The country was on the edge of revolution. The Egyptians cursed their Pharaoh and shouted at him to keep his word, and the Pharaoh sat ashen-faced in his palace, changing his mind with each passing hour and threatening death to anyone who disagreed with him. It would have been easy for God to snap his will, to force him to give way. But the plagues were a lesson in obedience, to the Israelites as well as to the Egyptians, and the lesson would not be learned until both peoples acnowledged God of their own free will and admitted that he was Lord.*

Exodus

Moses and the Pharaoh confronted each other, their tempers at knife-point. "For the last time," said Moses, "let my people go."

"The last time!" jeered the Pharaoh. "If you see me face to face again, you die."

"I'll never see you face to face again," said Moses. "God speaks. At midnight he will go into the land, and all the first-born in Egypt will die, from the first-born of the Pharaoh to the first-born of the millhand and the first-born of every animal in stall or field. The crying of your people will reach the stars. But against the first-born of Israel not even a dog will bare its teeth. You will see the difference God makes between Egyptians and Israelites. Your people will grovel at my feet and say, 'Take your people. Go!' – and then, at last, God will lead the Israelites out of Egypt."

Moses walked from the palace in a rage, and went to a room in the city where the elders of all the slave-villages were waiting. "Do this," he said. "Tell every household to take an unblemished lamb; poor householders should share with their neighbours. In the evening of the fourteenth day of the month, tell them to kill the lamb and smear its blood on the door-posts and lintels of their houses. They must roast the lamb that night, eat it and burn the remains. They must wear travelling clothes and have staffs ready in their hands. For that same night God will go out into Egypt, and kill all the first-born of humans or animals. His angels will see the lambs' blood smeared on your doors and will pass over your houses and spare you. Tell the people."

The elders hurried back to their villages, and the people did as Moses ordered. And at midnight on the fourteenth day of the month God killed all the first-born of Egypt, from the first-born of the lowest prisoner in the dungeon to the first-born of the Pharaoh, and the first-born of every animal. The Pharaoh started up out of bed in the night, and the crying of his people reached the stars. The Pharaoh sent mesengers to Moses saying, "Go. Take your people, your flocks, your herds and everything else that is yours. Go now, before God kills us all."

The Israelites were waiting in their houses, dressed for a journey. They sat the women and children on donkeys, and shouldered packs as heavy as they could carry. They laid Joseph's mummified body in its four-hundred-year-old sarcophagus reverently in a cart in the centre of the procession. The Egyptians pressed gold and silver into their hands, begging them to take as much treasure as they wanted if only they would get out of Egypt before first light. Moses and Aaron led the line of people and animals from the delta to the desert, and there were so many of them, a whole nation on the march, that few mortal armies would have outnumbered them.* They walked all day, camped at evening and ate the flat, unleavened loaves they had baked for the journey. Next morning they set out again, marching east. At first the ground was flat and stony, no hindrance to walking. But by noon, when the sun was blazing overhead, they had reached a wasteland of reedbeds, marshes and water-channels infested with crocodiles. They waded and struggled across as best they could, until their way was blocked by deep water: an arm of the sea stretching out of sight on either side. Moses called a halt, and his people sat grumbling in the sun while he sent riders north and south along the coast to find a possible crossing-place.

All this time, the Pharaoh's spies had been shadowing the Israelites, and they now galloped back to their master shouting that Moses and his people were trapped, pinned between the marshes and the sea. Once again God hardened the Pharaoh's heart. The Pharaoh ordered his war-chariot, and galloped after the Israelites with six hundred charioteers riding at his heels. Moses' people heard the roar of hooves, like surf on a distant shore, and were terrified. Some cowered by their animals, cloaking their heads and clutching their screaming children. Others shouted at Moses, "What have you done to us? Were there no graves in Egypt, that you had to drag us here to die? Why did we listen? We were better off as slaves."

Moses said, "Fear nothing. God brought you this far, and he will protect you. Trust God, and see."

He went to a spur of rock on the seashore, held his stick out over the water and prayed to God. At once God blackened the sky with storms. An east wind folded the sea aside before the Israelites' eyes. It was as if the water had been combed. A channel of dry land appeared, from coast to coast across the sea, and on each side waves towered like walls. "Hurry!" shouted Moses. He, Aaron and the elders began urging the trembling people into the water-tunnel. At first the Israelites howled with fear. But when they felt dry ground underfoot, and realised that the water-walls were as safe as stone, their confidence grew and they marched to the other side singing hymns of joy. By the time the Pharaoh and his men reined in their chariots on the Egyptian shore, the whole column of Israelites, men, women, children and animals had passed safely across and was hurrying into the desert. "After them!" shouted the Pharaoh. He whipped his horses into the channel, and his charioteers galloped after him. As soon as they were all clear of the shore, the ground which had been firm under the Israelite's feet turned into soft, deep mud. The Egyptians' chariot wheels stuck and their horses sank thigh-deep. The wind dropped, and the water-walls toppled. The Pharaoh and his men were engulfed. For a moment their screaming filled the air, but then the water stilled them and there was silence. The sea was as whole as it had been before the miracle. Of the Pharaoh, his men, his six hundred chariots and his horses nothing remained but a flotsam of spears, helmets and broken chariot-poles. As the storm subsided, bodies began bobbing to the surface, and the waves laid them like sacrificial victims on the Egyptian shore.*

The Wilderness of Sin

At first, the Israelites were full of glee at their own safe sea-crossing and the Egyptians' fate. For the first three days of desert wandering, they danced as they walked, played pipes and drums and sang God's praise. They camped at the oasis of Elim, where there were water-springs and palm-trees. Then, with their water-skins full and their hearts high, they set out to cross the Wilderness of Sin.

The Wilderness of Sin was the last low-lying ground before the uplands of Sinai. The ground was hard-baked earth broken by rocky outcrops. There were a few spindly tamarisk trees. There were insects, lizards and occasionally hawks in the sky overhead. But for forty days, as the Israelites trudged in the heat, they saw no other signs of life. At first the only sounds were the chirping of cicadas, the bleating of the Israelites' animals, and the shuffling of their own feet on the dusty plain. But after a while a new sound was added: discontented voices, murmuring against Moses. "We were better off in Egypt. At least we had food there. We sat by bubbling stew-pots; bread filled our bellies. What made us follow Moses here, to starve?"

At last Moses called a halt. He stood on a rock, head and shoulders above the grumbling crowd. He said, "God speaks. Have you no faith? Endure this hunger for five more days, and you will have meat in the evening and bread in the morning. God is the Lord; he won't let you die."

The people muttered in disbelief. But they eked out their food for five more days, shuffling endlessly on in the baking, energy-draining heat. On the evening of the fifth day, without making camp, without even tethering their animals, they sat on the ground like children, waiting for a miracle. The sun slid towards the horizon, and in the long shadows a flock of quails appeared from nowhere, darkening the sky. They fluttered around the Israelites' heads; they settled on the ground, on the bags and packs, even on the animals' backs and the Israelites' own arms and shoulders. They were unafraid. Even when the Israelites built fires and began sharpening spits, the quails stood placidly watching. They made no resistance as the people began knocking their heads on stones, spitting their bodies and roasting them over the fires. It was as if they were offering their own lives to save the Israelites'. It was a miracle. And next morning, an even greater miracle appeared. The people had slept late, gorged on quail, and when they woke the sun was already high and hot. But the ground was covered with what looked like hail. The people looked at it in amazement. "What is it?" they asked. "Where did it come from? Why doesn't it melt?"

"Pick it up," said Moses. "Gather it. Make cakes of it."

Distrustfully, one person after another picked up a pinch of the substance and tasted it. It was hard, like oatmeal or coriander seeds, and as sweet as honey. They gathered it in pots, and began grinding it to flour and moulding it into cakes, to bake in the embers. "Eat all you want," said Moses. "But throw the rest away. It won't keep till morning. God will send more tomorrow." Most of the people did as he said – and those who disobeyed, who crammed cakes of the substance into their packs or hid them in the sleeves of their clothes, found next morning that maggots had grown in it and it had begun to stink. But there was a fresh layer on the ground. The people nicknamed it manna (the whateveritis), and it and the quails appeared to feed them day after day, month after month, all the time they were in the wilderness.*

There was still the problem of water. There was enough moisture in the quails and manna to keep the Israelites alive, but as the waterless days passed their mouths burned, their tongues swelled, and in cracked, parched voices they began once more to curse Moses. By this time they had reached the edge of the Wilderness of Sin, and were walking along the foot of a line of cliffs, the ramparts of Sinai, looking for a pass that would take them to the hills. They walked for days, moaning and muttering, and at last Moses lifted his arms and cried to God, "Lord, help me! If I find them no water, they'll stone me. Both they and I will die, here in this wilderness."

"Walk on ahead of the people," said God. "Take the stick you held out to part the sea. Hit the rock with it."

Moses did as God said. He took the elders of the old slave-villages, and walked with them out of sight of the rest of the Israelites. He took his stick in his hand and hit the rock. At once the rock split open, and clear water fountained out and filled a pool at the elders' feet. The elders ran to fetch their people, and the Israelites brought pans, jars, bowls and water-skins. They drank; they watered their animals; they splashed like sparrows in a pond. Moses fell on his knees and thanked God for yet another miracle.

The Golden Calf

Glorying in the water, the Israelites camped for months at the foot of the cliff.* Moses divided them into groups, and appointed leaders from among the elders of the old slave-villages and the heads of each of the twelve tribes. He set up an altar to God, and made the people worship. He sent riders to spy out the land and find a way up the cliffs. They reported a stony gully a day's walk to the north, and Moses ordered the Israelites to fill their water-skins, gather their animals and break camp. They followed the line of the cliffs to the gully, and began driving their animals towards the uplands, sliding and stumbling among the stones. At last they came to a high, grassy plateau ringed by hills. The place was cold and wet, and the longer the Israelites stayed there the more terrified they grew. It was as if the mountains themselves were uneasy. Cloud swirled overhead; lightning flared; the ground shook; thunderclaps pealed like trumpets from peak to peak. The Israelites stood in the rain, looking mutinously at Moses. "Stay here," he said. "God is on the mountain. Tether your animals. If you, or they, stray into God's presence, you die."

He left the people and set off up the mountain. He passed the place where he had long ago seen the burning bush, and climbed higher, till he was enveloped in clammy cloud. He

was close to the centre of the storm. Lightning sliced past him
or rolled along the ground at his feet. Rain tore his face.
Thunder was above him, round him, in him, beating in his
brain. He fell on his knees on the jagged, streaming rock, and
prayed. As he knelt, the sounds in his mind formed words,
God's commandments. "I am the Lord your God. I brought
you out of slavery. You will have no other gods before me.
You will make no images to worship, of animals, people or
other living things. You will not swear in God's name, and
break your word. You will keep the seventh day holy, and
rest as God rested on the seventh day of creation. You will
honour your parents. You will not kill. You will not commit
adultery. You will not steal. You will not make lying accusa-
tions. You will not envy your fellow human beings or long
for anything that belongs to them."

The sound ebbed, the storm stilled and the mountain was
quiet again. Moses stumbled back down to the plain, and
found the Israelites still huddled in the rain, forlorn and
terrified. "Make camp," he said. "God is here: the place is
safe. Build an altar of earth and stones, and sacrifice. God will
come down to us here, and speak to us."

When they heard this, the people trembled even more.
"Moses, speak for us," they begged. "Climb the mountain
and speak with God. Leave us down here. If we see God's
face, or hear his voice, we'll die."

Next morning Moses cloaked himself against the rain and
once more climbed the mountain. He took Joshua with him,
but left him on guard halfway up the mountainside, and went
on alone to speak with God. He knelt in the same place as
before, in a cleft between two tall, flat stones. Once more
clouds swirled, lightning flickered, thunder rolled and God's
words filled Moses' brain. God told him that the way to the
Promised Land lay clear ahead. God himself would come
down to lead the Israelites. They were to make him a tabernacle*, a sanctuary in the centre of the camp where no human
beings but priests might tread. God's presence would live in
the tabernacle, and would guide the Israelites to the Promised
Land. God gave Moses exact instructions for making and
furnishing the tabernacle, for choosing priests, and for the

services and worship they were to perform. When the words
ceased, the storm cleared and the clouds lifted, Moses was
astonished to find the two flat stones on each side of him
covered with writing, God's words burned into the rock with
fire. He lifted the stones, and they were as light as pebbles in
his hands. He hurried down the mountain to take them to his
people.

To Moses and Joshua, their stay on the mountain had
seemed no more than hours. But for the Israelites on the
plain, whole days and weeks had passed. At first they had sat
in desolate groups inside their tents, waiting for the rain to
stop. But when the drizzle continued, day after day, and there
was no sign of Moses or Joshua, their panic turned to impatience and their impatience turned to rage. "Moses has gone,"
they shouted at Aaron. "He's brought us all this way, and
deserted us. We'll never see him again. What shall we do
now?"

"Sacrifice to God," said Aaron. "Ask his help, as you've
always done."

"What use is a God we can't see?" shouted the Israelites.
"Make us a god, and then we'll sacrifice."

Aaron knew nothing of the commandments God had given
Moses on the mountain-top. He remembered Moses' order:
to build an altar of earth and stones, and sacrifice. Now
Moses had gone, leaving him to lead the people. What harm
would an image do? "Give me your ear-rings, your bracelets,
and the rest of the gold the Egyptians gave you," he said. The
people gave him the gold, and he melted it into a single mass
and fashioned it into a creature with four legs, a tail and wide,
staring eyes. He set it on a boulder in the centre of the camp,
and told the people, "There's your God, who brought you
out of Egypt. Build him an altar; sing and dance to honour
him."

Later that day, as Moses and Joshua hurried across the
plain, they heard shouts, drum-beats and the clash of metal.
"There's fighting in the camp," said Joshua.

"Not fighting, singing," said Moses, and quickened his
steps. As he and Joshua came in sight of the camp, they saw
fires blazing, and naked figures prancing in the rain. The

golden calf stood in the centre of the camp, ringed by fires, and the Israelites were dancing round it in a long line, clapping, shouting, clashing pots and pans. Aaron stood alone on God's altar, fully dressed, with his stick held high in his hands.

Moses threw the stone writing-tablets down so hard that they shattered on the ground. He ran forward, elbowing the revellers aside, picked up the golden calf in both hands and hurled in into the fire on God's altar. The flames leapt up, as if the gold had been straw, and burned the calf to ash. Moses shouted, "Who is on the lord's side?" Joshua, Aaron and a dozen young men from Aaron's tribe, the Levites, ran to him. "God speaks," said Moses. "Take your swords. Go through the camp. Kill."

The men ran about their business. They hunted their fellow-Israelites through the rain-soaked camp, pulling them out of their tents and butchering them. They killed three thousand guilty men and women, and heaped their bodies by the rock where the calf had stood. When the slaughter was over, Moses ground the embers of the golden calf to powder. He filled a cauldron with water and sprinkled the golden ash on top. Then, one by one, he forced the survivors to cup their hands, scoop up the water, and drink their god.

The Promised Land

So, in God's name, Moses punished the Israelites' idolatry.* The people spent the rest of that day burying their dead, scattering the ashes of the fires and praying to God for mercy. Moses picked up the stone splinters with God's writing still burned on them, and God miraculously renewed them, making his orders plain for all to see. The Israelites hurried to obey him, building a tabernacle and establishing priests (from the tribe of Levi, the only people who had refused to worship the golden calf), ceremonies and ways of worship.

At first none of these signs of obedience satisfied God. The Israelites had made an idol and worshipped it. Unknowingly or not, they had broken his first commandment; the punishment was death. But gradually God's rage lessened, and he spared the Israelites' lives. He sent a pillar of smoke to hover over the tabernacle by day and a pillar of fire at night, signs of his presence. He told the people that he would lead them to the Promised Land. But that was all he promised. He was still alert for disobedience, and quick to anger.

The people reached the borders of the Promised Land in a few weeks' wandering, and sent Joshua, Caleb and ten other young men to spy out the land and its defences. The spies brought back bunches of ripe grapes, and reported rich, fertile countryside, the land of milk and honey God had guaranteed. But they also spoke of fortified villages, walled towns and armies of defenders, and the Israelites panicked. In their terror they forgot God and turned instead to Moses, begging him to lead them straight back across the desert to Egypt, and crying that slavery was preferable to death. God punished them by keeping them in the wilderness, lost, not for days or weeks but for forty more years, trudging from oasis to oasis across empty sand. One by one, all those who had left Egypt as adults fell ill and died, except only Joshua and Caleb; none but the children were allowed to set foot in the Promised Land. This was the Israelites' punishment for distrusting God. They spent their lives struggling to reach a goal none of them lived to see.

In the end, even Moses himself was punished for disobeying God. When the people were dying of thirst in the Negev sand-desert, Moses begged God to send water as he had done before, in the Wilderness of Sin. God told him to stand before a rock and order it, in God's name, to gush water. Instead of obeying God exactly, Moses took his stick and struck the rock. God sent water, as he had promised. But he punished Moses' one small act of disobedience by barring him from ever setting foot in the Promised Land. Moses saw it, looking down into the Jordan valley from the peak of Mount Pisgah northeast of the Salt Sea. But in that same moment God ended his mortal life, and the people buried him on the mountain-side and mourned him.

4 · WARRIORS

Joshua

Moses' death left his people bewildered. They were like children without a parent. They stood on the mountainside and waited for a miracle. God called Joshua secretly aside and said, "Take Moses' place. Lead the people down the mountain, across the river Jordan and into the Promised Land. Be ready for war. I have promised your people the land, till the end of time. But there are already settlers there, and none of them will welcome you. If you want your rights, you'll have to fight for them."

Joshua stood on a boulder, surrounded by the group of young warriors loyal to him. He ordered the people to follow him down the mountain. The Israelites were terrified. Their parents had told them Joshua's own report of the Promised Land, forty years before – and the story had lost nothing in the telling. They believed that the Promised Land was fertile and fruitful, that its rivers flowed with milk and its trees dripped honey. But they were also sure that it was ruled by giants, who gorged on living flesh and crunched the bones.*
The Israelites might have followed Moses, a gentle, peaceable old man they had known and respected all their lives. But Joshua was a soldier, hard-faced and unflinching – why should he care if hundreds of people died, so long as the Promised Land was won? How gladly they would have scurried back to the safety of the desert, as their parents had done in Moses' time! But their terror of giants was surpassed by their fear of Joshua and his armed young men. Muttering and mutinous, they straggled down the mountain and set up camp in a rocky gorge of the river Jordan, with the mountain at

their backs and the fast-flowing river in front of them – too swift and deep, they hoped, even for giants to cross.

While the people put up tents and lit fires for the evening meal, Joshua called to two of his young men and said, "Cross the river. Go to Jericho. See whether its people want peace or war."

The men walked obediently out of camp, to a bend in the Jordan where the river was broad and the current weak. Bundling their clothes on their heads to keep them dry, they waded and swam across. Then they made their way stealthily to Jericho, a town built on a palm-fringed hill and surrounded by high brick walls. The men slipped inside the city gates, and asked for shelter at the first house they came to: a flat-roofed lean-to against the city wall. Rahab, the house's owner, welcomed them and gave them a meal. But when they asked for a bed for the night she said, "No. The whole town's alert for strangers. The gate-guards will have noticed you slipping in. Later, when the gates are locked for the night, soldiers will come searching, and if they find you they'll kill you. Come with me. You'll need to hide."

She took them by a ladder to the flat roof of the house, just below the parapet of the city wall. Flax was spread on the roof to dry in the sun, and Rahab's distaff lay beside it, with a basket of spun linen thread. Rahab told the Israelites to lie down on the roof, and then she spread flax over them, scattering it smoothly as if it had never been disturbed. When the soldiers came searching, they found no one at home but Rahab, spinning on the roof in the evening sun. The soldiers clattered away to report that the spies had fled, and a party of horsemen rode out of Jericho to hunt the Israelites down.

Rahab waited until darkness, then pulled back the flax-stalks and rescued the cramped, half-stifled Israelites. "Go back to Joshua," she said. "Tell him that all Jericho is terrified. We've heard how your God sends plagues and parts seas to help you. How can Jericho stand against you? I ask only one favour. When you and your God destroy the city, pay for your lives by saving mine. Ask Joshua to spare every living soul inside this house."

The spies eagerly agreed. They told Rahab to hang a line of scarlet thread from the window, to mark the house. Then, whatever the fate of the rest of Jericho, the Israelites would spare her house and everyone in it. Rahab took the men up to the city wall, and let them down on ropes into the darkness. They fled to the hills, and hid in caves for three days till the hue and cry died down. Then they forded the river and went to tell Joshua everything they'd seen and heard.

Joshua gathered the people on the river-bank. In his hand he held the stick God had given Moses to part the sea and strike water from the rock. "God speaks," he said. "Wherever the Ark of the Covenant goes, follow it. Make no sound; ask no questions; follow the Ark."

The Israelites looked at him distrustfully. What new plan was this? How would the Ark protect them, if giants attacked? Their distrust turned to alarm, as Joshua told the priests to pick up the Ark of the Covenant and carry it to the river-bank. Holding the Ark by its carrying-poles, the priests stood waiting on the very brink of Jordan. Joshua beckoned the people to draw near. He chose twelve young men, one from each tribe, and told them to pick up twelve large boulders from the river-side. Then he signed to the priests to move on, into the water. The people gasped in horror. But as soon as the Ark-carriers' feet touched the river-surface, the water drained away under them. The torrent became a brook, the brook became a trickle, and the trickle soaked into the mud and disappeared. Where there had once been a fast-flowing river, there was a bed of muddy gravel, strewn with boulders and with floundering, grounded fish. Joshua urged the Ark-carriers across, until they were standing where the centre of the river, the deepest and widest stretch of water, had once been. Then he shouted to the Israelites, "No questions. Follow the Ark!", and began leading them across. The twelve young men went first carrying their boulders, and the rest of the people followed. Timidly, testing the mud for firmness, they began to cross slowly and reluctantly, driving their animals. But when they came to the middle, and realised that they were half-way across, they quickened their steps and ran to the other side, gasping and hysterical. When they were all across, Joshua signed to the Ark-carriers to join them – and as soon as the last man's feet were clear of the river-bed the water appeared again, welling up till the river was as fast-flowing and impassable as ever.

Joshua called to the boulder-carriers. "Make a stone-pile here on the bank," he said, "then in future years, when our children's children ask us 'Why are those stones there?', we can answer 'To remind us that God is all-powerful, and that we must obey him always.'"

After that, the people thought that they understood at last. God was not remote and terrifying, as he had seemed in Moses' time. He was like an army officer: they were his soldiers, and he was their general. He had drained the river and led them into the Promised Land – and he would go on leading them, whatever enemies they faced and whatever battles they had to fight. They were safe; not even giants could hurt them now. So they thought, as they bustled about on the shore of the Jordan, making camp, building watchfires, setting guards. But they were mistaken; they still had lessons to learn about obedience. Next morning, instead of arming them and leading them into battle, Joshua ordered them to dress in holiday clothes, and make a procession. They were to take no weapons: neither knives, sticks nor stones. Their children and animals were to wait in camp, while the procession made its way to Jericho. Seven priests playing trumpets would lead the way, and the Ark of the Covenant would follow them. And once again, whatever the people thought, they were to ask no questions. Until he ordered differently, they were to follow the Ark and make no sound at all.

The baffled Israelites followed Joshua inland to the hill where Jericho stood sweltering among its palms. The city's brick walls shimmered in the heat. The gates were shut and barred; there were no signs of life. Instead of marching up to the gates and demanding surrender, Joshua turned to one side and began leading the procession round the outside of the city, at the foot of the wall. The Ark-carriers and trumpeters followed him. The shuffle of feet and the occasional blare of trumpets were the only sounds in the hot morning air.

When the Ark and trumpeters had completed one circuit of the walls, Joshua turned, still without speaking, and led the procession away from Jericho and back to camp. For the rest of that day he sat in the shade, gripping Moses' stick in his hand and talking with his officers, and none of the Israelites dared to question him. Next morning he led the Ark-carriers, the trumpeters and the people on a second procession, and spent the rest of the day cheerfully talking, as before. The same thing happened on the next day, and the next, and for two more days after that. By this time the Israelites were making jokes of it. "The sun's up," they called to one another. "Time to take that walk." The people of Jericho, inside their fortress-walls, had grown equally used to what was happening. On the first two days, as the Ark of the Covenant followed the trumpeters round their city, and the brightly-dressed, silent line of Israelites shuffled after it in the dust, the townspeople had hidden in their houses, terrified. On the third day, they had begun to peep out of their windows, and a few curious children had even gone to look through the city gates before their parents ran out and hurried them home to safety. By the sixth day, when the procession had passed at the same time each morning and nothing else had happened, they were openly mocking the Israelites and their God, and on the morning of the seventh day they ran in crowds to the city walls, jostling to get the best view of the ridiculous spectacle underneath.

On the seventh morning the air was hot and still. The sky was the colour of dead leaves. No breezes stirred the palm-trees. No birds sang. The people of Jericho stood on their city walls and watched the Israelites gathering on the plain below. They saw Joshua climb on to a rock, and heard him giving the people orders in the Israelites' incomprehensible language. They saw the procession forming, and the Ark-carriers moving off, led by the seven trumpeters as usual. They watched the Israelites marching out of sight round the walls, and waited for them to reappear and turn back to camp as usual. But this time, instead of stopping, the silent procession walked a second time round Jericho, a third, a fourth, and on for seven times. By the end of the seventh circuit, as the exhausted, dusty Israelites were approaching the city gates for the last time, the heat overhead was stifling. The sky was the

colour of copper. The Israelites bunched outside the city
gates, footsore and sweltering. The carriers rested the Ark on
the ground. For a moment there was silence. Then Joshua
signed with his stick, the trumpeters blew fanfare after fanfare, and the whole crowd of Israelites lifted their arms and
began shouting in praise of God. At once, as if the sudden
noise had ripped the air apart, the sky boomed, dust covered
the sun and the ground began to heave and shudder, shoul-
dering Jericho aside as a person shakes off a cloak. The brick
walls crumbled; the beams of the houses splintered; tiles fell
like rain. For a while, as their city crashed around them, the
people screamed, their cries blending with the earthquake-
rumble and the Israelites' trumpet-calls and triumph-shouts.
But by the time the air had cleared and the dust had settled, all
sound had ceased. The Israelites stood where they were, and
gaped. Where a prosperous, fortified city had once stood,
there was a hill of rubble. Dust bowed the trees and choked
the water-channels. Except for a terrified donkey, still tethered to the stump of a shattered tree, there were no signs of
life. In a city that had once held thousands, only one house
was left standing: the wooden lean-to that was the home of
Rahab and her family. The city wall had crumbled away from
it, leaving it open to the sky. But the house itself was
untouched: the flax-covered roof, the wooden walls, the ladder, the window with its line of scarlet thread. Inside, Rahab
stood protecting her parents, with the rest of her family
huddled beside her. Like Joshua and the Israelites outside the
city, they stood without moving or speaking, dazed by the
power of God.

Gideon

At first, the fall of Jericho gave the Israelites confidence. They
trusted God, and were sure that if they kept his commandments he would protect them against all enemies. They
trusted Joshua too, and followed his orders without question.
For several years he kept them together as a single group, too
large and well-organised for enemies to overwhelm. They

tended their animals; they sowed and harvested; the other peoples of the Promised Land left them in peace. But then Joshua, thinking that the Israelites were secure at last, that unfaltering belief in God would guarantee prosperity wherever they went, decided to divide the Promised Land among them. He allotted a different region to each of the twelve tribes, and told them to conquer the local people or live in peace with them, as they chose; all that mattered was that they kept faith with God.

So long as Joshua lived, this scattering of the people caused no problems. But after his death a new generation of Israelites grew up, people who had not been alive to see the fall of Jericho, people to whom God's power was little more than an old wives' tale. One by one, they began to turn from God and to worship the same nature-spirits and idols as their heathen neighbours. There was a whole family of these gods, called Baalim, and their leader was Baal. Baal-worship involved not merely prayer and sacrifice, but orgies of drink, sex and ecstatic dancing when the priests gashed themselves with knives.

As the Israelites turned from God, their power weakened. One by one, their communities disappeared. Some people intermarried with their neighbours, went to live in heathen farms and villages, and abandoned God for Baal. Others tried to keep to their own religion, but were conquered and enslaved by idolators, so that the only time they spoke to God was to blame him for their plight. A few, led by descendants of Joshua's young warriors, turned to guerrilla-warfare, swooping on heathen settlements and carrying off booty to the hills. The whole Promised Land was in confusion; there was no peace in it. Earthquakes, floods and storms might have terrified the people back to God. But the Israelites had to choose him for themselves, to worship him not out of fear but of their own free will. Accordingly God decided, from time to time as the years passed, to inspire one man or woman to bravery, to lead true worshippers against the heathen; God hoped, each time, that victory would make the Israelites remember the Ten Commandments and abandon Baal.

Sometimes God's plans worked perfectly, because human beings did exactly as he hoped. When Eglon, the grossly fat tyrant of the heathen Moabites, conquered the Israelite settlement built in the ruins of Jericho, enslaving the people, God roused an Israelite called Ehud to save them. Ehud hid a dagger under his clothes, went to Eglon's palace and announced that he had a secret message which could be delivered to the king alone. The fat king, as bloated as a barrel, shooed his servants out of the room and waddled from the throne to hear Ehud's words more closely. When he was near enough Ehud stabbed him in the belly, so hard that the whole dagger disappeared, its blade and hilt engulfed in fat. Ehud slipped out of the room, locking the doors behind him, and hurried into the hills before Eglon's courtiers discovered the body. Then, as soon as the heathen began wailing and panicking, Ehud blew his war-trumpet, rallied the Israelites and slaughtered the idolators. This victory encouraged the Israelites to worship God once more, and there was peace for eighty years.

At other times, God's chosen champions failed him. They saved the people, but in their zeal they went too far, behaving more like bloodthirsty idolators than true believers. When Sisera, captain of the Canaanite army, went with a force of nine hundred charioteers to enslave the Israelites, God gave Israel the victory – and human over-eagerness turned it to disaster. Sisera, alone of all his army, survived the battle, and took refuge in the tent of Heber the Kenite, an ally he thought he could trust. Heber's wife Jael gave Sisera milk to drink and a pillow to rest on – and then, when he was asleep, took a mallet and drove a tent-peg through his skull. This bloodthirsty and unnecessary act was surpassed only by Jephthah, an Israelite war-leader many years later, fighting the heathen Amorites. Jephtha prayed to God for victory, and promised, if his prayer was answered, to sacrifice the first creature he saw when he went home from the battle. The first creature was not a chicken or a lamb, the usual sacrificial animals, but Jephthah's own beloved daughter – and still Jephthah kept his promise, so insulting God by human sacrifice, an act even Baal-worshippers despised.

The most unlikely Israelite hero was Gideon. He was a farmer's son, no fighter, and lived at a time when God sent

raiders from Midian to attack the Promised Land. The Midianites were desert warriors from beside the Red Sea, and they
swarmed like locusts into the Promised Land. They plundered the Israelites' farms, killed their animals, ate the crops
in the fields and the seed-corn in the barns, and murdered
anyone who stood in their way. The Israelites took to the
hills, skulking in caves and wailing for Baal to help them. At
last, when the people had suffered for their idolatry for seven
years, God's angel went down to Gideon and said, "The Lord
be with you, General. God has chosen you to drive the
Midianites out of Israel."

"Why me?" asked Gideon. "I'm a farmer, my father's
youngest son. How can I save Israel?"

"God has chosen you, and God will help you."

"If God has chosen me," said Gideon suspiciously, "show
me a sign to prove it."

For answer, the angel touched the meal of bread and meat
on the rock between them. Fire billowed from the rock and
charred the food to ash, and when the flames died down the
angel had disappeared. Gideon fell on his knees and prayed
to God. That night, as soon as it was dark, he called ten loyal
servants, took a bull from his father's byre and went down the
mountainside to a grove of trees sacred to Baal. In the darkness the servants attacked the trees with saws and axes, and
felled them all. Gideon built an altar of boulders, piled it with
branches and sacrificed the bull to God. The noise of axes and
the smell of fire roused Gideon's father and his neighbours.
The neighbours crowded round Gideon and the terrified
servants, stones in their hands and fury in their eyes. "They
cut down the sacred grove," they shouted. "They insulted
Baal. Kill them!"

"No," said Gideon's father. "It's you who insult Baal, if
you do his work for him. If he's offended by Gideon, let him
punish my son himself."

This speech saved Gideon's life. The people dropped their
stones and instead started spitting and jeering at him. "Fool!"
they shouted. "You've challenged Baal, greatest of gods.
Stand here and die!" Then they ran back up the mountain to
their caves, leaving Gideon and the servants by the still-
smoking altar, waiting their fate.

Gideon fell on his knees, and the terrified servants knelt beside him. "Oh God," he said, "please help me. If you truly mean me to lead the people against the Midianites, send a second sign. Let me spread a sheepskin on the ground, and in the morning when the dew has fallen, let the ground around be dry and the fleece alone be wet." He spread a fleece on the ground, and he and the servants crouched beside it, waiting for dawn. As soon as the sun rose Gideon picked up the fleece. The ground all round was dry, but the fleece was so wet that Gideon was able to wring a bowlful of water out of it. Gideon's servants ran whooping up the hill to report the miracle. But Gideon was still not convinced. "One more sign," he said to God. "Tomorrow morning let the ground be wet and the fleece be dry." He spent the day praying and the night watching, and took no notice of the crowds of people who gathered to see the miracle. Next morning at sunrise, though the ground was sodden with dew the fleece was so dry that Gideon could shake dust from it in handfuls. The people fell on their knees, worshipping God and honouring Gideon as their leader who would save them from the Midianites. In the days that followed messengers galloped to all the Israelite hill-strongholds, calling the tribes to war. People began gathering, by tens, hundreds and and even thousands. At the end of a week it seemed to Gideon that the entire population of Israel, men, women and children, was standing in front of him waiting to be led to war. And in the valley below, drawn up and ready to fight, was the Midianite army: well-armed, well-trained, never yet defeated.

"Oh God," said Gideon, "what can I do with all these people? We're unarmed, untrained: what chance have we?"

"Tell them to look at the Midianites, and count the cost of a battle. Then if anyone's afraid, let them go home."

Gideon gave the people these orders, and the crowd soon thinned to half. "Lord," said Gideon. "There are still thousands of them. What do I do next?"

"Take them to the river, and tell them to drink. Send away any who kneel or bend to drink, like animals. Keep only those who scoop up water in their hands."

Once again Gideon passed on God's orders, and this time, out of the whole nation of Israel, only three hundred men remained. By now it was dark, and down in the valley the Midianites were camping for the night. Gideon's three hundred men crowded round him. "Sir, we're ready," they said. "Give us our weapons; we'll attack at dawn."

"No," said Gideon. "You need no weapons – and we attack tonight."

He divided the men into three companies of a hundred. He gave each man a ram's horn, a jug and a lamp. Then, when he was sure that they understood their orders, he sent two companies down the hill, and gathered the third group round himself. "Light your lamps," he said. "Then hide them in the jugs, and follow me." He crept down the hill in the darkness, and the men followed him. Each man held his ram's horn in one hand and his jug in the other, with the lamp hidden inside it. Gideon led them to one side of the Midianite camp, stealthily so as not to alert the guards. As soon as his men were in position, he put his ram's horn to his lips and blew. At once his hundred men smashed their jugs on rocks, held their lamps high, blew the rams'-horn trumpets and shouted, "The sword of the Lord, and of Gideon!" – and on the other side of the Midianite camp, and in the hills above it, the other two Israelite companies did the same. The Midianite soldiers, roused from sleep by what they took for army fanfares, saw lights and heard battle-cries all round them. They panicked. Stumbling over one another in their haste, they snatched their weapons and ran about in confusion. In their terror they mistook one another for the enemy, and began hacking and stabbing in the darkness. Soon the whole camp was filled with cursing, struggling men, slipping on the corpses of their own dead comrades while Gideon's three companies stood where they were, blowing their horns and shouting their war-cries. The struggle was quickly over. The surviving Midianites suddenly gave in to their panic, streamed out of camp and began floundering and splashing downriver to make their escape. But whenever they tried to scramble up the banks to safety, they found Israelite farmers waiting, encouraged by darkness and carrying knives. The river ran red with blood, and at sunrise next morning messengers galloped to Gideon with the heads of Oreb and Zeeb, the enemy commanders. God had helped Israel defeat the Midianite hordes, and not a single Israelite had been harmed.*

Samson

God's angel appeared to a childless man and woman who lived in southern Israel. The angel promised to end their childlessness, and said that if they dedicated their son to God and marked the promise by never letting him cut his hair, from birth to death, the boy would grow up to be the strongest man in the world. The couple gladly agreed. When their child was born they named him Samson ("little sun"), and as he grew up they never cut his hair, but instead parted it in seven long locks to show that he belonged to God. All through his childhood, Samson was the strongest boy in the village. At three he could lift water-skins twice his own size; at seven he could run from bottom to top of the mountainside before his friends were halfway up; at twelve he used to yoke himself in place of a pair of oxen, and plough three fields unaided in a single afternoon. But his strength had a dark side, too. When it was time for sacrifice, instead of handing the lamb or kid to the slaughterer in the normal way, he picked the animal up barehanded and tore it limb from limb.

Samson's village lay on a hillside overlooking the wide plain-country of the Philistines. His people's fields bordered on Philistine land, and often Israelites and Philistines, sowing or harvesting, were separated by no more than a cart-track or a line of boundary-stones. But the two peoples despised each other, and never mingled. The Philistines bowed down to Dagon, an idol; the Israelites worshipped God. The Israelites drove cattle to market or took produce to sell in Philistine villages, and the Philistines tolerated them; but the relationship was never more than wary politeness, and both sides carried arms. Samson, however, cared nothing for such ideas. When he was fifteen he started going to the plain not to market but for pleasure, and spent his time with Philistine girls. When he was sixteen he said to his father and mother, "I want to marry a girl from Timnath. Please arrange a wedding."

"Timnath!" said his parents, horrified. "That's a Philistine town. Why can't you marry one of your own people? Why must you choose a foreigner?"

They argued and pleaded. But nothing would change Samson's mind. In the morning he set out for Timnath with his parents. The parents rode on donkeys, trembling at the thought of visiting idolators; Samson walked beside them. They reached the foot of the hill and began to cross the plain towards the vineyards of Timnath. Gradually Samson's eagerness overcame him and he lengthened his steps, leaving his parents and the donkeys far behind. He was just coming out of the vineyards on to the village road when a lion leapt out at him. It had been tempted from the mountains by the flocks and herds pasturing on the plain below, and now took Samson for easy prey and sprang at him. He snatched it in mid-air, tore it limb from limb as he was used to tearing lambs and kids, and threw its carcase into the weeds beside the road. Then he waited for his parents to catch up, and led them into the village without mentioning the lion. They rode to Samson's girl's house, and although at first the two sets of parents, Israelites and Philistines, were stiff and distrustful, they finally shook hands and the wedding was arranged. A few weeks later, when Samson went down to Timnath again to fetch his bride, he passed the lion's carcase beside the road, and found that wild bees had made a nest in it and filled it with honey. The sight gave Samson an idea. When the young men of his bride's family climbed the hill for the wedding feast, he met them on the way and said, "I've a riddle to ask you. If you guess the answer, I'll give you thirty sheets and thirty new suits of clothes; if you don't, you give sheets and clothes to me."

The young Philistines cracked their knuckles and said, "Ask any riddle you like. We'll answer it."

Samson said, "Out of the feeder came food, and out of the strong came sweetness. How?"

For three days, through all the wedding celebrations, the young Philistines racked their brains to answer the riddle, and could think of nothing. At last they took their relative, the bride, aside and said, "It's up to you. Trick the answer out of him. If you don't, we're ruined."

For the next four days, instead of laughing and dancing as before, Samson's bride stamped her foot and sulked. No one could make her smile; when anyone spoke to her, she screamed. At last Samson took her aside and asked what the matter was. She looked into his eyes and said, "Tell me the answer to the riddle."

"I've told no one," said Samson. "Not even my mother and father know. Wait; you'll hear it with the others."

"No," shrieked the girl. "Tell me now!"

Samson sighed and told her about the lion and the bees – and she ran straight to her relatives with the answer. The young men immediately demanded the thirty sheets and thirty new suits of clothes, and Samson ran furiously down the hill, picked a quarrel with the first thirty Philistines he saw and took their sheets and clothes. After that no one dared to face him. The Philistines married their daughter to someone else – and when Samson knocked at their door and demanded his bride, they insultingly tried to fob him off with her younger sister, a child of six. Samson gathered three hundred wild dogs, tied firebrands to their tails and sent them running through the Philistines' fields and farms. The fire destroyed everything: corn, vines, olive-trees and walnut-groves – and the Philistine farmers, too afraid to attack Samson himself, retaliated by burning the farm-buildings of their own kinsman, Samson's father-in-law, with the farmer and his family inside. At this Samson's fury overflowed. He rounded up the murderers and killed them – and when the Philistines sent an army to deal with him, he ran out armed with an ass's jawbone and killed a thousand men.*

After that, it was only Samson's existence which guaranteed peace between Israelites and Philistines. The Philistines realised that however many men they sent they would be no match for Samson; the Israelites knew that unless he led them they would be overwhelmed by the enemy – and Samson refused to fight. He was ashamed at the deaths his strength and his temper had already caused, and he vowed to spend the rest of his life quietly, serving God. For twenty years he patrolled the fields of the hillside and the plain, huge as a bear, and fear of his anger kept Philistines and Israelites from each other's throats.

Samson had only one weakness: women. He usually fell in love with Israelite girls from nearby farms and villages. But sometimes Philistine women caught his eye, and he spent weeks courting them, visiting their houses in the plain, taking them presents, spending days and nights with them while his people wrung their hands at the danger and the Philistines tried to think of ways to use his weakness to topple him.* At last they formed a plan. They bribed a woman called Delilah to trap him. "Make him fall in love with you," they said. "Make him promise to tell you anything you ask. Then find out the secret of his strength, and leave the rest to us."

Delilah was the most beautiful woman Samson had ever seen. She had no trouble making him fall in love. But at first not even she could charm him into telling the secret of his strength. She asked him three times, and he told her three different stories: that if he were tied with green willow shoots, or with new ropes, or had his hair woven into the cloth on Delilah's loom, he would be helpless. But each time, when Delilah took him at his word, bound him and then called soldiers to arrest him, Samson broke free of the bonds and scattered the men as easily as a bull flicks flies. After the third time Delilah said angrily, "Samson, don't you trust me? If you love me, prove it by telling me the truth."

To her surprise tears ran down Samson's face. "Of course I love you," he said. "But the truth makes me ashamed. Before I was born my parents dedicated my life to God. I should be on my knees praying, not making love with an idolator. My parents promised that I would never cut my hair as long as I lived, and in return God made me the strongest man in the world."

"Poor Samson!" said Delilah. "Kneel now, and pray. I won't interfere."

But when Samson finished praying, before he could get up, she took his head in her lap. She combed his beard with her fingers; she stroked his forehead and kissed his eyelids, murmuring words of love. Before long Samson was asleep in her lap – and at once she signed for her servant to bring a razor, and shaved the seven locks of hair from Samson's head. The servant ran to fetch the soldiers, and this time when they burst into the room and Delilah shook Samson awake, he was as weak as a baby in their arms. Whooping with delight, the Philistines bound him and threw him into an ox-cart. They took him for trial to the town of Gaza, and the magistrates sentenced him to blindness and the corn-mill. The soldiers gouged out his eyes, fettered him with brass chains and manacled him to a grindstone attached to an enormous pole. Then they forced him to walk round and round in a circle, endlessly pushing the pole to grind the corn. Day in, day out, he worked in the glare of the sun, while the Philistines gathered to mock his sightless eyes and the tufts of hair sprouting on his skull. "Look at him!" they jeered. "Samson the Strong, our enemy! Lord Dagon saw him burn our crops and murder our people, and gave him to us for punishment. Praise be to Dagon, god of gods."

After a few months, instead of running to jeer at Samson in prison, the Philistines took to dragging him out at dances and festivals. They set him feats of strength – wrestling calves, carrying boulders, challenging the strongest men in the kingdom to tugs-o'-war – and mocked him when he failed. All this time, for month after month, Samson said nothing. He turned his sightless face towards the jeering, spitting crowds, did whatever he was told and made no complaint. But all the time, while his hair grew long again, he prayed to God to give back his strength. The time came for the Philistines' main festival of the year, to honour Dagon at harvest-time. Thousands of them crowded into Gaza to praise their god. They set up a wooden statue in the courtyard of Dagon's temple, and crowned it with flowers. For six days priests sacrificed, musicians played and dancing-girls twirled while the watching crowds filled the courtyard and the balconies all round it. On the last day of the festival the people began stamping their feet and calling for Samson to be brought from prison to entertain them. Guards led him into the temple, and he stood in the gateway, his body filthy and his hair knotted and straggling to his shoulders. He ignored the jeering crowd and the soldiers' whips, and turned his face to heaven, praying silently for strength. Then he stretched out his arms, and the crowd fell silent to see what he would do. There were two pillars supporting the balcony above the temple gate: whole tree-trunks, set in stone. Samson stood between them with his arms outstretched, took hold of them, bent double and began to pull inwards with all his strength. The people jeered. "Who does he think he is? What's he trying to do? A blind man, a weakling – does he really hope to pull a whole temple down?" Samson took no notice. He tugged at the pillars till the veins knotted on his arms and the blood thudded in his chest. Crumbs of plaster fell from the balcony; fragments of stone broke away where the pillars were set into the ground. At first there was nothing else. But then Samson shouted, in a voice which echoed round the temple and made the Philistines look at one another in wild alarm, "O God, give me strength! Let me punish the Philistines who stole my eyes. Let me die with them!" At once, with a crack of splitting timber, the wooden pillars shattered in his hands. The balcony collapsed, dragging blocks of masonry from the temple roof and funnelling the spectators, helpless as netted fish, down on to the heads of the crowd in the courtyard below. The temple was filled with screaming people, scrabbling free of the rubble and the broken corpses of the dead. And under them all, in the heart of the destruction, lay Samson, his hands still clutching the splintered pillars. God had answered his prayers and restored his strength. In his death he killed more enemies than in all his life; he triumphed over the idolators, and showed God's power.

5 · RUTH

Ruth and Naomi

Once, when there was famine in Bethlehem, a poor farm-labourer took his wife Naomi and his two young sons across the river Jordan to look for work. After six days' walking they came to a bowl of fertile land: grain-fields and sheep-pastures on a plateau east of the Dead Sea. The people were Moabites, idolators, but they welcomed the family and found them work. The Bethlehemites stayed for ten years, and when the boys grew up they married two local girls, Orpah and Ruth. It seemed as if they would settle for good in Moab. They kept the Ten Commandments and prayed three times a day to God, but in every other way they followed the customs of their neighbours. But then, in their eleventh summer away from home, the father and both his sons fell ill and died. Naomi, Ruth and Orpah were widowed in a single morning. The women mourned their husbands for seven days as custom demanded, and then Naomi said, "It's time I went home to Bethlehem, to my own people. It's their duty to look after me in my old age. But you stay here, with your own people and your own gods. You're young; you'll find new husbands here."

Orpah kissed her mother-in-law, packed her belongings and went sadly home to her parents. But Ruth said, "Naomi, let me go with you; let me live with you and die with you. Make your home my home, your people my people, your God my God."

The two women wrapped their belongings in shawls and began the six-day walk to Bethlehem. They slept each night in caves or under trees, huddled together against wild animals, and came into the village early in the morning, just as gangs of reapers were setting out to harvest the barley-fields. Separate groups of men and women were hurrying to work, carrying sickles and long-handled wooden rakes. Naomi and Ruth veiled their faces and drew back to let them pass. "Good morning, mistress," said one of the women cheerfully. "Aren't you Naomi, who went with your husband years ago to look for work?"

Naomi was embarrassed. How could she face her old friends and neighbours, now that she was a widow and a beggar? "Call me Bitterness," she said in a low voice. "After everything I've suffered, what other name should I have?"

Ruth and Naomi set up house in a disused donkey-stable which Naomi's husband had owned before he went to Moab. It was a single room, made of stones piled loosely together and roofed with straw. The ground round it was as hard as rock; they had no tools to dig it, and no seeds to sow in it. With tears in her eyes, Naomi put down her bundle and took out a jug to fetch water from the public well. Ruth said, "Naomi, let me go to the reapers in the fields. Perhaps they'll give me food."

"Ask them to let you glean," said Naomi. "When grain-heads fall from the bundles, the law says that beggars can pick them up and keep them. Gather them in your shawl; see if you can bring back enough for us to eat tonight."

Ruth walked to the fields and began gleaning, in a corner apart from all the other women. The field had already been gleaned, but there were still a few scattered grain-heads, left by kind-hearted people to feed the birds. Ruth spread her shawl and began to glean. By mid-day she had collected a double handful of barley-grains. Her back ached and she was dry with thirst, but she was afraid to stop working in case someone else came up and stole her gleaning-place.

The fields' owner was a wealthy farmer called Boaz, a bachelor. God put it into his mind to saddle a donkey and ride out to see how the harvest was progressing. He asked the overseer of his reapers, "Who is that woman, gleaning in the far field? She's never been here before."

"Sir," said the overseer, "That's Ruth, who came from Moab to look after her mother-in-law Naomi."

Boaz rode across the field to Ruth. She veiled her face and bent her head. "Don't be afraid," he said. "Go where the women are reaping, and glean there. Ask them for water when you're thirsty, and for food at meal-times."

"Sir," said Ruth, "I'm a newcomer, a stranger – why are you so kind to me?"

"Why shouldn't I be?" said Boaz. "For your mother-in-law's sake you left your own village and your own people. You chose us; you put us first. God saw, and God rewards."

Ruth bent her head, and Boaz wheeled his donkey and trotted away. He told the reaping-gangs to let Ruth glean where she liked, and to drop grain-heads for her on purpose. By the end of the afternoon her shawl was full of barley, and when she stripped it from the stalks and took it home there was enough to feed her and Naomi for several days.

Ruth and Boaz

Ruth gleaned in Boaz's fields throughout the barley harvest and the wheat harvest that followed it. Every day Boaz rode past on his donkey, to check that his reapers were treating her well and leaving her plenty of grain to gather. He often reined in at the side of the field to speak to her, and Ruth blushed each time, bent her head humbly and veiled her face. She knew that Boaz was a cousin of Naomi's dead husband, and therefore her own distant relative by marriage. But he was rich and she was poor, he could throw her off his land any time he chose – why did he go on being so kind to her?

When Ruth went home on the last day of harvest Naomi said, "Boaz and his men have been winnowing all afternoon. He'll spend tonight on guard on the threshing-floor beside his barn. As soon as it's dark and everyone's asleep, go and lie at his feet."

"Why?"

"God is helping us, Ruth. He's telling us what to do. Don't argue: do exactly as he says."

That night, as soon as it was dark, Ruth crept through the empty streets to Boaz's farmyard, and into the threshing-

floor beside the barn. She found Boaz asleep beside a high pile
of grain. Without a word, as Naomi had told her, she wrapped herself in her cloak and lay down at his feet. Just before
dawn, God woke Boaz with a sudden start. He sensed someone at his feet, sat up stealthily and reached for his stick.
"Who's there?" he whispered. "Who are you? What d'you
want?"

Ruth answered with the words Naomi had taught her. "My
lord, your servant speaks. In God's name I beg you: help me,
protect me, grant my prayer."

Boaz's heart was filled with love. But he stood up, coldly
and firmly as a master should before his servants, and said,
"Go home, Ruth. This is no place for you to be alone at night.
In the morning, I'll do all you ask."

He told Ruth to hold out her shawl, and began filling it
with winnowed grain, as much as she could carry. Then he led
her to the gate, watched her hurry home in the pale dawn
light, and knelt down to ask God what to do.

Later that morning Boaz sat down in the market-place, in
the shade of the wall beside the village gate. Everyone who
went in or out of Bethlehem passed that way, and each time
Boaz saw one of the village elders he called to the man to sit
down: there was business to discuss. When ten elders were
gathered, Boaz sent a boy to fetch an eleventh man, the head
of Boaz's own family and the closest living relative to
Naomi's dead husband. As soon as the man arrived, Boaz
called for cool drinks and said, "My friends, you know the
law. Ten village elders make a council, a court of law. Any
decisions made before you are legal, and must be kept. I have
a distant cousin by marriage, Naomi. She owns a patch of
land just big enough to hold one small donkey-stable. She
wants to sell it, and I say that her husband's nearest relative
should have first chance to buy. If he refuses, I'll buy the land
myself."

The relative sipped his drink and said, "Boaz, the law says
that the nearest relative always buys a dead man's land, and
looks after his widow. I know Naomi well; I've no objection.
I'll buy the land."

"There's just one thing," said Boaz. "There are two widows
in this case, not one: Naomi and Ruth, her daughter-in-law.

If you buy the land, it's your duty not only to look after Naomi, but also to marry Ruth and give her children."

The relative jumped up in alarm. "I can't do that!" he cried. "I've a wife and children already. What would they say if I brought two more women home?"

"So you give up all claim to buy this land?"

"Exactly!"

Boaz turned to the elders. "Since my friend gives up his claim," he said, "I promise before you all to do everything myself, as the law demands. I'll buy the land; I'll look after Naomi; I'll marry Ruth."

Not long afterwards, the village filled with dancing and singing to celebrate the wedding of Boaz and Ruth. Ruth and Naomi moved into Boaz's house, and Boaz's donkey settled in the stable, their former home. In a year's time, God blessed Ruth and Boaz with a son. They called the baby Obed, and gave him to his grandmother Naomi to hold. As Naomi smiled down at the child, the bitterness of her husband's and sons' deaths left her heart at last, and she thanked God for sending her such happiness.

6 · THE COMING OF THE KINGS

In all their years of exile in Egypt, and throughout their desert wanderings, the Israelites had always looked forward to the Promised Land as a pleasant, fertile country, a place "flowing with milk and honey" – and so it was. It might be ringed by desert and ribbed by high, bare hills, but in the river-valleys and oases, wherever there was water, it was like a second Garden of Eden. Trees anchored the soil; the paths were bright with flowers; crops flourished; sheep, goats and cattle browsed, their bells tinkling in the hot, still air.

For the first few years after the Israelites crossed the river Jordan, the other inhabitants of the Holy Land had treated them with suspicion. But gradually the twelve tribes and their neighbours had come to live in peace. Their interests were the same: they were all shepherds and farmers, not fighters, and guided their lives by the cycles of sowing and harvest, lambing and marketing, rather than by war. After a while, even religious differences began to disappear. The Baal-worshippers treated God as just another nature-spirit, and the Israelites corrupted their own worship with such idolatrous practices as paid priests, wine-drinking and dancing-girls. In the end, even at their most sacred place, the shrine at Shiloh where the Ark of the Covenant was kept, the few true worshippers were often elbowed aside by drunks who went there less to pray to God than for orgies of drink and sex. If the priests had been strong-minded, they might have stopped it. But for generation after generation they were either terrified of their own congregations, or interested in nothing but profit. One man, Eli, survived as priest for over sixty years, unable to control either the visitors to the sanctuary or his own sons, who boasted of the fortunes they would make as

priests when their father died, and who in the meantime sold
their services, charging worshippers fees and demanding a
share of every sacrifice.

All this time, while the people of the Promised Land had
been growing soft and complacent, their enemies the Philistines had been planning war. The Philistines meant to rule
the entire stretch of land from Egypt to Syria. Until now they
had concentrated on conquering the desert peoples to the
south, as far as the Egyptian border. Now they were ready to
move north, and they expected no trouble from the peaceful
farmers and animal-breeders of the Promised Land. It was
time for God to warn his people.

Samuel

A devout hill-farmer – one of the few true worshippers left in
the Promised Land – had two wives, Peninnah and Hannah.
Every year for a dozen years, Peninnah had borne a son or a
daughter; the farm bulged with her children, laughing, playing, filling the house with noise. Hannah, by contrast, was
barren. Although she was devoted to her husband, and he to
her, they had produced no children in eleven years of marriage. "It's your fault," Peninnah jeered at Hannah. "Look
how many children he's given me. You must have offended
God – why else should you be barren, except as a punishment?"

Every year, the farmer and his wives went on pilgrimage to
Shiloh, to see the sanctuary and to pray to God. The farmer
and Peninnah stood facing the wall of the shrine, he with the
men and she with the women, and prayed aloud as custom
was. The farmer thanked God for his help in the past year,
and asked for continued prosperity for the farm and everyone
who worked there. Peninnah reminded God of the names of
all her children, thanked him for keeping them healthy and
happy, and told him how they'd grown and everything they'd
done in the year just past. As for Hannah, she crept to a dark
corner of the shrine and begged God silently to end her
childlessness. If he blessed her with a boy, she said in her

2

heart, she would not bring the child up as a farmer, but would dedicate him to God and send him to serve in the shrine.

One year Eli, the aged priest of Shiloh, was sitting sunning himself beside one of the pillars when he saw Hannah alone in the shadows, tears streaming down her cheeks and her lips moving soundlessly. "Go outside," he shouted. "God's shrine is no place for drunks."

"Oh sir," she said, "I was praying to God, not drunk. I was too ashamed to speak out loud."

Eli's heart filled with pity. He touched her gently on the cheek and said, "Go in peace. May God grant your prayer."

Soon afterwards, back at the farm, Hannah realised that she was pregnant, and the following summer she gave birth to a baby boy. Overjoyed, she called him Samuel ("named for God"), and as soon as he was old enough she took him to Shiloh, dedicated him to God as she'd promised and asked Eli to bring him up. The little boy grew up as a servant of the shrine, and when his mother visited Shiloh each year – now surrounded, like Peninnah, with children, for Samuel's birth had ended her barrenness – she brought him new clothes and shoes. But although she longed to take him in her arms and cuddle him, she never dared. He belonged to God now, not to her, and she contented herself with kneeling at her own son's feet and asking his blessing like a stranger.

From the time of Joshua, when the Ark of the Covenant had crossed the river Jordan and been carried to Shiloh, it had been customary for watchers to stay in the sanctuary, day and night. Originally they had been guards, looking out for thieves, but by Eli's time they were ordinary temple servants, and their duty was less to protect the Ark than to honour it, watching and praying. The sanctuary was dark and quiet, and for several years Eli thought Samuel too young to stay there on his own. But by the time the boy was seven or eight he was regularly taking his turn on watch, often unrolling a mattress and sleeping in the still, cool room, where a single lamp burned in the shadows. One night, just before dawn when the lamp was low, Samuel woke up to hear a voice calling his name. He ran to Eli's bedroom, and startled the old man awake by saying eagerly, "Here I am."

"What is it, child?"

"You called me. Here I am."

"I didn't call. Go back to bed."

But as soon as Samuel lay down in the sanctuary, the same voice called his name again. He woke Eli a second time crying "Here I am", Eli sent him back to bed, and exactly the same thing happened. By now Eli realised that Samuel was hearing more than dreams or imagination, and said, "If the voice calls again, answer it. Say 'Speak, Lord; your servant hears' – and tell me what happens next."

Samuel lay down again, and this time when the voice called his name he answered as Eli had told him: "Speak, Lord; your servant hears." At once the voice began filling his ears with terrible words. It said that Eli was old and weak, powerless to end his own sons' wickedness. The sons' blasphemy would bring destruction to all their family. Both they and Eli would die, and neither prayers nor sacrifices could prevent it. Samuel was terrified. In the morning, rather than face Eli and tell him what the voice had said, he decided to pretend that nothing had happened. He opened the sanctuary doors and began sprinkling the ground with water as usual, to lay the dust. But after a while he heard another voice calling "Samuel", and this time knew that it was Eli's. He went to the old man's room, dragging his feet, and said reluctantly, "Here I am."

"Child, tell me what God said."

"I daren't."

"Don't be afraid. The truth can't hurt. Tell me what God said."

Samuel burst into tears, and told Eli every word of the prophecy. The old man sighed. The words must truly have come from God – for how could an innocent child invent such things? Samuel was God's true prophet: when he grew up he would end the Israelites' idolatry and lead them back to God.* As for Eli and his sons, the course of their lives was set, and there was no changing it. The old man patted Samuel's head and said, "Don't cry, child. When God speaks, we must obey, not question. His will be done."

From that day on, throughout Samuel's childhood, he was terrified of standing alone in the sanctuary, in case he heard the voice again. What if he was mistaken? What if the words he'd heard came not from God at all, but from some evil spirit laying a trap for him? Twenty years passed, and no disaster happened to Eli or his sons. Samuel began to relax. Perhaps he was not to be a true prophet after all. He prayed to God daily to spare the old priest's life, to turn the sons from evil and prove that Samuel's own prophetic gifts were false.

But although twenty years pass slowly to mortals, to God and his angels they are no more than the blink of an eye, a moment in eternity. The time came when the Philistines at last thought themselves strong enough to attack the Promised Land. They swept east into the hills of Judah, overlooking the Dead Sea, and when the Israelites sent an army against them they killed four thousand men. The Israelite leaders, in panic, sent to Shiloh to ask God's help – and before Samuel could say a word to stop it, Eli's sons picked up the Ark of the Covenant and carried it on mule-back to the Israelite battle-line. "Why not take God to the battle?" they shouted. "Why wait till the battle comes to God?" At first the Philistines were terrified. But then they rallied their army, surged forward and attacked. The Israelites fled; Eli's sons were cut to pieces where they stood, and the Philistines picked up the Ark, carried it away shoulder high, and spent the night dancing and singing victory-songs. An Israelite messenger ran all the way to Shiloh. He found Eli sitting on a stone by the gate, anxious for news – and instead of telling him gently what had happened, blurted out, "The Ark's been captured! Your sons are dead!" Eli jumped up in horror – and his foot slipped on a stone so that he fell backwards, broke his neck and died. In this way God's words of twenty years before came true, and Samuel was proved a true prophet after all. He listened with tears streaming down his face as the people acclaimed him their priest and leader. He was priest of a God whose Ark had been captured by idolators, the leader of a people who fled from enemy attack.

Saul

The Philistines carried the Ark of the Covenant in procession to Ashdod, and set it up in Dagon's temple, in front of the statue. And when they went into the temple next morning, they found that the Ark was untouched, but that the idol had toppled over and was lying face-downwards in the dust before it. They set Dagon upright – and next morning he was grovelling before the Ark again, and his head and hands had been snapped off, so that he was no more than a splintered stump. At the same time plague ran through the town, infecting anyone who had touched the Ark, their families, their neighbours and everyone they met. In terror for their lives, the people of Ashdod moved the Ark to Ekron, another Philistine town – and the same thing happened there, the population gradually dying of plague. For seven months the Philistines shifted the Ark from one town or city to another, and wherever it went plague followed it. Rats ran through the streets, and people and animals swelled with boils and died. At last the survivors crawled to their kings and said, "Get rid of it! Send it back to Israel, to spread plague there." The kings ordered their trembling servants to lay the Ark on an ox-cart, and surround it with golden images.* Then they harnessed two cows to the cart, and penned the animals' calves in byres. "Let no one drive the cows," they said. "If they hear their calves lowing and turn back, that means that the plague is just a coincidence: the Ark is harmless and we'll keep it. But if the cows turn from Philistine land to Israel, it means that the Israelite God has caused the plague, and we'll be well rid of both it and him." As soon as the cows were harnessed to the cart they bent their heads and began lumbering towards Israel, ignoring the weight of the cart, ignoring their own calves' lowing in the byres. They dragged the Ark to the Israelite village of Bethshemesh, and stopped in the farm of a man called Joshua. He sent for priests, and they unloaded the Ark and the gold, broke up the cart to make an altar-fire and sacrificed the cows to God.*

Samuel spoke to the people. "You see God's power," he said. "Give up idolatry, keep his commandments and he will protect you always." The Israelites, terrified by what had happened to the Philistines, at first did as Samuel said. They gave up worshipping God as if he were a heathen idol, and lived their lives according to the Ten Commandments.

They made no kings or princes: God was their leader, they said, and Samuel spoke God's words. For forty years Samuel travelled from town to town settling arguments, judging quarrels and teaching the will of God. It was a peaceful, placid time, and the Israelites prospered. But a new generation was growing up, young people bored with their parents' unexciting lives. They began to take more and more interest in the idolators who lived all round them, and to contrast their gaudy, noisy lives with the sober existence of those who worshipped God. Even Samuel's own sons were corrupted. When they went round the towns as judges, they spent the time drinking and dancing; there were even rumours that they took bribes to slant God's commandments the way their rich friends wanted. Finally the elders of the twelve tribes went to Samuel and said, "We can't go on like this. Every town is making laws to suit itself. Give us a king, like every other nation on earth. He'll have God's authority; everyone will obey him. Make Israel one nation, under a single king."

Samuel tried to persuade them that they were wrong. A king would feed on the country like a parasite. He would need servants, a palace and an army. Even if he had enough personality to unite the people and make them follow him, such power was dangerous. What if he turned out to be a fool, a tyrant or a blasphemer? If they gave a man power, they would be his servants and not his equals. Only God deserved such honour; only God's authority could be trusted. So Samuel argued. But whatever he said, the elders gave the same uncompromising answer: "Make Israel one nation, under a single king."

"Lord, what shall I do?" prayed Samuel.

"Do as they ask. Give them a king."

"How shall I choose?"

"Go about your business: the king will come to you."

A rich farmer from the smallest of all twelve tribes, the Benjamites, had a son called Saul. The young man was strong, handsome and head and shoulders taller than anyone else in Israel. One day his father said to him, "Some of our asses have strayed. Take a servant, and ride out to look for them." Saul and the servant rode through the Benjamites' farms and villages, looking for the asses. They went east as far as Gilgal on the banks of the Jordan, north to Bethel, south as far as the next tribe's borders, and in a week's riding they found no trace.

"We'd better go back," Saul said. "We'll never find them now."

"Sir," said the servant, "There's a holy man staying in the next town, a prophet. He'll know where the asses are."

They found a man standing by the town gate, leaning on a stick. Saul bent down from his horse and asked, "Sir, can you please tell me where the prophet lives?"

The man at the gate was Samuel, and as soon as Saul spoke to him God filled his mind with certainty that this was the future king of Israel. "I'm the prophet you're looking for," he said. "Come home with me; tomorrow I'll tell you where your asses are."

He took Saul and the servant home, and gave Saul the place of honour, much to the young man's surprise. The servants brought food and drink, serving Saul before all the others. And the following morning, even more bewilderingly, when Samuel led Saul and the servant back to the city gate, he sent the servant on ahead, took Saul aside and anointed his head from a flask of scented oil. "What does it mean?" asked Saul.

"It means that you're God's chosen king," said Samuel. "He calls you to rule; all Israel will bow before you."

"I don't believe you."

"God speaks. Ride home; two of your father's servants will meet you on the way and tell you that the asses are found after all and that now your father's looking for you instead. You'll meet three men going to sacrifice, with goats, loaves of bread and a bottle of wine. Finally, on the very outskirts of your village, you'll join a procession of worshippers, with pipes, drums, harps and other instruments. God's spirit will enter you, and you'll dance and sing. These will be God's proofs that what I say is true; you're the chosen king of Israel.

But tell no one else. Go to Mizpeh, and wait till I tell you what to do."

Saul believed not a word of it. But when he rode off along the road to his own village, everything happened exactly as Samuel had described. His father's servants met him and told him that the asses were found. He met three men on their way to sacrifice, with bread, wine and goats. As he was riding into the village he found a procession of people singing hymns to God and playing musical instruments, and he jumped off his horse and joined them. He felt possessed; God's spirit flowed into him, and he knew that he was a changed man. The people of his village, however, were amazed to see him dancing and chanting with the others. "What's got into Saul?" they said. "No one would have thought him a holy man."

The next day, Saul went to God's shrine at Mizpeh. He still felt God's spirit filling him, possessing him. The sensation frightened him, and instead of greeting people openly he hid in a barn, waiting for Samuel to tell him what to do. He waited for several days, coming out only after dark – and as the time passed he was surprised to find the town filling with visitors, as if every tribe in Israel had sent pilgrims to worship God. On the seventh day Samuel himself arrived, and the crowd gathered round him. From the barn Saul watched Samuel talking to the people, gesturing at the sky and banging his stick on the ground. Finally, Samuel stepped down from his rock, the crowd parted to let him pass, and he came straight to the barn and fetched Saul out. Saul stood in front of the people, head and shoulders taller than anyone else there, and Samuel cried in a loud voice, "Men and women of Israel, behold your king." The people waved their arms and shouted, "God save the king!"

King Saul

So the choice was made, and Saul became the Israelites' anointed king. But he was a king without a country. The people were still divided: each tribe, each village went its own way, and for every one person who supported Saul, another two ignored him. He was a farmer's son, they said, a yokel – how could he unite the Israelites or defeat their enemies? In the end, God settled their doubts. Invaders from Ammon, the desert kingdom east of Jordan, besieged the Israelite town of Jabesh, and the people of Jabesh, peaceful farmers with no experience of fighting, said, "Tell us your peace-terms: we'll surrender."

"Certainly," said the Ammonite leader. "You can have peace, if you gouge out the right eye of every man, woman and child in Jabesh, as a sign of slavery."

"Give us a week," said the people of Jabesh. "If we can't find help in a week, we'll do it."

The Ammonite leader sat his soldiers in a ring round the town, to wait till the week was up. The men drank, diced, played ball-games in the sun. They set no guards. What had they to be afraid of? It had been fifty years since any Israelite had been known to fight. Where could the people of Jabesh go for help?

Inside the town, the panic-stricken Jabeshites met in council. "We'll have to ask Saul for help," they said. "Who else is there? He's our king: let him prove it by saving us."

When the Jabeshite messengers reached Saul, he was ploughing his fields with a team of oxen. As soon as he heard the messengers' story, fury boiled up in him as water overflows a pan. He sent for an axe, unyoked his oxen from the plough and hacked them to pieces. Then he sent gobbets of meat to every town in Israel with the message, "Come and fight. Obey your king, or see your own oxen butchered like this before your eyes." The Israelites were terrified. They could not decide whom to fear more, the Ammonite invaders or their own furious, raging king. In the end they followed Saul, and he led an army of farmers and shepherds, armed with scythes, axes, sticks and stones, against the startled Ammonites. The Ammonite soldiers threw down their dice and snatched weapons to defend themselves. But they were no match for the Israelites, led by Saul with rage in his eyes and God's spirit billowing in his brain. The fight lasted all day, and at dusk the Ammonites turned tail and ran. One by one, the Israelites bowed before Saul: he had proved himself their king in reality as well as in name.

In the next twenty years, guided by God's spirit, Saul united the twelve tribes of Israel into a single nation. So long as he listened to Samuel and obeyed God's word, he was like a castle to his people, and they loved and respected him. He and his son Jonathan led their armies against enemies on all sides, safeguarding the frontiers; even the Philistines, the biggest and best-armed nation in the area*, were powerless against them. But as the years passed Saul began to rely less and less on God. He put his victories down to his own brilliant generalship, and began to think of himself as a being set apart from ordinary mortals, the founder of a royal dynasty that would conquer and rule the world. When Saul was in this proud mood, no one dared challenge him. At other times, plunged in despair, he slumped like a sick animal for hours on end, snarling at servants or courtiers who went too close. He was a divided man, a living battle-ground.

In the end Saul threw away his own royal destiny by disobeying God. God ordered him to take an army south to fight the Amalekites, desert raiders who had attacked the Israelites on their way from Egypt to the Promised Land. God promised Saul victory, and ordered him to blot the Amalekite nation from the world. He was to slaughter every man, woman, child and animal, burn every tent, house and barn, plough up every pasture and sow it with salt. Saul disobeyed. He drove the best sheep and goats home to Israel, claiming that he meant to sacrifice them in triumph on God's altar; he spared the life of Agag, king of the Amalekites, and led him home in chains. He sent for Samuel, and waited like an eager child to hear his praise. But when Samuel sighed and said, "Saul, Saul, what have you done?", Saul at once realised his sin. His face crumpled, he slumped on his throne and said, "Help me, Samuel! Tell me how to put this right."

"It's too late," said Samuel. "You've disobeyed God, and lost the right to rule. God will anoint a new king, and favour a new royal house. Your dynasty will end with you."

He turned to go, and Saul stretched out a hand and caught hold of his coat. The coat tore in two and Samuel said, "There's no more to say. As this coat tears, so Israel will be torn by civil war."

He took a sword and stabbed Agag, king of the Amalekites, dead as God had ordered. Then he walked sadly out of Saul's house, through the yard where servants were hurriedly lining up Amalekite sheep and goats for sacrifice. He never spoke to Saul alive again: it was as if their twenty-year friendship had never been.

David and Goliath

God said to Samuel, "Go to Bethlehem, to Jesse's house. Take a horn of oil. Anoint Jesse's son the new king of Israel."

"If Saul hears of it, he'll kill me."

"Take a cow, and say you're going to sacrifice."

Samuel and his servant, leading a cow, went to Bethlehem, a village in the hill-country of Judah. The town councillors came out anxiously to meet them. "What is it?" they said. "Don't ask us to help you make war on Saul."

"Gather the people, answered Samuel. "I want to sacrifice this cow to God."

The whole village went to watch the sacrifice. Among the people were Jesse and his grown-up sons. After the sacrifice Samuel walked among the crowd, blessing them. He came to Jesse's eldest son Eliab, a tall, handsome man, and asked God in his heart, "Is this the man?"

"No. Mortal eyes see only a person's surface. God's eye sees the soul."

Samuel moved on to Eliab's brother Abinadab, to Shammah, and to seven other of Jesse's sons. Each time he asked God in his heart, "Is this the man?" and God answered, "No." Finally Samuel took Jesse aside and said, "Are these all your sons?"

"There's only the youngest left: David. He's out in the hills, looking after the sheep."

"Send for him," said Samuel. Servants hurried to fetch David, a fresh-faced boy of about fourteen. He stood before Samuel in the courtyard of his father's house, and Samuel anointed his head with oil. The spirit of God flowed into David, and his own father and brothers bowed to him as the future king of Israel. But Samuel told them to say nothing: while Saul lived, it was not yet time to claim the throne.

At the exact moment when Samuel sprinkled oil on David's head Saul, sitting in his house, felt a sudden emptiness of spirit, as if a gulf of darkness had opened inside him. Depression engulfed him, and he sat huddled in his stiff royal robes, refusing to eat, move or speak. "Fetch musicians," the servants said. "Music always soothes him." But this time, when the pipers piped and the singers sang, their music enraged Saul instead of calming him. Roaring with fury, he hurled a footstool at the terrified musicians. They scattered like frightened birds, and the servants said, "Who can we find to soothe Saul now?"

God put the answer into their minds. "There's a boy shepherd in the hills near Bethlehem," said one of the men. "He sings and plays at local dances. Fetch him for Saul. He'll be a new voice: perhaps he'll soothe the king."

So they fetched David from Bethlehem, and sent him in to sing for Saul. At first the king sat hunched in his chair as before, but gradually David's music began to soothe him. The frown left his forehead, the depression lifted for the first time in days and he called for food and drink. From then on David was Saul's most trusted servant, playing his lyre and singing whenever depression clouded his master's face.

News of Saul's sickness reached the Philistines. "He's gone mad," they said. "He lives with his head in his hands; he hardly eats or sleeps; leading soldiers is the last thing on his mind. Now's the time to attack!" They swept their army east, into the hills of Judah. They camped on a slope overlooking a narrow valley, and the Israelite army hastily gathered on the hill at the other side. Without Saul the Israelites fretted and fidgeted, like schoolchildren waiting for their teacher. Their uncertainty soon turned to panic. A huge man climbed on to a rock on the Philistine side of the valley. He was so tall that his squire, holding a spear like a sapling and a man-sized shield, looked no bigger than a child. The giant took off his helmet, and his hair and beard glowed like a lion's mane in the sun. He cupped his hands to his mouth and shouted, in a voice which sent echoes bouncing round the valley, "Israelites,

Goliath speaks: Goliath of Gath. Choose a champion to fight me, man to man. If he wins, Israel will rule the Philistines; if I win, you'll be our slaves."

He dropped his hands and waited for an answer. For a long moment echoes crashed backwards and forwards along the hillside, and then there was silence. The Israelites looked at one another in despair. What could they do? How could any ordinary man face Goliath, let alone kill him in single combat? Suddenly there was a stir at the back of the army. Saul was coming! The king and his servants reined in on the crest of the hill, and looked down at the silent soldiers, and at Goliath facing them across the valley, glittering in bronze. Saul said, "What's the matter with them? How can one man snatch the fight from them with words alone? Why does no one answer him?"

"Sir," said David, "I'll answer him."

"You, lyre-player? You're a boy; he's a grown warrior. How can you hurt him?"

"Sir, with God's help I've killed lions and bears that attacked my father's sheep. With God's help I'll kill this giant."

Saul looked at him. "If you must fight, lyre-player, wear my armour. Carry my sword and spear."

"No thankyou, sir. I have weapons of my own."

David walked down the hillside, barefooted and bareheaded, wearing a plain cloth tunic and carrying nothing but a shepherd's stick in one hand and a leather sling and pouch in the other. At the foot of the hill there was a pebble-filled gully, the course of a dried-up stream. He chose five smooth stones and pouched them, then walked up the hill at the other side, towards Goliath and the Philistine army. "Fool!" Goliath roared. "D'you think you can chase me away like a dog, with stones? Come closer: I'll feed you to the birds."

He drew his sword and began bounding down the hill towards David. David stood where he was. He took a stone from his pouch, whirled it twice round his head in the leather sling and sent it flying towards Goliath. The stone hit Goliath between the eyes, so hard that it embedded itself in bone. The huge Philistine toppled like a tree. His body rolled down the hill in a shower of stones and lay still at David's feet. David took Goliath's own sword in both hands, hacked off the Philistine's head and held it up by the bloodstained hair. The Philistine soldiers dropped their weapons, turned and began scrambling up the hillside for dear life – and the Israelites drew their swords and pelted after them, driving them like cattle to the borders of their own country and slaughtering all they caught.*

David outlawed

David's triumph over Goliath turned him from shepherd-boy to warrior. He spent his days training with the army, learning riding, sword-fighting and other war-skills. He made friends with the army commander, Saul's son Jonathan. Jonathan was two or three years older than David, and passed on to him clothes, armour and weapons he had grown out of – and because people grew used to seeing the two young men together, dressed alike, they began to think of them almost as brothers as well as friends. Jonathan even encouraged David to think of marrying into the royal family, to ask Saul for his daughter Michal as wife. David laughed and said that he would need to save for the bride-price for a hundred years.

The only dissatisfied person was Saul himself. He was jealous of David, and his jealousy was fanned when he overheard two palace women singing a snatch of song in the palace yard: "Saul kills thousands, David kills ten thousands." The words darkened Saul's mind with rage. He ripped his clothes to rags, he hurled footstools at any servants who tried to calm him, and he refused to see David or to listen to his singing. He promoted the young man to be captain of a thousand men and sent him against the Philistines, hoping that they would kill him in battle – and David came home triumphant, with his own soldiers singing the song about thousands and tens of thousands. Saul ground his teeth and growled, "What else does he want – my throne?" He tried once more to have David killed, when the young man asked him for Michal's hand in marriage. "The bride-price is – one hundred Philistine

foreskins", he snapped, knowing that the only way to cut off
Philistine foreskins was to kill the Philistines first. But David
went out into the hills of Judah, above the Philistine plain,
and came home with two hundred enemy foreskins in a
basket. Saul had no choice but to allow the marriage. But his
mind was given over to plans for David's death. In the end he
feigned a fit of depression, and when David came to play and
sing as usual he hurled a spear across the room at him. David
jumped out of the way, the spear jarred into the wall, and Saul
howled like a dog and shouted for his guards. David hurried
to his own house, and his wife Michal let him down on a rope
from a back window, and then delayed the guards by telling
them that David was sick in bed, and showing them a bolster
humped under the bedclothes to prove it. Saul punished
Michal by cancelling her marriage to David and giving her to
another husband; he punished David by declaring him an
outlaw, to be hunted down and killed.

David went first to Samuel, and the aged priest took him
for safety to the village of Naioth in the mountains. Naioth
was a holy place. Its people all wore bright-coloured robes,
and sang and danced for God. When Saul's soldiers looked
for David there, they were soon entranced themselves, threw
down their weapons and joined the dance – and when Saul
went looking for his soldiers, the same ecstasy came on him,
so that he tore off his clothes, rolled on the ground and
shouted and laughed hysterically for a whole day and night.
In the meantime, David escaped to another holy place*, the
town of Nob where he had long ago given Goliath's enormous sword to the shrine as a victory-offering. The priest of
the shrine, Ahimelech, gave David food – five loaves from the
bread on God's own altar – and armed him with Goliath's
sword. David fled into exile.* He lived for months in the cave
of Adullam, high in the hills, and collected a whole band of
followers: outlaws, debtors, escaped slaves, men and women
on the run from Saul. Before long there were six hundred of
them, and they moved from the cave to a forest lower down
the mountainside. Making this their headquarters, they
ranged far and wide across Saul's kingdom, keeping one step
ahead of Saul's soldiers and snapping their fingers at the law.

David stayed in hiding for four years, and Saul was power-less to find him. The king poured out his rage on Ahimelech, the priest who had helped David escape from Nob. He ordered the execution of Ahimelech and eighty-five of his family and servants, hoping that news of the massacre would draw David out of hiding to take revenge. When Samuel died and was buried in his home village of Ramah, Saul blockaded the roads and forbade anyone to help David or feed his followers, on pain of death. But David easily avoided the guards, paid his respects at Samuel's grave and slipped back into the hills before Saul's men even knew he had been there*. On another occasion, Saul thought he had David trapped in the hills near Ziph – and David showed his scorn for the royal army by stealing Saul's spear and water-bottle as he slept.*

All this time, while Saul and David were circling each other, wary as cats, the Philistines were watching for a chance to attack Israel and complete the conquest broken off after Goliath's death. But each time they invaded, Saul and David laid their private quarrels aside and turned their fury on the enemy. It was not till David and his six hundred followers settled in the town of Ziklag, on the edge of Philistine land, that the Philistines thought that their chance had come. King Achish, the Philistine ruler of Gath, made a treaty with David, promising that neither side would attack the other and that they would help to fight each other's enemies. Achish thought that this meant David's help against Saul, and stirred up his fellow-kings to make war on Israel. But the other Philistines refused to have David in their army, and David took his men instead to fight desert raiders who were attack-ing Ziklag from the south. The desert war took weeks, and carried David and his men deep into the south, sacking the raiders' fortified camps. In the meantime the Philistines invaded Israel, and Saul and his three grown sons Jonathan, Abinadab and Malchishua led the Israelite armies out to war.* There was a pitched battle, and Saul's three sons were killed. Despair clouding his mind for the last time, Saul begged his servant to kill him – and when the man refused he stuck his own sword in the ground point upwards, and fell on it. The triumphant Philistines hacked off his head and hung his and his sons' bodies on a wall, like butcher's meat drying in the sun.*

7 · KING DAVID

Civil war

David set up his royal court in the hill-town of Hebron. All the people of the area, tribesmen and tribeswomen of Judah, welcomed him as king. But the other eleven tribes were still loyal to Saul and the dynasty he had hoped to found. Saul and his three warrior-sons were dead, and the only surviving male member of the family was Saul's fourth son Ishbosheth. He was a gentle, placid person, with an adult's body but the mind of a child of six. He sat in his throne-room playing with toys while others ruled in his name. Their leader, Abner, commanded a gang of armed young men who swaggered through Ishbosheth's kingdom and terrorised the people into obeying orders and paying taxes. The country was at their mercy; they did as they pleased, and no one dared to challenge them.

For two years David's and Ishbosheth's followers lived in peace. There was plenty of land for everyone; each side had wars enough to fight with idolators, without picking quarrels with one another. But Abner's young men were always alert for the chance to make trouble, and in the end they found it. On a hot day, a group of them were swimming in a palm-fringed pond in Gibeon, a neutral town whose people favoured neither David nor Ishbosheth, and welcomed both sides equally. As Abner's young men bathed, a group of David's followers rode into town, hot and dusty, and ran to the water to join them. Abner sat in the shade with Joab, the commander of David's men. After a while he said, "My men challenge yours. Let twelve wrestle twelve, and see who's better trained."

"Agreed," said Joab.

The two commanders called their followers out of the water, and each chose twelve men. The wrestlers oiled their bodies and faced each other on a flat patch of sand beside the pond. For some time they circled each other, trying to get a grip on their opponents and a foothold in the hot sand. But as soon as the first man fell, rivalry turned to war. The wrestlers ran for swords and began stabbing and slicing each other, and their comrades ran eagerly to join the fight. The duel lasted for an hour, the men panting and staggering in the sun. But in the end Joab's followers, servants of King David, got the best of it, and Abner's men turned and ran. Most of Joab's followers dropped their weapons and flopped on the sand, too exhausted to give chase. But Joab's young brother Asahel, who prided himself on being the fastest runner in David's army, now set off in pursuit of Abner, eager for the honour of capturing the enemy commander. Abner swerved and ducked through the alleys of the town, trying to shake Asahel off, but the boy kept behind him as surely as if he were dragged by ropes. In the end Abner turned and shouted, "Why don't you find someone your own age to chase? You're no match for a grown man. What good will it do me to kill Joab's little brother?" But even as he was speaking, Asahel caught up with him. Abner held out his spear, butt-end outwards, to ward the boy off – and Asahel was running so fast that the blunt spear-shaft pierced his belly under the ribs and stuck out an arm's length behind his back. The breath whistled out of Asahel's body, and he fell dead at Abner's feet.

Asahel's death opened the gates of civil war. Neither David's nor Ishbosheth's followers were strong enough to risk pitched battle; but for five years they stalked one another in the hills, setting ambushes, stealing cattle, sacking towns and burning villages. The two sides were equally matched. Ishbosheth's army outnumbered David's by five to one, but David's soldiers were hill-tribesmen, used to guerrilla war, and were convinced (as Isbosheth's men were not) that God was on their side. Gradually the self-confidence of Ishbosheth's supporters drained away, and in the end even Abner, their war-leader, began looking for an excuse to desert to David's side. His chance came through an unexpected quarrel with Ishbosheth. Abner had been making love with one of the palace women, a former concubine of King Saul, and Ishbosheth (whom Abner had wrongly imagined too child-minded to care about such matters) sent for him and ordered him to leave her alone. Abner stormed out of the palace with twenty of his young men to offer his loyalty to David. David would have accepted this service gladly, as a way of stopping the war, but Joab met Abner at the town-gate of Hebron, took him into a dark corner as if to speak to him and stabbed him dead in revenge for Asahel. This outrage was surpassed only when two other followers of David crept into Ishbosheth's palace at night, found the child-man sleeping, hacked off his head and carried it back in triumph to David. David was furious. There was some excuse for the murder of Abner: blood-for-blood revenge was common, and if David and Joab sacrificed to God, honouring Abner before all the people, they might escape God's rage. But the murder of Ishbosheth was different. He was an unarmed, sleeping man, innocent as a child; his death tainted David's whole state with guilt. David ordered the murderers to be executed, and gave Ishbosheth and Abner ceremonial burial in Hebron.

Jerusalem

The leaders of all twelve tribes begged David to take power before civil war destroyed the state. There and then, in a ceremony in Hebron, priests anointed him king of Israel and Judah before them all, in the name of God.* He ruled from Hebron for seven years. But as time passed and the Israelites' enemies, Philistines, Moabites, Syrians, Ammonites, began gathering for war, David decided to settle in a new capital city, a stronghold no enemy could ever sack. He chose the Jebusite hill-fortress of Zion. It was protected by razor-cliffs and walls of stone blocks as big as barns; the Jebusites stood on their battlements and jeered, asking David what he hoped to gain with the cripples and beggars he called his army. But instead of direct attack, David took Zion by cunning. He stood with the main part of his army in front of the fortress, in full sight but just out of range, and while the defenders pelted them with stones and arrows, Joab led a small group of men to the only vulnerable part of the fortress, where an underground tunnel, carved from solid rock, carried water into Zion. The tunnel was narrow, jagged-walled and flooded; there was a wooden grille across its mouth to stop animals straying inside and drowning. Joab's men dragged the grille away and swam into the fortress. They came up in a water-cistern behind the jeering crowd on the battlements, overpowered the guards and threw open the gates. David's army poured inside: the citadel was theirs.

Most of David's followers put the capture of Zion down to David's own cunning or to the bravery of Joab's men. But David gave God the glory. He was convinced that his only claim to kingship was that God had chosen him, had sent Samuel to pick him out of all his brothers and anoint him king. He planned to persuade everyone in the twelve tribes, all his people, to give up their idolatry and return to God. He decided to transport the Ark of the Covenant to Zion and make Zion the city of God as well as his own royal capital. Two generations before, the Philistines had captured the Ark and been punished for it by plague. The Ark had been kept ever since in the town of Kirjath-jearim, and now David sent word that it was to be brought in procession across the hills to Zion. The people of Kirjath-jearim laid the Ark on an ox-cart and set out to trundle it through the hills. David and his people went to meet it in the valley below Zion.* They wore holiday clothes, danced, sang and played cymbals, trumpets, flutes and lyres as the Ark trundled behind them along the valley. When they came near Zion, and the track was too steep for the cart, priests lifted the Ark on poles, as it had been taken long ago from Egypt to the Promised Land, and carried it into the fortress, led by the singers and dancers and by David himself, leaping and dancing in holy joy.*

The coming of the Ark brought prosperity to Zion.* Secure in God's worship, the people began to spread outside the walls, pasturing sheep and goats on the scrubby hillside, farming the valley, digging irrigation-ditches and laying out fields and roads. Soon Zion was the heart of a much larger settlement; its neighbours called it Jerusalem and its inhabitants proudly named it the City of David and Citadel of God. As the city grew, people flocked to it from all parts of the Promised Land, and even idolators began to respect it. Some, like King Hiram of Tyre, made peace-treaties and sent David carpenters, stone-masons, goldsmiths and other craftsmen to beautify the city. Others set their faces against the Israelites and their God, plotting to wipe them from the earth. But as the years passed David's armies, led by Joab, defeated would-be invaders one by one, until all the surrounding peoples, Moabites, Ammonites, Philistines, Syrians, respected the Israelites' boundaries, and David's traders and ambassadors spread as far as Egypt in the West and Babylon in the east. By the time David was fifty, he had turned Israel into a single, God-fearing nation, honoured and respected throughout the area.

David and Bathsheba

The prophets of Jerusalem preached that God's laws must be obeyed to the letter: even the slightest wrong-doing was like the first step down a ladder to disaster. Not even kings could avoid this teaching. One cool evening, David was standing on the flat roof of his palace when he saw a beautiful woman washing in a courtyard below. Servants told him that she was Bathsheba, the wife of Uriah the Hittite who was an officer in the royal guard. Uriah was on army service in the desert, fighting the Ammonites, and David invited Bathsheba to eat with him – an unheard-of honour for the wife of a junior officer – and before the evening was over took her to bed and made love with her. He would have forgotten the matter immediately afterwards, but a few weeks later Bathsheba sent to tell him that she was pregnant. David's foot was on the ladder, and he had no choice but to continue down it. He sent a letter to Joab, the army commander in the desert, and ordered him to send Uriah home – and as soon as the young man arrived in Jerusalem David called him to the palace, stood him at ease and asked him for news of the war, smiling and joking as if Uriah were a friend instead of a subordinate. Stiff and embarrassed at speaking face-to-face with his king, Uriah stammered out his news, and when it was done David clapped him on the shoulder and said, "Well, it's time you were going home, to sleep in your own bed. Bathsheba should be delighted to see you, after so many weeks away."

"Oh no, sir," said Uriah, horrified. "I'm a serving soldier. I must spend the night on guard with the others."

Nothing David said would persuade him to go home to Bathsheba. He spent the night rolled in his cloak on the floor outside David's bedroom, and next morning reported to the king, saluted, and asked if there were messages to be carried back to Joab in the desert.

"Wait till tomorrow," David said. "Spend the day with me. I'd like to hear more about the war. Would you say that pitched battles or sieges are the best way to beat the Ammonites?"

Flattered, Uriah spent the whole day discussing military affairs. He glowed with the honour David was doing him, and even relaxed enough to eat and drink in the same room as his master. David kept sending servants to fill Uriah's wine-cup, and soon the young man's head was reeling with drink as well as self-importance. Finally, late in the evening, David stood up and said, "You can take a message to Joab in the morning. Go home now. Spend the night with Bathsheba; you've earned a twelve-hour leave."

Uriah stood up carefully, took a last drink of wine and tried to salute David with the cup still in his hand. "Sir," he said, "My comrades are sleeping in tents under the stars. The General's in a tent. The archers are in tents. The spearsmen are in tents. Even the cooks and the sword-sharpeners are in tents. Why should I sleep in my own soft bed, with my own soft wife beside me?"

He sat down suddenly, laid his head on his hands and began to snore. David left him to sleep, called for a secretary and dictated a letter to Joab. "Uriah's a brave man," it said. "Put him in the front line, where heroes stand." Next morning, David gave Uriah the letter and sent him on his way. Uriah rode to Joab in the desert, still bewildered at his king's unexpected kindness – and he was even more surprised when Joab read the letter and at once promoted him to the front line, among the assault-troops who besieged each Ammonite town.

Not long afterwards, Joab sent David a report on the progress of the war. "My lord, the Ammonites are falling before us like corn at harvest. Only a few Israelite lives have been lost, chiefly those of front-rank troops. I regret to report that they include Uriah the Hittite, whose promotion you commanded." David said nothing. But he sent a message of condolence to Uriah's widow Bathsheba, and as soon as the days of mourning were over he took her into his harem and married her.

So far no other human being but David knew of his descent down the ladder of crime, from adultery through treachery to murder. But God sent Nathan the prophet to check him. "Sir, God speaks," said Nathan. "There were two men in a city, one rich and one poor. The rich man had sheep and goats in thousands; the poor man had one ewe lamb, a pet hand-reared from birth. A traveller came to the city, and the rich man entertained him. But instead of killing one of his own sheep or goats for the banquet, the rich man stole the poor man's ewe lamb and slaughtered it."

"As God lives," David said furiously, "that rich man will pay for what he did. Who is he?"

"Sir," said Nathan, "God spoke in a parable. You are the man. Not content with a harem of wives and concubines, you stole Bathsheba and murdered her husband. God will punish you. Bathsheba's child will die, and quarrelling between your wives, sons and daughters will divide the royal household. You'll wish you'd never been born. God speaks."

The rape of Tamar

Not long afterwards, Bathsheba's child was born. It was puny and sickly, and although David prayed for its life for seven days, fasting and sleeping on the ground, the baby died*. David realised that there was no way even for God's anointed king to escape his destiny – and soon afterwards, the trouble Nathan had predicted flared in the royal house. David's son Amnon fell in love with his own half-sister Tamar. Their mothers were David's wives Ahinoam and Maacah, but they had the same father (David), and God's law said that any love-making between them, or just one fond look, was incest. None the less, Amnon said to his friend Jonadab, "Tamar's the most beautiful girl I've ever seen. I'll die unless I make love with her."

"Why don't you, then?" asked Jonadab. "You're the king's son: do as you please."

"She'll never make love with her own brother."

"Pretend you're sick, and when she comes to look after you, do what you like with her."

That same day Amnon lay down on his bed and began sighing and panting as if he had a fever. He refused to get up, he refused to eat any food the servants brought. "Fetch Tamar," he groaned. "If she brings food, I'll try to eat." But when Tamar bent over him to ask how he felt, he pulled her into bed and raped her. Then he shooed her out of the room and went whistling about his business. "It was just a fever," he told anyone who listened. "I'm better now."

But if Amnon thought nothing of the rape, Tamar was heartbroken. She tore her clothes; she streaked her face with ashes; she ran sobbing to her father David and told him everything. David heard her out, stony with rage. But then he said, "Child, what can I do? The punishment for rape is death. Am I to accuse the crown prince of Israel? Am I to condemn my own son to death?"

Weeping even more bitterly, Tamar asked help from her elder brother, Absalom. At first he seemed even less comforting than David. "Forget it," he said. "It's not as if it were some stranger. It was your brother; it's not important." But as soon as Tamar went back to the harem, hysterical with sobbing, he began to make revenge-plans. Absalom was ambitious, and Amnon was David's heir; punishing the rape, claiming a brother's just vengeance for a dishonoured sister, would clear Absalom's own path to his father's throne. Absalom waited for two years, smiling at Amnon and hiding what he planned. Then, in the second summer after the rape, he organised a sheep-shearing festival in a village far from Jerusalem, invited all David's sons, and in the midst of the dancing sent servants to drag Amnon aside and cut his throat. David's other sons ran for their lives, shouting that Absalom was planning to seize the throne – and Absalom himself fled into the desert, to live in exile till his father's fury had run its course.

Absalom

Absalom stayed in exile for three years, and it was as if his absence were a drug, turning his father from middle-aged to senile. White-haired, wild-eyed, David sat alone in his throne-room, twanging his lyre and sighing "Absalom, O Absalom" as if the words began a song he had no idea how to end. Joab, the army commander, worried about his old friend's sanity. He remembered how the madness of Saul, the previous king, had swept the whole country into civil war, and when he thought of Absalom, gathering followers in exile and feeding on ambition, he was afraid for Israel. But there was no way to discuss it with David directly. Whenever anyone mentioned Absalom's name, the old man strummed his lyre and shouted like a child, trying to drown out the conversation while tears streamed down his face. Accordingly, instead of going to David himself, Joab found a gypsy woman, a dancer used to playing parts, and sent her to the palace disguised as a peasant from one of the villages. The woman streaked her face with ash, wrapped a shawl round her head and ran into the palace sobbing and shrieking, "Help me! Oh help me save my son!"

The words "save my son" drew David from his misery for the first time in three years. He asked the woman gently, "What is it, granny? How can I save your son?"

"O sir," the woman sobbed, in the words Joab had carefully taught her, "I'm a widow, and I had two beloved sons. But they quarrelled, and the younger killed the elder. Now the whole family want my younger son dead as well: they want him hanged for murdering his brother. How can I let him die? How can I live when both my sons are dead? Sir, give orders: make the killing stop."

"As you ask, so it shall be," said David. His voice was as firm, as sure as it had been in his youth. "No one will kill your son. One tragedy's enough. Let him live in peace." He broke off suddenly, and looked hard at the woman. "Did Joab send you here?" he asked.

"Yes, sir, Joab sent me," said the actress. "He taught me this talk of sons."

She knelt trembling in front of David. The old man sat for a long time in silence and then said gently, "Go in peace." He washed himself, changed his clothes and sent for Joab. "Fetch Absalom back from exile. He can live in Jerusalem, free from arrest, so long as he keeps away from the palace. He's my son and heir, and I won't harm him. But I never want to see his face again."

Absalom rode back to Jerusalem in triumph, and David peeped out at the procession from a palace window, weeping with happiness to see his son. At first Absalom stayed away from the palace as agreed, but after a few weeks he slipped into David's throne-room and grovelled on the floor before his father. The old king ran to him and hugged him. It was as if Absalom had done good, not harm; it was as if Amnon's murder had never happened.

In the months that followed David sent for Absalom every day. He ate with him, laughed at his jokes, basked in his company as people soak up sun. Absalom smiled and put up with it. But all the time he was hiding his real impatience. He ached for the old man to die, longed for the day when the people would acclaim him king in David's place. He swaggered in royal robes, sewn with gold; he surrounded himself with bodyguards, and rode through the city with fifty servants to clear the crowds. He turbanned his head in silk, and once a year celebrated the ceremony of the Royal Locks. A crowd waited in the palace courtyard while barbers went in to cut the royal hair. Every year, without fail, the barbers showed the crowd a sackful of hair, the weight of five large loaves, and Absalom's courtiers cried that this was a sign of

God's approval, that the Israelites would flourish under Absalom's rule as the hair flourished on his head. Finally, four years after his return to Jerusalem, Absalom fled once again, this time to David's old capital city of Hebron, gathered an army of followers and prepared to march on Jerusalem and seize the throne.

The threat of invasion split David's court. Some people advised David to withdraw to Zion, the fortress at the heart of Jerusalem, and sit out a siege. Others, including the old priest Ahitophel whose advice had never failed, tried to persuade him that his reign was over, that he should give Absalom royal power, retire, and so avoid civil war. For David, neither choice was possible. He was God's anointed king – how could he give up the throne unless God ordered it? On the other hand, if he barricaded himself in Zion, thousands of men would die on both sides, attacking and defending it, and Absalom's army would fall on the rest of Jerusalem, the undefended streets and squares below the citadel, as wolves tear sheep. He crossed the valley and climbed the Mount of Olives on the other side. He meant to stop on the summit and pray to God for help – but he was appalled when hundreds of people set out to follow him, as if he were abandoning the city. Even Zadok and Abiathar, the priests who guarded the Ark of the Covenant, followed with servants carrying the Ark. "Go back!" said David. "Ask God for a sign. If he wants me still to reign, send messengers to call me back to the city. If he chooses Absalom, leave me to die in the desert." The priests turned back, and David and his followers pulled the hoods of their cloaks over their heads, passed over the Mount of Olives and settled for the night in the village of Bahurim on the other side, to wait for news.*

As soon as Absalom heard of David's flight, he rode into Jerusalem in triumph and called for his counsellors. "We are now king of Israel," he said. "What steps should we take, to prove it to all the people?"

"Majesty," said Ahitophel, the old priest, "occupy your father's harem, in the heart of the citadel. If you take his women hostage, no one will risk besieging it. Then send me out with twelve thousand soldiers. I'll terrify David's followers into deserting him, and kill him: that way, one death will save us all from civil war."

"No, Majesty," said Hushai, another counsellor. "Half the country still supports David. The only way to secure your throne is to gather an army, hunt David down and exterminate him and all his followers in a single battle. Total war is the way to win."

As soon as Absalom's hot-headed young warriors heard this, they began stamping their feet and shouting for total war. Absalom waved his arm in agreement, and his officers ran to arm their men. But Hushai, who was secretly loyal to David, and who had suggested total war as a way of flushing Absalom out of Jerusalem, of removing him from the safety of the citadel, sent word to David to arm his men for battle. As for Ahitophel, he was so dismayed that his advice had been ignored that he saddled his ass, went home, put his affairs in order and hanged himself.

Absalom had hoped to catch his father by surprise, to cut him to pieces before his followers had time to collect themselves. But Hushai's warning gave David time, not only to gather and arm soldiers but to move to battle-ground of his own choosing, a stretch of flat land not far from the river Jordan, bounded on one side by a wood and on the other by the walls of the David's headquarters, the town of Mahanaim. David called his commanders to council. "Make your own battle-plans," he said. "I'm too old to fight; I'll wait here at the town gate for news. Kill as few people as possible – and above all, for my sake, deal gently with the young man Absalom."

He sat by the gate and watched his men march out for war. The battle was uneven. David's soldiers were veterans, led by generals like Joab, who had been commanding troops since the time of Saul. Absalom's followers were a rabble, mincing young courtiers and their servants, slaves, farm-hands and apprentice-boys who had never fought in their lives before and who were so dazzled by Absalom's promises of the rewards of victory that they never for a moment stopped to think how that victory might come. Absalom led them in

person, wearing golden armour, carrying a golden shield and
with his hair piled high under a golden helmet with scarlet
plumes. His followers sauntered from the wood, laughing and
talking as if they were on their way to a picnic; David's men
swept grimly out of Mahanaim to meet them.

It was less battle than butchery. At the first sight of blood,
the front line of Absalom's men turned and ran, hacking at
their own comrades who stood in their way. The rear ranks
tried to defend themselves, and soon both groups were at one
another's throats, slipping and stumbling over the bodies of
their own dead comrades. David's men drove them inexora-
bly back towards the wood. Finally, as suddenly as starlings
whirl and scatter from marauding hawks, Absalom's men
dropped their swords and ran, unbuckling their armour and
dropping it at their pursuers' feet. Absalom himself found a
mule in a field and galloped for the safety of the wood. He
came to an oak-tree with low, overhanging branches, and his
neck caught in a fork. The collision knocked off his helmet
and twined his long hair round the branches, leaving him
dangling while the mule ran blindly on. David's pursuing
soldiers found him there, swaying and cursing, and stood in a
bewildered group wondering what to do. One of them ran for
Joab, and he took three arrows, sharp as daggers, and stabbed
them into Absalom's heart. David's treacherous son was
dead; the rebellion was at an end.

The end of David's life

David was standing at the town gate, looking anxiously across
the plain. He saw two young men, running, picking their way
between the bodies. It was as if they were racing to bring him
news. The first man knelt before the king and panted, "Sir,
praise God. We've won."

David asked, "Is Absalom safe?"

"Sir, I saw fighting, confusion . . . nothing else."

The second man ran up. "News, my lord!" he cried. "God
has routed our enemies!"

"Is Absalom safe?"

"My lord, may all your enemies, all who revolt against you, end like Absalom."

David's eyes filled with tears. He brushed past the two young men into the guardroom beside the gate. He sat weeping, alone, and no one dared approach him. As the day wore on, survivors from the battle began straggling into the town, and each time they passed the guardroom door they could hear the king inside, sometimes sobbing, sometimes singing in a quavering voice the grief-song he had begun for Absalom years before: "O my son Absalom, my son, my son Absalom! Would God I had died for you, O Absalom, my son, my son!" At the end of the day Joab strode from the battlefield and went briskly in to see the king. The listeners outside heard him shouting at David that the battle was won and it was time for joy, not tears; they heard David's mumbled answer; finally Joab opened the door and called for servants, and they picked the old king up in a litter and carried him gently home.

From that day on, it was as if David was shrivelling before their eyes. He sat in his throne-room, a grey old man, and shivered. The servants brought fire-baskets, and covered their master with fleeces and blankets, but still he sat red-eyed, white-faced, twisting his bony fingers and shivering. They sent a young girl, Abishag, to warm him, as the palace women had always quickened him in the past. She put him to bed, covered him with blankets and settled beside him, snuggling him in her arms. But he lay cold as iron, staring with unseeing eyes and whispering "Absalom, O Absalom!" in a voice as quiet as corpse-breath.

While servants scurried about the palace, fetching wood for the fire-baskets and hot drinks to try and thaw their master back to life, David's courtiers gathered in anxious groups. Their care was not for David, but for the royal succession. There were two contenders, Adonijah, David's son by Haggith, and Solomon, his son by his beloved Bathsheba. Adonijah was the elder, and many of the royal advisers, including Joab, were convinced that the throne was his by right. Adonijah thought so too. He remembered how his half-brother Absalom had ingratiated himself with the people, and began to walk the same road himself. He surrounded himself with a royal bodyguard, went everywhere with fifty servants to hold back the crowds, and began judging lawsuits and scattering favours as if he were already king. From the windows of the harem, Bathsheba watched and scowled. There was nothing she could do: Adonijah's soldiers controlled Jerusalem, and to argue with them meant death. Her only hope was to catch David in one of his few lucid moments, and persuade him to grant royal power not to Adonijah but to her own son Solomon.

At last Bathsheba's moment came: Adonijah's own impatience toppled him. Tired of waiting for David's death, the young man invited his supporters to a banquet, sacrificed to God before them all and proclaimed himself king. The celebrations lasted long into the night – and in the dark of the evening Bathsheba and Nathan the prophet hurried through the deserted palace to David's bedroom. Shooing Abishag out of the room, they stood beside David's bed and waited till the old man woke up and focused watery eyes on them. At first it was as if he failed to recognise them: he turned his head away and called feebly for Abishag. But when Bathsheba knelt beside the bed and spoke his name, he suddenly propped himself up, looked into her eyes and said in a clear voice, as unexpected as the flicker of flame in the ash of a dying fire, "Bathsheba, tell me. What is it you want?"

"My lord," said Bathsheba, "have you forgotten your promise to make Solomon king? Has no one told you how Adonijah is sacrificing, feasting with his followers, stealing power? Act quickly: name the rightful heir."

"Sir," said Nathan, "Your loyal followers are waiting. Name your heir."

David sank back on the pillow. His eyes were closed. Nathan leaned over him to hear his answer. "Go to Zadok the priest," David whispered. "Tell him to take Solomon to the pool at Gihon. When the trumpet blows, let him name Solomon my heir. Then bring Solomon to me."

Nathan hurried to Zadok, and the priest and the prophet took Solomon to the pool of Gihon. There, in front of God's altar, Zadok anointed Solomon king of Israel from a horn of oil, and he and Zadok knelt before him. Then they took the young man to the palace, to David's room, and the old king raised himself in the bed and bowed his head in homage to his son. It was David's last act on earth. He had ruled his country for forty years, seven in Hebron and thirty-three in Jerusalem. He had united Israel, and extended its boundaries from the Red Sea to Syria, from the Mediterranean coast to the shores of the river Euphrates. When David had succeeded Saul, he had become king of a small warrior nation; when Solomon succeeded David, it was as ruler of half the world.*

8 · KINGS AND PROPHETS

Solomon

Solomon's subjects thought him the wisest person in the world. They believed that all the time he was growing up he had gathered knowledge from his father David, from wise men and women from foreign countries, and even from God himself. He hoarded ideas as other people store coins or jewels; his head was a treasure-house of thought. His subjects boasted about his knowledge. They called it as limitless as sand; they said that he knew three thousand proverbs and one thousand and five holy songs; they claimed that he understood the language of every bird, insect and animal on earth. Scribes gathered many of his ideas in books and read them to the people*; he revealed others himself in speeches and judgements, often in simple, unexpected ways. Once, two women who shared a house each gave birth to a baby on the same day. One of the babies died, and its mother secretly exchanged its corpse for her friend's still-living child. Both women appeared before the king. Each claimed the child; they begged Solomon to choose between them. Any other judge would have asked questions, called witnesses and listened to hours of argument. But Solomon told his guards to cut the baby in two and give the rival mothers half each. At once, although one of the women smiled in agreement, the other cried, "No, sire! It's hers, not mine. Spare its life! Give it to her" – and Solomon announced that she was the true mother and handed the child to her.

To ordinary people, judgements like this were almost magical. Solomon's knowledge seemed like a wizard's, a power far beyond normal understanding. His priests, however, explained it in a different way – as a direct gift from God. They said that just after Solomon became king, God appeared in a vision and offered him any gift he chose. Instead of asking for riches or long life, the priests went on, Solomon prayed for the wisdom to distinguish good from bad – and God was so impressed that he gave him riches and long life as well. Not long after this vision Solomon sent messengers to King Hiram of Tyre. He said that he wanted to build God a Temple in Jerusalem, an earthly palace to house the Ark of the Covenant and to declare God's glory to all the world. He asked Hiram for building-materials and workmen, and offered to pay twenty thousand measures of wheat and twenty of olive oil each year. Hiram sent workmen to fell cypress, cedars and fir-trees, and shipped the timber in barges down the coast, where it was loaded into ox-carts and dragged along the steep mountain roads to Jerusalem. Solomon conscripted forty thousand young Israelites as labourers. They quarried stone in the hills, carried it on carts to Jerusalem, and laid the giant blocks in place. The outer part of the Temple, a stone-paved courtyard, held an altar as high as a man, covered in beaten bronze, and a water-basin supported by twelve life-sized bronze bulls. Beyond this, up a flight of steps, was the shrine, made of stone blocks faced with cedar-boards. The shrine consisted of three houses, one inside the other. The walls of the outside house were a honeycomb of cupboards, storehouses and treasuries; the middle house held a golden incense-altar, a golden offering-table and five pairs of lamps on golden stands. The innermost house, the Holy of Holies, was forbidden to everyone except the High Priest, and even he could enter only once a year. The walls, floor and ceiling of this house were lined with cedar-wood, carved with flowers and flying angels and overlaid in gold. Window-slits let in light from the outer courtyard, and the dim glow of lamps was reflected in yellow gold.

Work on the Temple took seven years. As soon as it was finished Solomon called the leaders of Israel to a feast of celebration. The people of Jerusalem cheered the procession through the streets. First went trumpeters and singers; dancers followed, leaping and waving their arms in holy joy.

After them priests bore the Ark of the Covenant on its long carrying-poles, just as it had been brought from Egypt five centuries before. Behind them followed the king, the courtiers and the clan-chiefs, with servants leading sheep, goats and cattle for sacrifice. People and animals thronged the Temple courtyard, and priests began sacrificing the victims. The altar was ten strides long and ten strides wide, heaped with sweet-scented pine-wood. Sparks and smoke filled the sky. Then, as the people prayed and the musicians sang, priests carried the Ark into the Holy of Holies and laid it reverently in its place, under the outspread wings of two wooden cherubim covered in plated gold. At once the sanctuary filled with the dark, dense smoke of God's presence. The priests retreated to the courtyard and Solomon prayed before the people, asking God to bless the Temple, Jerusalem, and everyone who lived or worshipped in the Promised Land.

As soon as the Temple was complete, Solomon set his workmen to finish another lavish building, the royal palace. It was more like a village than a single building. As well as Solomon's court it housed a harem of seven hundred royal wives, together with their maids, children, cooks, entertainers, hair-dressers, gardeners and guards. Apart from the royal princes, Solomon's young sons, everyone in the harem was either female or a eunuch: for a grown man, to stray inside meant death. The harem was not only a sign of Solomon's own magnificence, it was also a guarantee against attack. All through the years of building-work, when the young Israelites were busy as stone-masons and carpenters, Solomon had avoided war. Instead, he made alliances with his neighbours, offering peace and trade instead of conquest – and he fixed each alliance, each trading-partnership, by welcoming another foreign princess as wife and taking her to Jerusalem. Which of Israel's neighbouring kings would declare war, knowing that his own sister or daughter could in an instant be turned from queen to hostage?

As the years passed, Solomon's power grew ever greater. He built fortified towns on every trade-route north, south, east and west through the Promised Land, and charged customs-duty on goods of all kinds from Egyptian chariots to

Syrian olive-oil. He turned the young men of his people from building-work to army service, and sent them to guard the mountain passes and protect the long lines of mules and camels that passed, laden, in and out of every trading-town. He built ports on the Mediterranean coast and at Eilat on the Red Sea, and trading-ships brought him trade-goods and treasures from every land on earth: apes, peacocks and ivory, spices from Arabia, and gold-dust heaped in the holds like corn. Every dish in Solomon's palace, every bowl, even the ceremonial shields of the royal guard, were gold. In that court, silver was as cheap as stone.

News of Solomon's glory brought visitors crowding to Jerusalem. They gaped at the wide, paved streets, at the tall buildings and at Solomon, riding in procession or sitting on his judgement-throne of gold and ivory. Many visitors were ordinary merchants or tourists; but Solomon's admirers also included the richest and most powerful monarchs in the world. His fame reached as far as Sheba, a fabulous desert kingdom in Africa, whose ruler was also a goddess, queen of their religion. She had often watched Israelite traders worshipping God, and now set out for Jerusalem in person, to question Solomon and talk to his God face to face, deity to deity. It took three months for her procession to reach the Promised Land. The queen and her attendants rode in golden litters, guarded by prancing horsemen. A thousand camels followed, laden with spices, gold and jewels. At every step of the journey, priests played lyres and flutes and eunuch-choirs sang hymns. The people of Jerusalem gaped as the procession wound through the streets. But the queen of Sheba, goddess or no goddess, was even more amazed at the glitter of Solomon's court. She had hoped to learn the secret of his wisdom, perhaps even to marry him and make their joint kingdom the most powerful in the world. But when she saw the food on his tables, the number and manners of his servants, the rooms, corridors and gardens of his harem, and when she watched him pass each day from bejewelled luxury to the ecstatic stillness of the Temple, humbling himself like a slave to God, she realised that she could offer him nothing more than he already had. The two monarchs exchanged presents and compliments; then the queen called for her attendants, her soldiers, her choirs, her mules and her camels and left Jerusalem as baffled as she had come.

Elijah and the prophets of Baal

Solomon ruled for forty years, and most of that time was a golden age, with greater peace and prosperity than his people had ever known. But at the end of his life he grew as feeble and foolish as his father David had before him. He sat drooling on his throne, with his embroidered robes stiff as a tent around him; he let his courtiers make judgements and sign papers in his name; his hands shook and his eyes were dim. In the end even his wisdom deserted him, and he broke God's first commandment, "You shall have no other gods but me". He built altars and ordered prayers and sacrifice to his wives' idolatrous gods. The furious Temple-priests predicted disaster for the royal dynasty if he persisted. But the king's word was law, and the foreign altars stayed.

God's punishment followed Solomon's death, exactly as the priests had warned. The people rebelled against Solomon's son Rehoboam*, and divided the kingdom as it had been at the beginning of Saul's reign a century before. Ten of the twelve tribes swore loyalty to King Jeroboam, who ruled from the mountain-citadel of Shechem; only the tribes of Judah and Benjamin stayed loyal to Rehoboam, ruling from Jerusalem. As for Solomon's former allies, the Egyptians, Moabites, Syrians and Ammonites, they saw his country divided, northerners and southerners squabbling like children, and began advancing on the frontiers and border-towns, alert for conquest. Time and again prophets warned the Israelites that their only hope was to abandon idolatry and trust in God. Sometimes the warning worked, and for a few years this king or that smashed the heathen altars and restored God's worship. But these changes were swept away in new outbursts of idolatry, each more vicious than the last.

A century after Solomon's death, King Ahab of Israel married the Phoenician princess Jezebel, a high priestess of

Baal who took her religion with her to Ahab's court. She ordered a massacre of four hundred priests of God, and replaced them with four hundred and fifty prophets of Baal and four hundred of other, lesser gods. The false prophets lived at court, casting horoscopes, muttering spells and sacrificing chickens, dogs, snakes, camels, apes and peacocks. God's priests looked on, appalled. Then a lord called Hiel decided to build a castle in the ruins of the old town of Jericho, and tried to win Baal's favour by cutting his own sons' throats on the foundation-stones. God acted. He sent a prophet, Elijah, to warn Ahab. Elijah stood before the king and queen, in the presence of the four hundred and fifty prophets of Baal and the four hundred prophets of lesser gods, and said, "God speaks. There is no god but God. He will prove it with drought. For three years, unless God orders it, there will be neither dew nor rain."

The court rang with laughter. The four hundred and fifty prophets of Baal and the four hundred prophets of lesser gods twisted their beards, pranced up and down and mocked Elijah with the sign of the evil eye. Elijah turned on his heel and walked out, scattering them as a man scatters cackling hens. "Let him go," said Jezebel. "Dance! Sing! Pray for rain!"

But for three years, no rain came. Streams dried. Rivers dwindled. Cisterns yawned. Sheep and cattle lay panting in the dust, or licked stones and fence-posts, desperate for moisture. At court, the Baal-prophets drew magic squares and circles in the sand, then ordered ever more exotic rain-dances and sacrifices: a hundred she-asses, two hundred leopards, a thousand dolphins, ten thousand swans. Day and night, the palace floors ran with the victims' blood, while the priests begged Baal to disembowel the clouds and send them rain. But the drought continued. Then, three years to the day since Elijah first appeared at court*, he walked back into the palace and bowed to Ahab. The Baal-prophets and the four hundred prophets of lesser gods growled in fury, and Ahab said, "Do you dare come back – you, the man who troubles Israel?"

"You are the man, not me," said Elijah. "You worship idols; you cause the drought. God speaks. Send messengers; call the people together on the slopes of Mount Carmel. And gather these false prophets there as well: four hundred and fifty prophets of Baal, and four hundred prophets of lesser gods."

The Baal-prophets began growling again, like a pack of hounds. Jezebel lifted a hand, to order her guards to kill Elijah where he stood. But Ahab stopped her. "What can it hurt to do as he says?" he asked. "Let him call on his god for rain. When he fails, we'll kill him." He sent messengers throughout the kingdom, calling the people together on Mount Carmel. They gathered in a thin-faced, muttering crowd, spitting their hatred of Elijah with dry, parched mouths. The four hundred and fifty prophets of Baal and the four hundred prophets of lesser gods gathered too. Sleek and silky in the sun, they stood in groups and watched Elijah.

Elijah climbed on a rock and shouted to the people, "How long must this go on? How long will you stagger between two opinions? Make up your minds! Choose God or Baal – and whichever you choose, worship him alone."

No one answered. The people shuffled their feet and looked at the ground. There was no sound but uneasy breathing. Then Elijah spoke again. "Let this be the test," he said. "I am one man alone, the only prophet of God left alive in Israel. There are four hundred and fifty prophets of Baal, and four hundred prophets of lesser gods. Bring two bulls: one for them, one for me. Let them slaughter their bull, lay it on Baal's altar, and put wood but no fire underneath. I'll do the same with mine. Then let them pray to Baal for fire; I'll pray to God. The god who sends fire – let him be your god, and him alone."

The crowd murmured agreement. Ahab's servants fetched two bulls. The prophets of Baal chose one, and Elijah took the other. The Baal-prophets heaped their altar with branches, killed their bull, cut it up and laid it on the wood. Then they began their prayers. They called Baal's name; they shrieked to him to send fire; they danced round the altar, chanting and beating drums. All morning they leapt and pranced and prayed, watched by the silent crowd, and no fire came. At noon, when the sun was high, Elijah began to mock them. "Shout louder," he said. "Perhaps he's day-dreaming, or hunting, or gone for a walk. Perhaps he's asleep. Shout louder, and wake him up!"

The Baal-prophets cried even louder. They began to call Baal's secret names, the ones usually only murmured in private, in riddles, rites and spells. They ran round the altar, leaping into the air. They sliced their own flesh with knives, and skewered their arms and cheeks. But nothing happened: no answer, no voice, no fire.

At last, as evening came, the prophets of Baal gave up their ritual. They stood in a sullen group, hoarse and exhausted. Flies buzzed round the bull's carcase on Baal's altar. There was no other sound. Then Elijah called to the people, "Gather round", and they gathered round. He showed them a broken altar made on the mountainside to God many years before. He rebuilt it, and topped it with twelve smooth stones, one for each of the tribes of Israel. Then he piled wood on the altar, sacrificed his bull and laid it on top. Finally, he dug a trench all round the altar, an arm's-length wide and an arm's-length deep, and said to the people, "Fill four barrels with water, and pour it over the sacrifice and over the wood."

Four barrels! In a time of drought! The people looked in horror at Ahab. But he nodded permission, and his servants brought the water and poured it. "Fetch four more barrels," said Elijah, "and four more after that." The servants did as he told them. The people watched wide-eyed, licking their lips and sighing as water sluiced out of the barrels, soaking the carcase, the wood and the altar-stones and splashing into the trench.

It was the time of evening sacrifice. Elijah stood by the dripping altar. He bent his head and prayed in a quiet voice. "O Lord, God of Abraham and Isaac, show these people today that you are the God of Israel, that I am your servant, and that all this was done according to your word. Hear me, Lord! Make these people worship you again."

There was a blaze, a fizz of light. God's fire fell from heaven, and the people, Baal-prophets, king and soldiers cowered and hid their eyes. When they uncovered them they saw that the fire had burnt bull, wood and altar-stones to ash. Flames had licked up every drop of water in the trench: there was nothing but charred, baked ground. The people grovelled in the dust and cried to God for mercy. Elijah said, "Take the prophets of Baal, and the prophets of the lesser gods, and kill them." The king's servants led the prophets to a dried-up river-bed. The prophets whimpered and whined, tearing off their gold bangles and silver-sewn robes to bribe the soldiers and calling in hoarse voices to Baal to save their lives. But the soldiers butchered every one of them and filled the river-bed with corpses. Elijah walked past the crowd of kneeling, praying people to the mountain-peak. He crouched down, put his face between his knees and said to his servant, "Look towards the coast, and tell me what you see."

"Nothing, my lord."

"Look again."

"My lord, nothing."

Seven times Elijah sent the servant back to look, and the seventh time the man came back and said, "My lord, there's a cloud rising from the sea: a little cloud, no bigger than a man's hand."

Elijah went back down to Ahab. "Get up," he said. "Go home: God is sending rain."

Ahab looked at him in disbelief. But the cloud was already gathering overhead: a thick, black storm-cloud ballooning in the wind to fill the sky. He jumped into his chariot and galloped home, and even as he did so the first drops began falling, darkening his clothes with rain. God had answered Elijah's prayers. The Israelites had turned back to him, and he had ended the drought and sent them rain.

Naboth's vineyard

It was all very well for Ahab and his people to abandon Baal for God. Their own eyes had seen the miraculous fire from heaven and their own backs had felt the rain. But for Jezebel, high priestess of Baal, news of what happened on Mount Carmel was less a proof of God's existence than an insult. Furious at the death of her four hundred and fifty prophets, and of the four hundred prophets of lesser gods, she sent a message to Elijah: "May the gods do the same to me, if I don't do the same to you before this time tomorrow." Terrified by the threat, Elijah ran into hiding in the desert*. Jezebel now turned her powers on Ahab. She felt that by giving way to Elijah, by letting the Baal-priests be slaughtered, he had lost face with his own subjects, and that they were mocking him behind his back. She became alert for disobedience, and was merciless with anyone who seemed to be paying the royal house less than maximum respect. A rich man called Naboth owned a vineyard. It was a small, walled area in the centre of the town of Jezreel, next to the walls of the royal palace. Ahab wanted it for a herb-garden, and asked Naboth to sell it. But Naboth said no: it was family land, not his to sell. Ahab thought this a perfectly reasonable reply, and would have let the matter drop. But Jezebel took it as an insult. She sent letters to two of her most trusted servants. "Call Naboth before the people. Accuse him of blasphemy against Elijah's God. Make it convincing; stir up the crowd to punish him." The two men did exactly as she ordered. Dressed as priests of God, they ran through the streets of Jezreel shouting that Naboth was a secret Baal-worshipper, a blasphemer against the one true God – and they were so convincing that the townspeople dragged Naboth out of his house and stoned him to death. "There, my lord," Jezebel said to Ahab. "Naboth refused to sell you his vineyard, and now it's yours for the taking. Forget God: with Baal, all things are possible!"

Ahab told his gardeners to plough up Naboth's vineyard and make a herb-garden. But before a single vine could be cleared, Elijah strode into the palace and said, "Ahab, God speaks. You agreed to blasphemy and murder, and your punishment is death. Your people will rise against you; your blood will soak the stones; vultures will feast on your soldiers in the fields. As for Jezebel, she will die in the street and dogs will gnaw her bones." He walked out of the palace as calmly as he had come, leaving Ahab cowering in terror. For three years the king covered his head with ash each morning and wore sackcloth as a sign of penitence. He ordered God's altars to smoke day and night with sacrifice – and just to be on the safe side, he paid a whole new generation of Baal-prophets to

chant, dance, skewer themselves and pray for his deliverance
from Elijah's curse. But it was not true repentance, and it
failed. His people despised him, and foreign kings gathered
their armies and rode to the attack. Ahab heard of the
approach of Benhadad, king of Syria, and sat trembling on his
throne, asking his prophets what to do. They told him that if
he rode out in disguise to face his enemy, Baal would protect
him. But as soon as Ahab's chariot came in bowshot of the
Syrian army, an unknown man fired an arrow that slid
between the plates of Ahab's armour and left him drowning
in his own blood on the chariot floor. Jezebel survived for
thirty-five more years, ruling through her sons Ahaziah and
Joram. She sat in the royal palace like a spider in a web, a grim
old woman veiled in black, and servants told tales of magic
rituals and ceremonies of blood and death at dead of night.
Finally, God sent an army commander called Jehu to kill
Joram and seize the throne, and the court eunuchs picked
Jezebel up like a bolster and threw her out of the palace
window. She lay on the ground, flapping like a wounded bat,
and wild dogs caught her scent and ran up to tear her to
pieces. When the civil war ended and King Jehu sent servants
to gather her body for burial, there was nothing left on the
blood-soaked ground but a gnawed skull, the bones of her
feet and the palms of her hands.

Elisha and Naaman

Elisha was a prophet, Elijah's follower*. Not long after
Ahab's death, when Ahaziah was king and Jezebel was still
brooding in her black-curtained palace in Jezreel, God carried
Elijah into Heaven in a chariot of fire*, and left Elisha to lead
the prophets. Elisha quickly became famous. Priests admired
his piety, princes respected his statesmanship, and ordinary
people spoke of him in awed tones as a man who worked
miracles in the name of God*.

In Syria, the desert kingdom far north of Israel, there lived
a man called Naaman. He was a general and courtier, second
in importance only to the king himself. He had a hundred

wives, five hundred children and ten thousand servants. The
floors of his palace were marble; the walls were cedar-wood;
the furniture was ivory; the hangings were cloth-of-gold. But
for all his riches, for all his army of followers, Naaman lived
alone in a single room, and his servants fed him at arm's
length and shuddered to go near him. The reason was that he
was a leper. His skin flaked; the flesh stank on his bones; his
fingers and toes were stumps. For months, while doctors sent
to the ends of the earth for potions, and priests wailed prayers
at the altars of a thousand gods, Naaman sat and suffered. He
would have given every penny of his wealth, every arrow-
head of power, to find a cure. Then one day a little girl, the
Israelite slave of one of Naaman's wives, whispered to her
mistress that she wished Naaman could go to Israel, because
there was a prophet there who could end his leprosy. Naaman's wife told one of the harem eunuchs; the eunuch told
the guard-captain; the captain told Naaman's butler; the
butler wrote the message on a wax tablet and handed it to a
trembling slave to give his master. As soon as Naaman read
the news, he ordered camels to be laden with gold, silver and
robes of cloth-of-gold sewn with jewels. Then he, his officers
and his bodyguard rode with the procession into Israel, where
he handed the king a letter from his master, the king of Syria,
ordering him to cure Naaman's leprosy.

As soon as the king of Israel read the letter, he tore his
clothes and wailed, "Who does your master think I am – a
god? How should I know how to cure disease? This is a trick!
Your master's picking a quarrel. He wants an excuse for war."

Naaman sighed. He told his servants to reload the treasures
and go back the way they had come. But before they could
move a ragged, wild-eyed man pushed through the crowd and
said to the king, "Lord, let Naaman leave his treasure and his
bodyguard and come alone to my master, driving his own
chariot. My master will cure his leprosy."

"Who is your master?" asked the king. "Who are you?"

"My name is Gehazi," said the ragged man. "My master is
Elisha, prophet of God."

Naaman climbed into his jewelled chariot with its tasselled
sunshade. Gehazi took the horses' reins, and led them out of

the city and along rutted paths to a small hill-village. Hens squawked out of their way; donkeys brayed in the olive-groves; dirty children watched as they passed; it was ordinary life, unlike anything Naaman had seen before. Gehazi stopped at the door of a small hut, tethered Naaman's horses and went inside, leaving Naaman standing in the chariot, watched by the wide-eyed children. After a moment Gehazi came out and said, "My master says, "Dip yourself seven times in the river Jordan, and you'll be cured."

Naaman was furious. He snatched the horses's reins, whirled the chariot and galloped away. "Am I a beggar, to be so insulted?" he stormed at his servants in the royal palace. "Are there no rivers in Syria? Why should I humble myself to dip in the trickle these people call the Jordan?"

"Lord," said the bravest of his servants. "If the prophet had told you to do something huge and terrible, like sacrificing a million sheep or building a pyramid of gold, would you not have done it? Why refuse, when all he asks you to do is wash?"

Naaman bent his head, humbled. He rode to the banks of the Jordan, and dipped himself in the river seven times as Elisha had told him. When he came out the seventh time, his flesh was whole and his skin was as pink and pure as a baby's: his leprosy was cured. He galloped back to Jerusalem, gathered his bodyguard, his servants and his treasure and rode to Elisha's village. Soldiers, camels and chariots choked the streets, as Naaman dismounted from his chariot, knelt at Elisha's feet and said, "Now I know that the God of Israel is the only god. Take all I have: a thank-offering."

"No," said Elisha. "Believe in God, the God I serve, the God who cured you. He asks for nothing else."

"I believe," said Naaman. He bent his head for Elisha's blessing, climbed into his chariot and signed to his men to ride away. But before the tail of the procession had passed out of the village Gehazi, Elisha's servant, was leaping up and down at the head of it, signalling Naaman to stop. "Is all well?" asked Naaman.

"Lord, all's well. But my master says, there are two hermits in the village, holy men who worship God. They spend their days praying and reading holy books. They have no time to earn their living; they depend on charity. Give them a thousand silver pieces each, and a suit of clothes."

"Gladly," said Naaman. He ordered his servants to take the silver and the clothing and follow Gehazi back to the village, while the rest of the procession went on its way. Gehazi took the bags, dismissed the servants, and hid the money and clothes under the mattress on his bed. Then he went in to serve Elisha's dinner as if nothing had happened.

"Where have you been, Gehazi?" asked Elisha.

"Nowhere, lord."

"You went after Naaman. He stopped and spoke to you. What does a servant of God want with money or fine clothes? Your greed has earned you another present, one you never asked for. Look at your hands."

Gehazi lifted his hands to look at them, and gave a sob of horror. His fingers had twisted into stumps, his knuckle-bones jutted like lumps on a log, and his skin was dry, flaking, and transparent as onion-skin. He had cheated God, and his crime had turned him into a leper, white as snow.

9 · GOD AND HIS PEOPLE

For 250 years, from the time of Ahab onwards, there was a struggle in the people's minds. They had to choose between God and Baal. God demanded constant, strict obedience; Baal-worshippers could indulge themselves. Although there was always a handful of true believers, devoted to God's commandments, generation after generation of kings preferred idolatry, and even some prophets distrusted the word of God.

Jehu and Athaliah

Jehu was an officer in the royal guard. He was a God-fearing man, one of the few true believers in a court of Baal-worshippers. God inspired him to end the idolators' rule and bring back true religion – but the taste for blood turned Jehu's head and made him drunk on death. He began by killing two kings who were also high priests of Baal, Joram of Israel and Ahaziah of Judah, and by ordering the death of the witch-queen Jezebel, whose corpse dogs ate. Next, from his headquarters in the royal palace at Jezreel, he wrote to the leaders of the people saying, "There are seventy royal princes in the kingdom. Unless you want me to rule you, crown any one of them, and fight for him."

"What can we do?" the trembling counsellors asked one another. "Look how he treated Joram, Ahaziah and Jezebel. If we fight, he'll kill us too." They sent Jehu a message saying, "Master, we're your slaves. Tell us what to do."

"Kill the seventy princes and send me their heads."

But when two basketfuls of heads arrived and were piled in heaps at the palace gate, Jehu pretended to be horrified. "I executed three criminals, as God commanded," he said. "But who murdered all these innocent young men?" He sent soldiers to round up the counsellors, and personally sliced off each man's head. In this way he cleared the court of everyone loyal to the old royal family, and filled it with his own followers instead. Then he dealt with the priests and worshippers of Baal. He declared himself high priest, decreed a victory-celebration in the Baal-house, and said that every Baal-follower in the kingdom was to be there on pain of death. But as soon as the Baal-house was full, and the priests were sacrificing before a throng of people (unarmed as custom was), he barred the doors, sent eighty men with swords in by a side entrance, and told them not to come out until they had killed every living soul. When the massacre was over his soldiers dragged Baal's statues from the house among the corpses, hacked them to pieces and burnt them. They tore down the hangings and prised the gold plating from the walls. They plundered the treasuries and smashed down the ornamental doors. Jehu presented the shattered Baal-house to the people, and cowherds and shepherds used it as a byre for animals.

So Jehu made himself king of Israel, drowning all opposition in a storm of blood. The prophets and priests were silent: none risked reminding the king of the sixth of the Ten Commandments. But for all Jehu's bloodthirstiness he was God's anointed king, the man chosen to rid the country of Baal-worship, and he ruled for twenty-eight years and died peacefully in his bed. Not so Athaliah. She was Jezebel's daughter, and the mother of King Ahaziah of Judah whom Jehu killed. As soon as news reached Jerusalem of her son's death, she proclaimed herself queen of Judah and sent soldiers into the harem to murder every prince or princess of royal blood. The children's bodies were laid in front of the queen in rows like lambs on a butcher's floor. Athaliah filled the palace with wizards and magicians, and for six years made it the centre of a black magic cult which sickened and terrified her people. Day and night, her guards dragged pretty children to the palace, forced them to take part in orgies of sex and torture and then sacrificed them to Baal. Anyone who so much as whispered against Athaliah's rule was beaten to death and left to rot like a dead cat in an alleyway.

But although Athaliah's subjects were too frightened to act against her, God had not abandoned them. Six years before, when the harem children were massacred, he had saved the life of one of them, a newborn baby called Joash. The wife of Joiada, high priest of God's Temple, rolled the child in a pillow-case and smuggled him past the guards. She took him to the Temple, and for six years nursed him there in secret. The Temple was a secure hiding-place. God's presence hovered over its labyrinth of corridors and storerooms; Athaliah's superstitious soldiers whispered prayers to Baal as they passed, and none dared to step inside. The little boy played happily in the dusty rooms, never seeing daylight, never knowing the friendship of another child.

All this time, the high priest and his supporters were plotting revolution. Men from Athaliah's own bodyguard, ranging from high-ranking officers to the humblest archers and spearmen, slipped into the Temple at dead of night, muttered prayers to God and told the priests the latest palace news. At last, on Joash's sixth birthday, the high priest gathered all the conspirators in the Temple courtyard and showed them the little boy, dressed in glittering royal robes. One by one the men touched their lips to the hem of Joash's garment and swore a loyalty-oath. Then they divided into companies. Some slipped into the dark courtyard and stood on guard behind the gates. Others armed themselves with the sacred shields and spears of David's army, hung in the Temple years before, and surrounded Joash with a wall of weapons.

The high priest anointed Joash king, and laid the royal crown on his head. This was the agreed signal. The Temple trumpeters blew fanfares, choirs sang, and every man on guard, every soldier in the Temple, crashed his weapons together and shouted "God save the king!" The racket ran through the dark streets, and all the people of Jerusalem flung open their windows, cheering and shouting till the sound beat on Athaliah's shutters, high in the palace above their heads. She ran down the spiral stairs in her nightdress, unveiled and with her grey hair straggling, shrieking "Treason!" and calling for her guards. The conspirators carried her, snarling and wriggling, into the Temple courtyard. "Kill her!" the high priest said. "But not here, not in God's holy place. Take her outside and kill her there!" The soldiers dragged her to an alley beside the palace, the way to the royal stables, and cut her throat – and as soon as she was dead the people of Jerusalem swarmed into the palace with torches and fire-brands. They carried light into corners that had been dark for six long years, dragged out Athaliah's Baal-priests, witches and magicians and slit their throats. They burst open dungeons and torture-chambers and freed the captives; they smashed the Baal-statues and burned Athaliah's spell-books and the foul ingredients of her magic. Finally, they carried their six-year-old king shoulder-high into the palace and sat him on the royal throne. By the time dawn streaked the sky, the memory of Athaliah's wickedness had already begun to fade, as the shadows were fading in the city streets.

Jonah

Jonah lived in a village near Nazareth in Galilee. He was clearing weeds in his bean-patch one morning, when the voice of God suddenly filled his ears. "Jonah, go to Nineveh. Tell the people that their wickedness is condemned. Unless they give up Baal and worship me alone, they and their city will be blotted from the world."

Jonah threw down his spade, furious with God. The people of Nineveh were some of Israel's fiercest enemies. Their city lay a month's walking east of Galilee, across trackless deserts and bandit-infested mountains. Even if he survived the journey, why should the Ninevites listen to him? Why should they not cut his throat and throw him in a ditch? God's duty was to protect his worshippers in Israel, not to send prophets to convert their enemies.

Jonah knelt in the dust and prayed. He spoke no words, but God knew exactly what thoughts were in his mind. The voice filled his ears a second time. "Go to Nineveh. Tell the people to give up Baal and worship me alone, or they and their city will be blotted from the world."

"I won't do it," thought Jonah. "Why should I save Baal-worshippers, God's enemies? I'll take a ship, and sail to Tarshish. Let God send someone else to Nineveh."

Tarshish was a trading-port in the Mediterranean Sea, as far west from Galilee by water as Nineveh was east by land. Jonah saddled a donkey and rode to the port of Joppa. He found a boat loading for Tarshish, sold the donkey to pay his fare, wrapped himself in his cloak and lay down on deck. The sailors finished loading, prayed to their gods for a safe voyage and hauled in the mooring-ropes. They rowed the boat into clear water and hoisted sail. For some hours a warm wind drove the boat like a knife through blue sea capped with white. Then dusk fell, and with the darkness God sent storms. Clouds billowed, lightning ripped the sky, winds from all sides played catch with the boat like children with a ball. The sailors ran to haul in sail, but the mast split and took sails, rigging and half a dozen men overboard. The helmsman, high on his platform, tried to turn the boat to rescue his companions, but the sea snatched the steering-oar and snapped it like kindling-wood. The boat wallowed, and waves slopped over the sides faster than the men could bale. The crewmen began calling on their gods to rescue them. They were sailors and fishermen from a dozen countries, with as many gods. Some begged Poseidon the Earthshaker to quell the storm; others called on Baal, others on Dagon the Fishfather, others on Osiris Lord of the Dead, on Succothbenoth, Nergal, Nibhaz, Tartak and Adrammelech. They tossed corn, cloth-bales, even bags of gold-dust and live chickens, over the side as offerings – and with each sacrifice the storm howled louder and the waves leapt higher to drown the boat.

All at once the ship's captain noticed Jonah, wrapped in his sodden cloak, cringing grey-faced against the boat's side and waiting for death. "Get up!" shouted the captain. "Haven't you a god to pray to? Who are you, anyway?"

"I'm an Israelite," said Jonah. "I worship God almighty, who made the earth, the sea and everything in them."

"In that case," snapped the captain, "You're a fool to run away from him. This storm's your fault. You caused it; you find a way to end it."

"Throw me over the side," said Jonah miserably. "If God is angry with me alone, and if you sacrifice my life to him, he'll end the storm."

"Human sacrifice?" said the captain. "What d'you take us for – barbarians?" He ordered his men to the oars again, and they bent them like bows to turn the boat. But they made no progress, and at last the captain lifted his hands to the sky and prayed, "God of Israel, save us! Don't kill us for this man's guilt, and don't punish us for murdering him. Let the guilt of his death be yours, not ours." He shouted an order, and the crew picked Jonah up like a bundle of washing and threw him over the side. At once the sea calmed, the sky cleared and the winds disappeared. The crewmen fell to their knees on the waterlogged deck and babbled prayers of gratitude, each in his own language, to God who had spared their lives. As for Jonah, he sank like a stone. Water filled his mouth and pressed on his eyes; he heard his own blood roaring in his ears. He made no effort to save himself, but hung his hands by his side and surrendered to the water, hoping that God would drown him quickly and without suffering. Then he felt a surge of fins in the sea beside him, scales as rough as sand scraped his skin, and a huge toothless mouth gaped open and engulfed him. God had sent an enormous fish to rescue him. The monster surged from the sea-surface, and the sailors on the boat gibbered with fear to see it; inside its cavernous mouth, Jonah took a long breath of air before the fish splashed back into the sea and dived to the depths.

For three days and nights Jonah clung inside the monster's mouth. The huge fish tried to shake him free, or to wash him out by gulping water. If it had stayed below the surface, Jonah would have drowned. But the monster, like Jonah himself, had to breathe air, and every few minutes, when it surfaced to gulp air and spout waste water through its vent-hole, Jonah snatched another breath. He was cold, sodden and terrified. He might have cursed God, and died for it. But instead he prayed for forgiveness, silently in his thoughts, and whenever the monster basked on the surface he opened his mouth and sang hymns of praise*. The sound boomed round the monster's mouth like the echo in a cave – and at last the monster, maddened by the noise as cattle are goaded by stinging flies, writhed from the depths of the sea to the shallows, opened its jaws and spat Jonah out on an empty beach. Jonah lay exhausted, clutching sand as if it were a lifeline, and as he lay there his ears filled with God's voice, speaking the same remorseless message as before: "Go to Nineveh. Tell the people to give up Baal and worship me alone, or they and their city will be blotted from the earth."

Jonah dragged himself to his feet and stumbled along the sand towards a village in the distance, the shacks of fishermen, with upturned boats in the sand and gutted fish drying in the sun. The fisherwomen gave him food to eat and a bundle of nets to sleep on, and in a day or two, when he was strong enough to travel, they put him on the road for home. As soon as he reached his own village he saddled a second ass and set off across the desert and through the hills for Nineveh. The donkey's feet sank in the hot sand or scrabbled on pebbly mountain-tracks, and Jonah kept looking over his shoulder for bandits, cursing his fate and praying to God to keep him safe. But he saw no one, until after a month's riding he came in sight of Nineveh. The city was enormous: it would have taken three days to walk through it from side to side, and its suburbs sprawled out of sight along the banks of a broad, slow-flowing river. Jonah groaned. "How can one man persuade a place this size to give up idolatry?" he thought. "How can I convert a million people? As soon as I open my mouth, they'll string me from the nearest tree."

He forded the river and drove the ass up the far bank. At once he was surrounded by inquisitive children, and soon adults joined them: women who had been scrubbing clothes at the river's edge, a couple of ferrymen, a soldier from the palace guard. Jonah cleared his throat nervously, like a schoolchild frightened of a teacher. "God speaks," he said in a low voice. "Unless you give up Baal and worship God alone, you and your city will be wiped from the earth."

To his amazement, instead of dragging him from the ass and stoning him, the people no sooner heard these words than they threw their arms in the air and ran away shrieking, "God's messenger is here! God speaks! Repent! Repent!" The same thing happened wherever he went. People ran into their houses to change their bright clothes for sacks and blankets; they smeared their faces with dust; they banged their foreheads on the ground, praying to God for mercy, or ran with tears streaming down their faces to warn their neighbours. In the end a group of soldiers galloped up and took Jonah, trembling, before the king himself. Once more Jonah repeated his message, and once more his words caused panic. The courtiers milled in all directions, tearing off their jewels and gold-sewn clothes; the king crashed his sceptre on the ground and proclaimed that all Baal's shrines in the city were to be destroyed and that sacrifices were to be made to God before nightfall, on pain of death.

At first, Jonah was pleased with the effect his words were having. But then he began to lose his temper. "All my life," he thought, "All my people's lives, we've worshipped God. We've followed his commandments, lived good and holy lives – and he's repaid us with disaster, misery and death. Now all these heathens have to do – people who have worshipped idols all their lives, who have broken every one of the Ten Commandments, who have committed human sacrifice and cannibalism – all they have to do is grovel on the ground and tell God how sorry they are, and at once he spares their lives. It's unfair! Why should wicked people be better treated than good ones?" He rode out of the city, past the groups of people eagerly chopping up Baal-idols to build altar-fires to God, and sat sulkily down in the dust beside the gate. He was on the eastern edge of Nineveh, the opposite side to the river. He could see nothing but desert: flat, tawny sand shimmering to the horizon. It was blisteringly hot. The sun beat on his head and there was no greenery, no vegetation of any kind, to shelter him. He bowed his head and sat, pouring sand through his fingers and sulking like a child. After a while, in the bare sand beside him, he saw a small green shoot. As he watched, it grew before his eyes: to finger-length, to shoulder-height, and finally to a tall plant with shiny, fern-like leaves. It was a miracle: God had provided a plant from nothing, to shelter him. Jonah lay down in the shade, and slept. But that night God sent a caterpillar to gnaw the stem of the plant, and by morning when Jonah awoke the stalk and leaves were lying on the ground beside him, already withered and yellowing. "Why, God, why?" shouted Jonah. "What had that plant done, that it had to die? Why do you always spare the guilty and punish the innocent?"

"Are you angry about the plant?" asked God.

"Of course I'm angry about the plant!"

"And are you sorry for the plant?"

"Of course I am."

"Well, if you're sorry for something you neither planted, grew nor cared for, why should I not take pity on Nineveh? There are a million people, most of them so innocent that that can't even tell left from right, and countless million animals. God's mercy is what it is. Don't question it: pray to receive it, and accept it when it comes."

Hezekiah

King Hezekiah of Judah was a fool and a coward. He was afraid of his wives, his bodyguards, his slaves, even the hawks in the royal mews and the shadows on the wall. He was afraid of God and afraid of Baal, so he worshipped both of them equally. In the fourth year of his reign the Assyrians overwhelmed the southern half of the Promised Land. They killed every man of fighting age, enslaved women, children and old people, and filled the towns and farms with settlers from their own country, barbarians who worshipped stones, logs, ploughshares, even the man in the moon and the wind that moans in hollow trees. Finally, as wolves fall on a sheepfold, they attacked Hezekiah's capital city Jerusalem. They besieged it with two hundred thousand men, and sat waiting in the sun to see if the inhabitants preferred to surrender, fight, or starve to death.

"What can we do?" wailed Hezekiah. He ran round his palace like a terrified chicken, squawking orders. He sent a messenger to gallop by secret ways to Egypt and to offer the Pharaoh half-shares in Judah's wealth if he would only send horsemen and chariots to defend it. He made the palace

astrologers count stars and pore over sky-charts to predict the
city's future. He sent slaves with crowbars to prise the gold
facings from the Temple walls; then he piled the treasure in
carts and sent it to the Assyrian commander, with a grovelling
letter admitted his guilt (whatever it was) and begging the
Assyrians to show them mercy and go back home. Hezekiah
watched from the battlements, biting his nails, as the treasure-
carts rumbled to the Assyrian lines. There was a long pause
while Assyrian soldiers unloaded the sheets of gold, glinting
like beacons in the sun, and stacked them in tents. Then
another procession formed and made its way back towards
the gates. Drummers and trumpeters split the air; behind
them soldiers surrounded a high-ranking officer on horseback; behind them more soldiers led Hezekiah's empty treasure-carts, and a single prisoner laden with chains. A trickle
of terror ran down Hezekiah's back: the prisoner was the spy
he'd sent secretly to Pharaoh.

The procession stopped at the city walls, and the officer
rode forward, alone. He signalled to his trumpeters to blow a
fanfare, and then shaded his eyes to look up at the people on
the battlements. "I am the Rabshakeh," he said. "I am the lips
and tongue of the Great King. The Great King speaks. Why
do you trust the Egyptians, those broken reeds? Why do you
send us bribes, water-drops in the ocean of the Great King's
wealth? People of Jerusalem, why do you trust Hezekiah – ?"

"My lord," interrupted Hezekiah hastily. "Wouldn't you
like to come inside the palace, and discuss this matter in your
own language? We have translators. It's wrong for two of the
Great King's highest-ranking servants, such as ourselves, to
negotiate where ordinary folk can listen and comment on
every word."

The Assyrian waved an arm for silence, and then continued
in his harshly-accented Hebrew as if Hezekiah had never
spoken. "People of Israel, hear your choice. Surrender to the
Great King, and he'll take you to live in a land like your own
land, a land of corn and wine, a land of bread and vineyards, a
land of honey and olive oil. That choice means life. Or choose
to stay with Hezekiah, and sit out the siege. That choice
means death."

He wheeled his horse and galloped away. The soldiers and musicians rode after him in a cloud of dust. The treasure-carts and the spy were left contemptuously at the foot of the walls. On the battlements, the people turned silent eyes on Hezekiah. Three times he opened his mouth to speak to them, and could find no words. In the end he turned and hurried into the palace, trying to look like a man with urgent matters to arrange. He ran into his private apartments and barred the door. A crowd of inquisitive servants gathered. They heard the king moaning and whimpering, and the creak of furniture as he flung himself from table to chair to bed. Then they were brushed aside, and a short, bushy-eyebrowed man pushed past, knocked on the door and said, "Hezekiah, open this door. I'll tell you how to defeat the Assyrians."

"Who is it?"

"Isaiah the prophet."

"What can you do? How can one prophet defeat an army?"

"I speak for God. Abandon Baal, trust God alone, and he will save the people."

"The people of Arpad, Hamath, Hena, Ivah and Sephar-vaim trusted their gods, and ended up as slaves. Why should our God help us?"

"Trust him and see."

Reluctantly Hezekiah opened the door. He walked with Isaiah to the Temple, and the silent crowd followed. Hezekiah bent his head and prayed, "O Lord God of Israel, who live between the cherubim, who made heaven, earth and all that lives or breathes in them, bow down your ears and listen; open your eyes and see. The king of Assyria has challenged you. His army has invaded your land and enslaved your people. Only we are left. Save us, Lord: show all people that you alone are God."

He finished, and waited for a puff of smoke, a clap of thunder, or some other sign that God had heard. But there was nothing. Sighing, he walked wearily along the corridor and up the spiral stairway to the palace – and when he was halfway up a messenger ran after him, panting the news that the entire Assyrian army, of two hundred thousand men, was dead. The soldiers' flesh had erupted in boils and sores; their camp was heaped with bodies, stinking and rotting in the sun.*

Hezekiah skipped upstairs to the palace, shouting with joy. He ordered every musician in Jerusalem to the Temple, to give thanks to God. He declared a thanksgiving banquet, and offered Isaiah any reward he cared to name. But Isaiah refused. "The Assyrians besieged Jerusalem, and God punished them," he said. "But what of you, my lord? You should have trusted God alone, and you bargained with Egyptians and offered bribes. You've condemned yourself."

That same evening, the inside of Hezekiah's thigh erupted in a foul-smelling, yellow boil, exactly like those which had killed the Assyrians. The king lay on his bed, whimpering, and sent for Isaiah. "Is there no cure?" he groaned.

Isaiah answered grimly, "God speaks. Set your affairs in order, for you will surely die."

Hezekiah turned his face to the wall and sobbed, "What crime have I committed? Am I to die simply for being a coward? Lord, I beg you, let me live a little longer."

Isaiah said, "God hears. Dry your tears. In three days' time, go to the Temple and worship him. You'll live a little longer."

"How much longer?" asked Hezekiah, eager as a child. "And how can I go to the Temple, with my leg like this?"

"Take a handful of figs and put them on the boil," said Isaiah. "You'll live."

"What proof is there?" asked Hezekiah. "How can I trust God's word?"

Isaiah sighed. "With every word you say, you condemn yourself again. Look at the sundial on the garden wall. If the shadow goes backwards one hour instead of forwards, will that make you trust God's word?"

"Yes!" cried Hezekiah. "One single hour!"

He sent a servant to the window, and the man ran back to say that the shadow on the sundial had moved back one hour. Isaiah said, "Hezekiah, mortal time means nothing to God. You have fifteen years more of life, and then you'll surely die. In one hundred years from now your people will be enslaved: their children's children will be taken away to be eunuchs, in the palace of the King of Babylon. Misery and hard labour will be their punishment for idolatry. But as for you, you'll live until you die."

Hezekiah joyfully wiped away his tears. What did he care about his people's children's children, a hundred years from now? He had never even heard of Babylon. But he himself was alive, not dead; his prayers had been answered. He thought he understood God at last. He sat up eagerly, and called for figs.

Captivity

God gave Hezekiah fifteen more years of life, exactly as he had promised. And in the first weeks, when the boil had lessened on Hezekiah's leg and he was able to walk with a stick, ambassadors from the king of Babylon brought presents and a letter congratulating him on his recovery. Hezekiah was delighted. "Let me show you my treasures," he said. Remember every detail, so that your master will realise that he's made friends with Solomon's heir, the greatest king on earth."

He limped from his throne and led the ambassadors round the palace, pointing out the bejewelled walls and gold-sewn tapestries, the storerooms heaped with spices, oil-jars and gold, the armoury, the chargers in the stables and the hawks in the royal mews: he left nothing out. The ambassadors went home to Babylon and reported everything they had seen – and the scribes of the king of Babylon duly noted on clay tablets that Jerusalem was worth conquering, and stored the information in the royal files. The Babylonians were in no hurry: they could bide their time.

In the century after Hezekiah's death, seven kings ruled in Jerusalem. Except, briefly, for Josiah* they were all idolators. Day and night the altars of a thousand gods* smoked with sacrifice. The Temple priests were stripped, shaved bald and flogged through the streets while the people pelted them with filth. In the time of King Manasseh newborn babies were dismembered at dead of night, and their still-throbbing hearts were used for magic rituals. God sent prophets, from Isaiah to Jeremiah, from Hosea to Ezekiel, to warn the people that he would bring such evil on Jerusalem that people's ears would sting to hear of it, that he would wipe the city clean as a person scours a plate – and their hearers kicked them away like dogs. At last, in the reign of Jehoiachin, the sixth king of Hezekiah's dynasty, God acted. In Babylon, scribes handed King Nebuchadnezzar the century-old tablets describing Jerusalem's riches, and the king gathered an army to plunder them*. As the Babylonians advanced, the kings of Ammon, Moab, Syria and the other states bordering on the Promised Land took chariots, horsemen and foot-soldiers to join them. Nebuchadnezzar ringed Jerusalem with a million men; his siege-weapons splintered the gates and his soldiers poured inside like ants. They plundered the palace and the Temple. They stripped the decoration from the walls and piled the sacred vessels in sacks for carrying. They enslaved King Jehoiachin, his mother, his courtiers, his bodyguard and ten thousand lords, craftsmen and army officers and took them to Babylon in chains. In Jehoiachin's place Nebuchadnezzar put a puppet-king, Zedekiah. He sat in a ruined palace on a wooden throne and ruled a rabble of peasants, kitchen-maids and those too old, young or feeble to be any risk to Babylon.

For a while, Zedekiah ruled docilely. But after eleven years, as if he could stand not another second of insignificance, he armed his people with sticks, stones and swords forged from ploughshares and pruning-hooks, and set this pathetic army against the might of Babylon. Nebuchadnezzar's forces wasted neither effort nor manpower in attacking Jerusalem; they sat quietly outside the walls to starve the inhabitants. After four months, when half Zedekiah's people were dead and the rest were too weakened by hunger to defend themselves, the king ordered the city gates to be thrown open to the enemy. The Babylonians sacked the city. What was wood, they burned; what was stone, they smashed; what was open space, they ploughed up and sowed with salt. They battered Zedekiah's children to death; then they gouged out his eyes, loaded him with chains and took him with the other slaves to Babylon. Jerusalem, the city founded by David and beautified by Solomon, was a ruin tenanted only by birds and dogs. Its pillars and walls were rubble, its doors, roof-beams and wall-panels were heaps of ash. The people who had once been the proudest in the world, whose arrogance had led them to snap their fingers at God himself, were scattered. The poor were dead, or cowered in the hills in caves and holes. The rich, who had mistaken worldly wealth for true riches, that is the fear of God, were slaves in Babylon, as their ancestors had been slaves in Egypt a thousand years before.

10 · BABYLON

God kept the Chosen People (the Jews) in exile for two generations. They were slaves in a foreign country; they wept when they remembered Jerusalem*; they had no possessions and no power. There was only one small hope. For all their years of idolatry, they were still God's Chosen People. If, of their own free will, they abandoned Baal, returned to God and kept his commandments, they might still be saved. The seeds of obedience were dormant: they could grow again. In each generation, God sent a handful of true believers to preach his commandments and keep the faith.

Feet of Clay

Every summer Nebuchadnezzar, king of kings, chose a hundred of the prettiest and most intelligent slave-children in his kingdom. The girls were sent to his harem, and the boys went to be educated in writing, languages, magic and astrology: skills which would one day make them judges, historians, soothsayers and royal advisers. In the year when the Jewish slaves arrived in Babylon Nebuchadnezzar's chief eunuch (the headmaster of the royal school) chose four children for such education. His servants bought the boys in the slave-market, bathed them, gave them the Babylonian names Belteshazzar, Shadrach, Meshach and Abednego, and sat them at a cedarwood table in front of silver dishes of all kinds of roast meat: lamb, goat, beef, swan. To their astonishment, the boys refused to eat.

"What's the matter?" the chief eunuch asked the eldest boy. "Don't you know it's treason to refuse the king's food?

What's your name – Belteshazzar? You must learn to do as you're told."

"Sir," said the boy politely, "My name's Daniel, not Belteshazzar. Your cooks kill animals for food in Babylonian fashion and not according to Jewish law. Neither I nor my friends can eat your meat."

"Belteshazzar – Daniel – our master the king (may he live forever) cares for the health of his slaves, as well as for their education. He sends food from the palace kitchens, one portion for each child in the school. If I send four portions back each day, and if you or your friends fall sick, the king will have me hanged."

"Sir," said Daniel, "For ten days give us nothing but lentils and cold water. Then let the doctors examine us – and if we look faint or feeble, deal with us as you please."

The chief eunuch reluctantly agreed. For ten days, while the other children fed on food and wine from the king's own kitchen, Daniel, Shadrach, Meshach and Abednego tasted nothing but lentils and cold water. On the eleventh day the king's doctors examined them, and found them as strong and healthy as any other children in the school. From that time on, the chief eunuch gave them a cook of their own, to prepare food after Jewish law, and divided their royal portions among his other pupils. He also allowed them to keep their hair long in Jewish style, and to pray to their own God three times each day, while the rest of the pupils sacrificed to the idols of Babylon. He even let Daniel keep his Jewish name. The four boys throve, and soon learned everything their teachers had to tell them. There were no others like them in all Babylon.*

In the year that the four boys were sixteen, King Nebuchadnezzar began to be tormented by nightmares. One dream in particular racked him, night after night, until he was too frightened of it even to go to bed. He sent for his astrologers and said, "I'm troubled by a dream."

"O king, live forever," answered the astrologers. "Tell the king's servants the dream, and we'll explain it."

But Nebuchadnezzar was afraid even to describe the dream. He said, "Find out the dream yourselves, by magic. If you explain it, you'll be second only to me in Babylon. If you don't, my guards will cut you in pieces and make dungheaps of your houses."

"O king, live forever," quavered the astrologers. "How can the king's servants enter the king's dreams? Unless we hear the dream from the king's own lips, how can we explain it?"

"Guards!" shouted Nebuchadnezzar, "Round them up and kill them! Kill every wise man in Babylon, and every pupil in the wisdom-school."

The astrologers scattered like frightened starlings. They scrabbled through spell-books, trying to find what the king's dream might be. They grovelled before the statues of their gods. The bravest loaded treasure-carts and made escape-plans; the most cowardly huddled beside their wives and children and waited, trembling, for the executioners. The pupils and teachers of the wisdom-school ran up and down in panic, snatching papers from cupboards, slamming doors, wringing their hands and whimpering. Only Daniel, Shadrach, Meshach and Abednego were unafraid. They prayed calmly to God as they did each morning, then rode out to meet the captain of the royal guard. "Sir," said Daniel. "Leave these people in peace. Take us to the king. We'll explain his dream."

Soldiers led the four boys to Nebuchadnezzar, and the wise men, soothsayers and astrologers crept out of hiding to hear what they would say. "Belteshazzar, whose name is also Daniel," said Nebuchadnezzar, "Can you tell me my dream?"

"Not I alone," answered Daniel. "No mortal can enter other people's heads and know their thoughts. But the God I serve, God who made the Earth and everything in it, sent this dream for a purpose, and has told it to me, together with its explanation."

"First tell the dream."

"You dreamed of a statue, an idol of idols. Its head was gold, its breast and arms were silver, its belly was brass, its legs were iron and its feet were clay. You saw a stone roll from a mountainside and smash the idol to pieces, so that the gold, silver, brass, iron and clay were like chaff at harvest-time. Wind scattered the chaff to the ends of the earth, until only the stone was left: a mountain that filled the world from horizon to horizon. That was your dream, my lord, and this is the explanation. You, sir, are king of kings: God has given you power, riches and glory. You are the statue's golden head. After you there will be a second kingdom, of lesser glory: this is the statue's silver parts. The third kingdom will be of brass and the fourth of iron. When iron gives way to clay, the kingdom will be at its weakest point, and will be smashed to pieces as the statue was. God will scatter its remains like chaff, and make a final, everlasting kingdom, strong as the mountain which destroyed gold, silver, brass and iron."

King Nebuchadnezzar stood up, ashen-faced. "That was my dream," he whispered. "That was my dream exactly." He knelt at Daniel's feet and kissed the hem of his robe. When the courtiers saw it – since no one was allowed to hold his head higher than the king's – they, too, grovelled on the floor. Nebuchadnezzar led Daniel up the golden steps, sat him on the footstool beside the royal throne and said, "Because you explained the dream, because you showed me God's power, you shall be courtier of courtiers, judge of judges, lord of lords. Be second to me in Babylon."

The Burning Fiery Furnace

King Nebuchadnezzar made a Baal-statue fifteen times human size and dressed in gold. Then he summoned every lord, judge, treasurer, counsellor and sheriff in Babylon and said, "Listen to the words of Nebuchadnezzar, king of kings. Whenever you hear the sound of the cornet, flute, harp, sackbut, psaltery, dulcimer and all kinds of music, you are to fall down and worship this statue. Anyone who disobeys will be thrown into a burning fiery furnace."

The princes, judges, treasurers, counsellors and sheriffs bowed like corn bending in the breeze. "O king, live forever," they said with a single voice. "As the king orders, so it shall be."

Some days later Nebuchadnezzar's Baal-priests went to him and said, "O King, live forever. The king decreed that everyone who heard the sound of the cornet, flute, harp, sackbut, psaltery, dulcimer and all kinds of music should fall down and worship the golden statue, and that anyone who refused would be thrown into a burning fiery furnace. There are three Jews, Shadrach, Meshach and Abednego. Lord, they ignore the king's orders. They say that they worship no god but God. They refuse to bow to statues."

Nebuchadnezzar sent guards to arrest Shadrach, Meshach and Abednego. "You have one last chance," he said. "When you hear the sound of the cornet, flute, harp, sackbut, psaltery, dulcimer and all kinds of music, fall to the ground and worship. If you don't, you'll be thrown into a burning fiery furnace – and then you can beg this God of yours to save you."

He signalled to his musicians. The sounds of cornet, flute, harp, sackbut, psaltery, dulcimer and all kinds of music filled the air, and everyone fell on the ground and worshipped the golden statue. Even Nebuchadnezzar grovelled. Only Shadrach, Meshach and Abednego stood where they were, waiting for the noise to end. "Is this your answer?" Nebuchadnezzar shouted.

"Sir, we'll never bow to idols. Do what you like to us. God will save us."

"Guards!" shouted Nebuchadnezzar. "Stoke the burning fiery furnace. Chain Shadrach, Meshach and Abednego and throw them in. Not even the king's favourites can disobey the king."

The guards loaded Shadrach, Meshach and Abednego with chains, and carried them like parcels to the furnace. The furnace was built in the palace yard: a thin-necked opening and a vast, brick-lined pit. The pit was full of pine-branches and pitch-soaked logs, and the heat was so fierce that when the soldiers carrying Shadrach, Meshach and Abednego reached the lip, their arteries burst and they fell down dead. Shadrach, Meshach and Abednego rolled over the lip of the furnace and fell into the fiery heart.

Normally, when people were executed in a burning fiery furnace, there were no sounds but a few brief screams and a hiss as the victims' body-fat melted in the flames. But on this occasion the watching princes, governors, captains, judges, treasurers, counsellors and sheriffs heard singing. They looked at Nebuchadnezzar. He was gripping the arms of his throne and staring rigidly ahead like a man in a trance. The guard-captain fell on his face in front of him and said, "O King, live forever. The king's orders have been obeyed."

"Look!" whispered Nebuchadnezzar, pointing a shaking finger at the pit. "How many men did you throw into the burning fiery furnace?"

"O King, live forever. Three, chained hand and foot."

"I see four men, walking in the flames and singing.* Three of them are Shadrach, Meshach and Abednego, and the fourth is an angel, the servant of their God."

Nebuchadnezzar walked as close as he dared to the lip of the burning fiery furnace and called, "Shadrach, Meshach, Abednego, servants of God, come out!" Then, to gasps from the princes, governors, captains, judges, treasurers, counsellors and sheriffs, Shadrach, Meshach and Abednego stepped out of the furnace, and the fire had melted their chains but left their clothes, bodies and hair unsinged. They stood silhouetted like angels in the fire-glow, and the perfume of flowers, not the stench of burning, filled the air. Nebuchadnezzar led them up the steps of his throne, sat them on stools, and made a new proclamation to his courtiers. "There is no god but God. Anyone who refuses to worship him will be cut in pieces and thrown on the dunghill. As for Shadrach, Meshach and Abednego, they are declared First Courtiers, Friends of the King, Chief Men in Babylon. Sound trumpets! Let it be done as I command."

Weighed in the Balance

Soon after the testing of Shadrach, Meshach and Abednego in the burning fiery furnace, Nebuchadnezzar began to be plagued with dreams again. First he dreamed that he was a tree in a field, and that angels came from heaven to lop him. Then he dreamed that his hair grew into feathers and his nails into talons; he pecked and strutted like a bird. Finally he

dreamed that he was not a man but a bull – and this delusion
lasted when he woke up, so that he ran into the palace
garden* and began eating grass and bellowing. His courtiers
kept his illness secret for seven years. He spent his days
browsing in the gardens, and his nights eating human food
and sleeping in the royal apartments – and all the time he was
under the twin delusions that his people were worshippers of
the Jewish god, and that he himself was a sacred bull. At the
very end his wits returned, and he walked into the throne-
room, upright like a human being, singing a hymn of praise to
God*. But madness had weakened his body as well as his
mind, and before he could be told about about his sickness, or
discover that his people were plunged as deeply in Baal-
worship as ever, he caught a chill and died.

There followed twenty years of civil war. Nebuchadnezzar's children squabbled for the throne, the priests shifted
their loyalty according to which prince offered them most
power, and all the while the Medes, Babylon's northern
enemies, were massing for final, total war. Time and again the
Jewish prophets warned their Babylonian masters that unless
the people repented and turned to God, their empire would
be destroyed; the Babylonians replied each time by redoub-
ling sacrifice to Baal. "We live in the most powerful empire in
the world," they said. "The Medes are a grain of grit in Baal's
eye. He has only to blink, and they'll be wiped from the
world. Who needs your God? What did he ever do for you?
Who let us make you slaves?"

So they jeered – and God ignored them for a whole human
generation. But then King Belshazzar gave a feast for a thousand of his lords, and at the height of it he called for wine and
said, "Bring the cups Nebuchadnezzar looted from the temple of that Jewish God. I want to drink a toast." His slaves
hurried to the storerooms, fetched out the gold, silver, brass,
iron, stone and wooden vessels from the Temple of Jerusalem
– the vessels which God allowed none but his priests to touch.
The slaves dusted them and handed them to the king.
Belshazzar poured wine into a golden cup looted from beside
the Ark of the Covenant, cried, "A toast to the god of gold!"
and drank it dry. The cup went from lord to lord, and each

man filled it, repeated the toast, and drank. The same thing happened with each of the other cups: wine was poured and toasts were drunk to the gods of silver, brass, iron, stone and wood. Belzhazzar and his lords began shouting, laughing, hammering on the tables and singing mocking songs about the God of the Jews and the slaves who worshipped him. They stripped God's priests naked and forced them to dance, while eunuch-musicians played tunes made from Jewish hymns and psalms.

The noise was at its height when suddenly Belshazzar dropped his wine-cup and jumped to his feet, sending his footstool clattering. When the king rose, the lords were bound to stand as well. They clutched the tables for support and peered at their master. Belshazzar, white with fear, was pointing at the palace wall. In the dim light the fingers of a man's hand had appeared and were writing words: four rows of letters that blazed like fire. There were no sounds in the room but the lords' terrified breathing and the hiss and scratch of the writing. Then the hand disappeared, the stench of burning faded, and only the words were left: it was as if the wall had been branded like an animal. Belshazzar and his lords sank down on their cushions. They looked at one another with wide, white eyes. "Fetch the wise men," croaked Belshazzar. "Let them read it. Let them explain."

The palace astrologers, soothsayers and Baal-priests stood in a gaggle, staring at the writing. "Look carefully," said Belshazzar. "Whoever explains it will have scarlet robes, a gold chain, and power over one third of Babylon."

The astrologers, soothsayers and Baal-priests whispered among themselves. Then one of them stepped forward. "O king, live forever," he said in a trembling voice. "This is a god's handwriting. What mortal can read it or explain it?"

"Daniel can!" exclaimed a voice from the side of the room. The lords shrank in horror. It was a woman's voice, the voice of Belshazzar's queen – and it was unheard-of for a woman to burst in on men while they feasted. Belshazzar's wife walked across the room, holding her veil across her face, and knelt before her husband. "O king, live forever," she said. "Send for the slave Daniel. Fifty years ago, he explained Nebuchadnezzar's mysteries; let him explain this one, now."

The lords waited for Belshazzar to order his wife's arrest. But he was like a person hypnotised. He told his guards, in a toneless voice, to fetch Daniel, and watched slack-eyed as the old man picked his way through the wine-puddles on the floor, while the astrologers drew their skirts away from him, the soothsayers hissed and the Baal-priests made the sign of the evil eye. "Are you Daniel?" asked Belshazzar. "Are you the slave who explained Nebuchadnezzar's dreams?"

"I am God's servant," answered Daniel.

"If you explain this writing, your rewards will be scarlet robes, a gold chain of office and power over one third of Babylon."

"Keep your rewards," said Daniel. "What point has mortal power? Nebuchadnezzar out-roared all human kings – and still he was humbled, made to eat grass like a bull, till he admitted that there was no god but God. And what of you, Belshazzar? You filled the sacred Temple vessels with wine, you drank toasts to gods of gold, silver, brass, iron, stone and wood, you mocked the God who made you, who gave you the breath of life. The writing says MENE, MENE, TEKEL, UPHARSIN. You are weighed in the balance and found wanting.* Your kingdom is given to the Medes."

Once again, Belshazzar's lords gasped with horror – not at the prophecy, but that a slave should dare so to address a king. But Belshazzar sprawled back on his throne, as arrogant as ever, and said in a bored voice, "You've explained, and now you'll be rewarded. Give him scarlet robes and a gold chain of office, and put him in charge of a third of the slaves in Babylon. Fetch mops; wash the wall. And pour more wine. The gods of of gold, silver, brass, iron, stone and wood will save us."

Slaves hustled Daniel out and began pouring wine. The palace filled with the drunken laughter of the king and his lords, even louder than before. And in that same night the Medes invaded Babylon, sacked the city, burned the palace and everyone in it and enslaved the people, exactly as God had said.

Daniel in the Lions' Den

Darius, king of the Medes, divided Babylon into three provinces. Each province had its own governor, and one of them was Daniel. By now Daniel was eighty years old, and frail; but still he visited every town and village in his province judging lawsuits, hearing grievances and preaching obedience to the Ten Commandments. Ordinary people spoke of him with awe, as someone halfway between a wizard* and a saint; the lords by contrast considered him a jumped-up slave and plotted to topple him. Day and night their spies watched for signs of feeble-mindedness or treachery which could be reported to the Great King, and found none. "Very well," said the lords. "If we can't find any other fault, we'll use his religion against him." They asked Darius to add a decree to the Laws of the Medes and Persians saying that for one month no one was to beg favours of any god or mortal except the Great King, and that anyone who disobeyed should be thrown into a den of lions. A few days later they reported to Darius that Daniel had been observed, three times each day, kneeling and praying to the Jewish God. Darius sent spies of his own, and they found Daniel praying exactly as described.

"What harm is he doing?" Darius asked the lords. "He's an old man and a loyal servant. Let him pray as he pleases."

"Great King, live forever," the lords replied. "The king decreed that for thirty days, whoever asked favours of any god or mortal but the Great King was to be thrown to the lions. No person on earth, not even the Great King himself, can change the King's decree. Daniel is guilty: he must die."

Darius sighed and gave the order. In the palace cellars was a lions' den, with seven lions. Darius' servants starved them for a week, and then the guards bundled Daniel into the lions' den, slammed the door and blocked it with a stone. Darius sealed the entrance with the royal seal, and each of the lords pressed his ring into the warm wax as witness that Daniel had been punished as the law decreed. Then they went upstairs and left Daniel to his fate. Darius passed a sleepless night. He threw off his bed-covers. He paced up and down. He shouted. He knelt on the floor and prayed. His slaves took him soothing drinks, and he sent them away untasted. Musicians tuned up to play, and the king drove them out, bellowing for silence. As soon as it was dawn, Darius ran to the lions' den and began tearing off the seals with his bare hands. Servants levered the stone aside and unbarred the door, while Darius stood in his nightshirt shouting, "Daniel, servant of God, are you alive or dead?"

For a moment, when the door was opened, there was silence. Then Daniel walked unharmed out of the lions' den. "Darius," he said, "God saw that I was innocent, and sent his angels to stop the lions' mouths. Kneel, and give thanks."

There and then, in front of the astonished servants, Darius king of the Medes knelt in his own cellar and gave thanks to God. Then he stood up and ordered the treacherous lords to be arrested and thrown to the lions. "From this day on," he said, "Let all people, in every province of my kingdom, tremble before Daniel's God, who performs wonders and miracles and who saved Daniel from the lions. Write this decree in the Laws of the Medes and Persians, where it can never be blotted out."*

Esther

Darius' decree gave the Jews freedom of religion. In the next twenty years they turned more and more to God – and many Babylonians, their masters and mistresses, began to be converted too. But there were others, idolators, who detested Jewish ways and let race-hatred rule their lives. In the time of King Ahasuerus, a merchant called Haman picked a quarrel with his Jewish neighbour Mordecai. It began when Mordecai refused to step aside for Haman in the street, and swelled until Haman loathed Mordecai's clothes, his house, even the flowers in his garden and the way he shaded his eyes or combed his beard.

On the third anniversary of Ahasuerus' coronation, the king gave a banquet of celebration. There were one hundred and twenty-seven provinces in his empire, and he invited the governors, their wives, their grown-up children and their courtiers. The palace courtyards were shaded with white, green and blue awnings hung from silver rings. The guests lay on cedarwood couches and drank from golden cups. Inside the harem, away from public gaze, Queen Vashti, Ahasuerus' senior wife, gave a banquet of equal magnificence for the visitors' wives and daughters. While the men feasted, the first talk was all of wealth: of treasure-houses, horses, racing-camels, hawks. Then the boasting turned to wives, and each man in turn described the most beautiful woman in his harem. Suddenly Ahasuerus banged his cup on the table and shouted, "None of these women outshine the queen! Chamberlain! Tell Vashti to come out and show these lords her charms."

After a while the chamberlain came back from the harem and said, "Great King, live forever. Her majesty says that it would be dishonour to show herself."

"Dishonour?" shouted Ahasuerus. "Her disobedience dishonours me! If the Great King's wife refuses him, what wife in Babylon will ever obey her husband? Hear the Great King's words. The woman Vashti is no longer Queen. If the Great King's eyes ever see her again, she dies."

In the weeks that followed, scribes sent Ahasuerus' decree to every corner of the kingdom. And with each day that passed, Ahasuerus more and more bitterly regretted what he'd done. He longed for Vashti; he moped in the palace gardens; he snarled at any courtier or bodyguard who went too close. The seven most senior courtiers, Abagtha, Bigtha, Biztha, Carcas, Harbona, Methuman and Zetha, discussed anxiously what to do. They decided to gather the most beautiful girls in Babylon, teach them the ways of royal wives, and then send each one in to spend a night with Ahasuerus. If the king sent for any girl a second time, she would be declared queen in Vashti's place.

Girls arrived at the harem from every part of Ahasuerus' empire: white-skinned city aristocrats, nomads on camel-back, falconers' daughters, fishergirls and the sisters, daughters and nieces of palace guards. Among them was Esther, adopted daughter of Mordecai the Jew. While servants packed her trunks with clothes and jewels, Mordecai took her aside and said, "Esther, whatever happens, remember our religion. Keep the commandments, pray three times a day, and God will look after you." He laid his hands on her head in blessing, and then took her the door, where harem litter-bearers were waiting to carry her to court.

Esther stayed in the harem for twelve months, until it was her turn to spend a night with Ahasuerus – and all that time Mordecai went to the palace gate each morning for news of her. At first the gate-guards were suspicious, but they soon heeded him as little as the horses tethered outside the guard-house or the spears propped against the wall. One day he overheard two of them plotting to assassinate Ahasuerus, and sent a warning to the guard-commander. The two men were arrested, interrogated and hanged, scribes wrote Mordecai's name on a list of people the king would honour at some future time, and the matter was forgotten. Ahasuerus still had citizens to honour from previous years – and one of them was Haman, Mordecai's neighbour and enemy. Two years before, he had covered the king's head against a sudden rain-shower, and now Ahasuerus rewarded him by making him Court Chamberlain, with the right to give his opinion before any other royal adviser. At the same time Esther's turn came to spend a night with Ahasuerus, and the king was so pleased with her that he called her back every night afterwards for a month. He named her First Wife and Queen, held a coronation banquet in her honour and decreed celebrations in every house in Babylon.

Neither Haman's nor Esther's new position did anything to end the rivalry between Haman and Mordecai. Even their slaves picked up the quarrel, and began snarling at each other like dogs in the street. "Stand aside! I serve the Great King's Chamberlain." "You stand aside! I serve the father of the Queen."

"What can I do?" Haman complained to his wife. "Mordecai irritates me more than anyone else in Babylon."

"Get rid of him," said Haman's wife. "Accuse him of some crime, and have him hanged."

"I can't accuse him personally," said Haman. "All Babylon knows we're enemies. There's a cleverer way: to attack the

Jews." He went to Ahasuerus and said, "Great King, live forever. May it please the Great King to think about the Jews? They infest our kingdom; they scorn our gods; they put commandments of their own above our laws. Great King, give the king's servant permission to wipe the world clean of Jews."

Ahasuerus cared nothing for the Jews. He gave Haman a royal signet-ring and said, "Do as you please. Write letters; seal them in my name. Let me know when the work's complete."

Haman wrote to the governors of every town and village in the empire: "On the thirteenth day of the twelfth month, attack every man, woman and child of the Jewish faith. Make no exceptions." He sealed the letters with Ahasuerus' ring: to disobey meant death. The news caused panic among Jews everywhere in the empire. They were forbidden by law to carry arms – how could they defend themselves? Convinced that God had deserted them, they wore sackcloth, daubed themselves with ash, fasted and filled the sky with prayers. Mordecai wrote to Esther: "Unless you save us, our whole nation is condemned to extinction. Go to Ahasuerus; beg him to spare our lives."

"I can't," Esther answered. "If anyone enters his presence uninvited, they die. It's been thirty days since last he sent for me."

"Risk it," said Mordecai. "Perhaps this is the moment for which God gave you life."

Esther veiled herself, and walked to a courtyard where Ahasuerus often walked in the afternoon. Soldiers ran to arrest her, but the king beckoned her closer and said, "What is it, lady? Ask whatever you like, even to half my kingdom."

"Great King, live forever," said Esther. "Will it please the king to dine with me tonight, together with Haman his chamberlain?"

"As you ask, so shall it be," said Ahasuerus. That evening he and Haman dined with Esther in the queen's apartments, and when the meal was done Ahasuerus said, "Esther, ask any favour. Whatever you want is yours, even to half my kingdom."

"Great King, live forever. If it please the king to come again tomorrow, with Haman his chamberlain, I'll ask my favour then."

"As you say, so shall it be," said Ahasuerus.

Haman beckoned for slaves to light him home. He scampered into the house and shouted to his wife, "All power is mine! I dine again tomorrow with the king and queen. I can persuade them to do anything I like. Now Mordecai, my enemy, is in my power!"

"Tell the servants to build a gallows," said his wife. "Then tomorrow, when you're alone with the king and queen, ask for Mordecai's death."

All that night, God tormented Ahasuerus with nightmares. The king tossed and groaned, and finally got out of bed and shouted for his officials. They hurried in, rubbing their eyes, and Ahasuerus said, "Fetch the lists of those whom the Great King delights to honour. If none of us can sleep, we might as well work instead." The sleepy officials began reading out long lists of names, and came at last to Mordecai. "What did he do?" Ahasuerus asked.

"Great King, live forever. He warned the Great King of a plot against the Great King's life."

"How should I honour him?"

"Great King, live forever. Let Haman, the chamberlain, think of a way tomorrow," said the yawning officials. Ahasuerus put Mordecai out of his mind till morning. Then he sent for Haman, who dressed in his best clothes and hurried to the palace, all but dancing with his own importance.

"Haman," said Ahasuerus, "What should be done to the man the Great King delights to honour?"

"He means me!" thought Haman. "He's offering me anything I choose!" Aloud he said, "Great King, live forever. Let the man the Great King delights to honour be dressed in scarlet robes and a golden crown, sat on a horse from the royal stables and led through the streets by trumpeters and a herald proclaiming his fame to all the people."

"As you say, so shall it be," said Ahasuerus. "The Great King delights to honour – Mordecai."

Haman had no choice but to obey. Grinding his teeth with rage, he gave orders for Mordecai to be led through the streets in scarlet robes and a golden crown, preceded by trumpeters and a royal herald. Then he went home and sulked till evening, when servants came to fetch him to dinner in the queen's apartments. The meal was as lavish as on the previous night, and when it was over Ahasuerus said, "Esther, ask your favour. Whatever you ask is yours, even to half my kingdom."

"Great King, live forever," said Esther. "I ask one favour only. Defeat my enemy, and save my life."

"What enemy?" asked Ahasuerus, astonished. "Who dares to threaten the Queen?"

"Great King, live forever," said Esther. "The enemy who threatens my life, as he threatens the life of every Jew in Babylon, is Haman."

Ahasuerus jumped up and ran to the door, shouting for guards. Haman grovelled at Esther's feet, clutching her dress and begging for mercy. Esther stepped back angrily, and Haman fell off-balance and knocked her to the floor. At that moment guards rushed in, and Ahasuerus turned back into the room and saw what was happening. The king's face purpled with rage. "Arrest Haman!" he shouted. "First he plots murder, and now he tries rape before my eyes!"

The soldiers stuffed Haman's scarf into his mouth to gag him. "Great King, live forever," said the captain. "There's a brand-new gallows on the city walls, which this man's servants built for Mordecai the Jew."

"Use it!" snapped Ahasuerus. "Hang Haman on it!"

The soldiers dragged Haman out, and as he went Ahasuerus snatched the signet-ring from his finger and gave it to Esther. "Give Mordecai Haman's place," he said. "Make him Court Chamberlain. And let him write letters, tonight, to every Jew in Babylon. The Great King smiles on the Jews. They are no longer slaves. They may carry arms; they may defend themselves. Let them have light, gladness, joy and honour. These are the Great King's words."*

Zerubbabel

It was time for the Jews to leave Babylon. They had served their punishment; they had returned to God, blessing him for his guidance and protection in exile; for the time being at least, idolatry had been driven from their hearts and minds. God began to work for their return to the Promised Land.

There were three young men in the Great King's bodyguard: two idolators and one true worshipper, Zerubbabel*. One night as they stood on guard, God put it into Zerubbabel's head to say, "Let each of us put an idea under the Great King's pillow. Then, in the morning he'll choose one of us as the wisest man in Babylon." The others eagerly agreed. They wrote words on three strips of papyrus and hid them under the Great King's pillow. Next day, when the king called his counsellors, he held up the first papyrus strip and said, "On this strip is one word: Wine. Who can explain?"

"Great King, live forever," said the first young man. "I can explain. Of all powers in the world, wine is the strongest. It turns everyone's head who drinks it, and makes even the mightiest warrior equal with a child."

The king held up the second papyrus strip and said, "On this strip is written Majesty. Who can explain?"

"Great king, live forever," said the second young man. "Of all powers in the world, none is stronger than the king. He gives life or death; he gives wealth or poverty; before him, even the mightiest warrior trembles like a child."

The king held up the third strip and said, "On this are two words: Woman and Wisdom. Who can explain?"

"Great king, live forever," said Zerubbabel. "Neither wine nor majesty are as powerful as woman. Wine turns a man's head for half a day; love of a woman turns it for a lifetime. Not even kings are exempt – for love of women, even kings stammer and tremble like children. But even women are not the strongest power in the world. That power is wisdom: belief in God. Time sours wine; it spoils women's beauty and the majesty of kings. But wisdom is the same forever. God is unchanging, and belief in him brings everlasting life."

Zerubbabel's fellow-guards rolled their eyes and groaned. "Another sermon!" they whispered to each other. "Whymust he always preach?" But the Great King beckoned Zerubbabel to kneel and said, "You're the wisest man in Babylon. Any gift you ask is yours, even to half my kingdom."

"Great King, live forever," said Zerubbabel. "Let my people go. Send me home to Jerusalem, with every true believer who chooses to go with me. Let us worship God in his own Temple, and the Great King's praise will be always on our lips."

"As you ask, so shall it be," said the Great King. "Let the people go!"

In the weeks that followed, the Great King's scribes sent a letter to every Jewish family in Babylon. Many Jews were settled and prosperous, and had no wish to return home. But others began rounding up their animals and loading their possessions for departure. The Great King sent presents for the Temple, and a string of asses laden with the sacred vessels looted by Nebuchadnezzar seventy years before.* He gave the Jews an escort of a thousand horsemen, and sent two hundred musicians to lead the procession across the mountains and through the desert back to Jerusalem. The Jews followed: forty-three thousand people, with uncounted flocks of sheep and goats. Their belongings were loaded on seven thousand asses, seven hundred horses, four hundred camels and two hundred mules. Ahead of the procession, Zerubbabel and the other leaders walked beside the musicians, singing and praying to God. After four months they reached Jerusalem. They pitched tents in the ruined streets and squares, and held a festival of praise and thanks to God. Then they took shovels, pickaxes and hand-carts, and began to build.*

11 · JOB

God tests Job

Job was a farmer in Uz, on the desert's edge*. He owned seven thousand sheep, three thousand camels, a thousand oxen and five hundred donkeys. He had seven sons, three daughters and a hundred servants. He was the most prosperous landowner in the area, and the most pious. He honoured God, respected strangers and loved his family. No one on earth had a bad word to say of him, and even God smiled when he looked down on him from Heaven.

God's courtiers assembled in Heaven to give an account of themselves. One by one they described everything they'd seen and done since last they appeared before God's throne. God said to Satan, "Where have you been?"

"Going to and fro on the earth, and walking up and down in it."

"Have you seen my servant Job? Is any mortal more honest or obedient?"

Satan said, "Is he not well rewarded? You protect his family and all he owns; you bless everything he does. If you took his prosperity away, he'd curse you to your face."

God said, "Everything he has is in your power. Leave Job himself untouched, but do what you like with all he owns."

That same day, Job's sons and daughters were feasting in their eldest brother's house. Job's servants had taken his flocks and herds to browse. His wife was busy with her maids. Job was sitting in the shade, pondering God's goodness. As he sat and thought, he picked up some sand and balanced it unconsciously in his hand. After a while his thoughts were interrupted. A man flung himself down before him, panting for breath and crying, "My lord, my lord!"

"What is it?"

"Sir, your oxen were ploughing and your donkeys were feeding – and raiders came down from the hills and took them away. When your servants resisted, the raiders killed them. Only I escaped."

He had hardly finished when a second man ran up and said, "Sir, your camels were browsing in the thorn-patch, and raiders came out of the desert and took them away. When your servants resisted, the raiders killed them. Only I escaped."

He was still speaking when a third and a fourth man ran up. The third man said, "Sir, fire fell from heaven and burned up all your sheep and the servants who were guarding them. Only I escaped." The fourth man said, "Sir, your sons and daughters were feasting in their eldest brother's house. A whirlwind blew the house down; only I escaped."

Job let the dry sand trickle from his hand. He stood up, took off his cloak and slowly tore it from hem to hem. He looked at the four men, and his eyes were wet with tears. "I came into the world with nothing," he said, in a voice shaking with self-control, "And I shall leave it in the same way. God gave; God has taken away. Blessed be his name."

In Heaven, God said to Satan, "Where have you been?"

"Going to and fro on the earth, and walking up and down in it."

"Have you seen my servant Job? Despite all his suffering, is any mortal more honest or obedient?"

"Skin for skin!" said Satan. "What do possessions matter, compared to a person's self? If you blister Job's own flesh, he'll curse you to your face."

God said, "He's in your power. Spare his life, but do what you like with the rest of him."

That same moment, every part of Job's body erupted in boils and sores. They covered even his scalp, the soles of his feet and inside his nose and ears. He took a piece of broken pottery to scratch with, covered his head, and knelt in the ash by the fire to pray. "Pious fool!" said his wife. "Will nothing change your mind? Curse God, and die."

Job said, "You're the fool, not me. We accept the good God sends – should we not accept bad as well?" He folded his hands, bent his oozing head and prayed.

Job's comforters

News of Job's suffering drew crowds. People came from all around to pity him. Three of his oldest friends, Eliphaz, Bildad and Zophar, sprinkled their heads with dust and sat down in the ashes beside him. For days the four old men rocked themselves on their heels in grief, while Job's wife tended the fire and the people watched. On the seventh day Job at last broke the silence, and filled his friends' ears with a stream of murmured, bitter words. "May the day die when I was born. May darkness possess it; may its stars and sun be blotted out. What use is a life of misery? I long for death: only the grave will end my suffering."

Eliphaz said, "Job, how often have you helped other people? Have you no comfort for yourself? Everybody suffers: the human race is born to trouble, as sparks from a fire fly upwards. God sends suffering to punish us for wrongdoing. Accept it! Take your punishment, and wait patiently until he forgives you."

"How can I be patient?" answered Job. "God's arrows breed maggots in my flesh. In any case, what have I done? All my life I've loved my family, respected my neighbours, honoured God. How have I earned this punishment?"

Bildad said, "How can you ask that? God is just: if you were truly innocent, he'd help you, not hurt you. Ask him what you've done. Beg forgiveness. Bless his name."

"How can I question God?" said Job. "His anger overturns mountains, shakes the earth till its pillars tremble. He can do as he likes: why should he explain? I'll ask no questions; leave me alone, let me go to the grave in peace."

Zophar said, "By claiming to be innocent, you question God. Of course you must be guilty. Admit your guilt, whatever it is, and pray for mercy before it's too late."

"What's the point of arguing?" said Job. "Every animal, every fish, every bird, even stones and plants know God's power. But I know, just as clearly, that I'm innocent. God has turned his face from me; he has abandoned me. Why else should an innocent man suffer so? Human beings are shadows, as frail as grass – why should God waste time being fair with us? He sends good luck or disaster as he pleases, whatever we deserve."

The watchers sucked in their breath to hear such words. Eliphaz said, "God may seem unfair. The wicked may seem to prosper. But their own wickedness is a millstone, a nagging tooth. They have no hope, and God will not let them rest. Your own suffering shows that."

"Why do you keep accusing me?" said Job. "If I were guilty, I'd accept God's punishment. But I'm innocent. Since God is just, if I pray to him, he'll declare my innocence."

Bildad said, "You're wrong. God is just, and only guilty people suffer. Therefore, if you're suffering, you must be guilty. Prayer can't change that."

"Where can I turn?" said Job. "God has tripped me, snared me like an animal. My wife, my neighbours, my own friends turn on me. My only hope is God. I know that one day, at the end of time when he judges all creation, when he punishes the guilty and rewards the good, he'll declare me innocent."

Zophar said angrily, "You keep saying you're innocent, and that we're no help to you. But you pay no attention to what we say. If you're suffering, you're guilty. Admit it, and beg God for mercy."

"What use is that?" asked Job. "You say God's justice means that the guilty suffer and the innocent are happy, always. But does it? Wherever I look, I see innocent people suffering, and guilty people growing fat and dying comfortably in their beds. How does that prove what you say? You misunderstand God completely."

Eliphaz, Bildad and Zophar looked at each other, wondering how to answer this attack. Then Eliphaz said, "Job, this is stubbornness, not argument. Of course you're guilty. You made every coin of your riches at someone else's expense. You sold things for more than they cost; you lent money; you charged rent; you owned slaves; you profited from other people's work. Was this blameless? Perhaps God knows more than you do – why should he listen when you claim you're innocent?"

"Why should he listen at all?" asked Job bitterly. "Where can I find him, to make my claims? All I know of him is the misery he sends. The innocent suffer; only the wicked thrive."

Bildad said, "Nonsense! If God is all-powerful, human beings mean no more to him than worms. Why should their goodness or badness cause him a moment's thought?"

Before Job could answer Zophar added angrily, "Whether God is just or unjust, giving in to him is the only wisdom. It is more valuable than gold, more precious than precious stones. The fear of God is the beginning of wisdom; to understand that is to give up sin."

"All I understand," said Job wearily, "is that once I was powerful and respected. I was eyes to the blind, feet to the lame, a father to the poor. Now I'm humbled to the dust: even my friends despise me. I was like a man riding on the wind: I soared high; I fell. All I ask, now, is that God should answer me. If I did wrong, I accept his punishment. But if I'm innocent, why does he torment me so?"

God speaks

Eliphaz, Bildad and Zophar turned angrily away. They were Job's oldest friends, and he rejected their comfort and scorned their arguments. The crowd was angry, too, and a man called Elihu put its feelings into words. "How long must this go on?" he asked. "They say that the old are wise, and that young people should keep quiet, listen and learn. But what have we heard today – wisdom or stubbornness? Job gulps misery the way a thirsty man drinks water. He's so busy complaining that he can't find God, that he gives himself no time to look. He says he's innocent, that God is punishing him unjustly – has anyone ever heard such arrogance? If God punishes us we're guilty, whether we know what we've done or not."

Job stood up to answer. But before he could speak a whirlwind began hurling sand from the sky like knives. The people huddled on their knees and cloaked their heads. The wind roared in Job's ears, and in the roaring he heard God's voice. "Who dares to question God? Instead of asking, answer. Where were you when I laid the foundations of the earth, when the morning stars sang together and God's children shouted aloud for joy? Who divided light from dark? Who sends sun and rain, till even the desert flowers? Can you make peacocks . . . ostriches . . . crocodiles? Like everything else on earth, you were created from nothing – what gives you the right to question God?"*

Job bowed his head. He understood at last – not God, not his creator, but himself. "Forgive me, lord," he said. "I knew nothing, and still I opened my mouth and spoke. You are far beyond mortal understanding: we should worship, not challenge or explain. Lord, I kneel before you. You made me; show me what to do."

Eliphaz, Bildad and Zophar heard Job's voice in the storm, and lifted their heads to listen. God spoke to them from the whirlwind, so that they covered their ears and cowered. "Fools! You thought you understood God. You cut me down to the level of your own intelligence. You can say nothing I want to hear. Sacrifice seven bulls and seven rams; ask Job to pray for you. If I spare you the miseries I heaped on him, it will be for his sake, and his alone."

The voice stopped; the whirlwind ceased. Trembling with terror, Eliphaz, Bildad and Zophar ran to sacrifice. Then they hurried back to beg Job to pray for them. They found him exactly as he'd been in the days of his prosperity. His skin was free from boils, his children and servants were all alive, his cattle, sheep and donkeys were restored. Except that Job's trust in God had been rewarded, and that his suffering had taught Eliphaz, Bildad and Zophar true understanding, everything was exactly as it had been before.

12 · TOBIAS AND THE ANGEL

The Two Prayers

In Nineveh once there lived a man called Tobit. He was powerful and prosperous, and gave half of all he earned to charity. But then he offended the king, lost his position and all his wealth, and was forced to depend on other people's kindness to support himself, his wife Anna and their son Tobias. Even then, Tobit still worked to help strangers. He was a devout Jew, and believed that unless Jewish people were buried according to the law of Moses, their souls were doomed to wander and wail forever. In that heathen city, Nineveh, he made it his business to see that every dead Jew was given holy burial, even tramps, criminals and victims of the state police.

It was the festival of Pentecost. Tobit's wife Anna had scraped and saved for weeks, and now she served a dinner of soup, meat and soft white bread. There was even a skin of wine. But before the meal began Tobit said to Tobias, "Go out into the streets, and see if you can find someone poorer than ourselves. We should share the good things God provides."

Tobias ran out, and Anna, tight-lipped, covered the dishes, wrapped them in cloths to keep the food hot, and set another place. After a while Tobias came back and said, "Father, there's no one. But they've just hanged a Jew in the market-place, and left his body on the gallows till morning."

Without a word Tobit stood up, put on his cloak and hurried out. He came back with the body, lugged it into the outhouse, washed and ate his meal. Then, as soon as it was dark, he dragged the body to an open space beside the city walls, dug a grave in the sand and buried it, weeping and praying to God to grant rest to the wandering soul. He levelled the sand, leaving no trace for the authorities, and slipped back through the empty streets.

By now it was after midnight, and when Tobit reached his own house, he found that Anna had locked the door and gone to bed. "I can't face an argument at this hour," he thought. "It's a warm night: I'll sleep outside." He rolled himself in his cloak and lay down beside the wall. The wall was old and crumbling, and sparrows had nested in a crevice. Tobit heard them rustling, looked up – and was spattered with warm dung. He wiped his eyes and thought no more about it. But next morning, when the sun rose and he opened his eyes, the world still seemed dark. A filmy skin had grown over both his eyes: he was as blind as stone.

In the next weeks Tobit went from doctor to doctor, and none of them could help. It was left to Anna to support the family. She went out every morning, grumbling, to sweep floors, wash clothes and mind the children of kindly neighbours. One day, she brought back a goat instead of wages, and Tobit heard it bleating and cried agitatedly, "Where did that come from? Is it stolen? You know it's against God's law to eat stolen meat."

Anna was furious. "God's law!" she shouted. "What do you know about God's law? You've lost everything we own. You're blind. People laugh at you in the street. Do you really think that's what God's law means?"

Instead of answering, Tobit fell on his knees and prayed. "Lord," he said, "if my own sins, or the sins of your Chosen People, have earned me this punishment, please kill me as I deserve. But if I'm innocent, if my life is to be spared, please hear me; help me now."

In the city of Ecbatana, two months' camel-ride across the desert, a second true believer was praying to God. Her name was Sarah, and although she had married seven husbands, one after another, she still lived like a child in her parents' house. The reason was that she was in the power of the demon Asmodeus. Asmodeus was the prince of darkness, shapeless and vast. He spent his time brooding in the gulf of space;

from time to time he squeezed himself into the form of a light-ray or a puff of wind and swooped to Earth to prey on God's creation: he meant to exterminate created things, one by one, till none was left. Seven times Sarah's friends led her and a new husband to the marriage-room and closed the door; seven times, when dawn streaked the sky and maids went to wake the couple next morning, they found Sarah weeping and her husband dead beside her. Now they mocked her. "Who'll márry you next?" they said. "Wedding-day, death-day – how many men want that? Why don't you hang yourself, join your seven husbands in the spirit-world, and leave us in peace?"

Sarah knelt and prayed. "O Lord," she said, "How have I deserved this punishment? If I'm guilty, please kill me as I deserve. But if I'm innocent, if my life is to be spared, please hear me; help me now."

What Happened in Ecbatana

The two prayers, Sarah's and Tobit's, rose up to God in Heaven. God called to his angels and said, "Both these mortals are innocent. All their lives they've kept the law, helped others and worshipped me. Why should they suffer? Their prayers are answered; their misery is over."

God sent the angel Raphael, the healer, the prince of light, to help Tobit and Sarah. Raphael disguised himself as a desert camel-driver, and sat in the market-place of Nineveh like a man looking for a job. Then God reminded Tobit of some money, twenty silver talents, which he had left for safekeeping years ago on a visit to a distant city, Rages, and forgotten. Tobit said to Tobias, "Go to Rages, find Gabael's house, and ask him for the money I left there twenty years ago."

"How can I, father?" asked Tobias. "I've never heard of Gabael; I've no idea where Rages is."

"Hire a camel-driver in the market-place, who knows the way. Say you'll pay him a drachma a day. Choose one of our own people: he'll have visited the Rages Jews before, and he may know Gabael's house."

In the market-place, Tobias hired Raphael (who claimed to be a Jewish camel-driver called Azarias, an old friend of Gabael's). The two of them set out for Rages, with Raphael leading a pack-camel and Tobias' dog trotting beside them. They walked for weeks. Every evening Raphael hobbled the camel to stop it straying, made camp and served Tobias a meal from the food in the camel-packs. On the first few days Tobias asked the angel to share his meal. But Raphael refused, saying that it was bad manners for servants to eat with their masters, and after a while Tobias sat down to eat alone, feeding his dog the scraps. The food and water lasted all the time they were in the desert, and on the evening of the last day they came to a wide river, with the domes of a city glowing in the distance. Tobias ran down the bank to wash, and a pink-finned, glittering fish jumped out of the water and lay gasping at his feet. Raphael handed Tobias three tiny pots, stoppered with wax, and said, "Keep the fish's heart, liver and gall-bladder: you'll need them later." Tobias had no idea what he meant, but he cut open the fish, took out the heart, liver and gall and stoppered them in the pots. Then he grilled the rest of the fish for supper, threw the skin and scraps to his dog and burned the bones. Raphael waited till he'd washed his hands in the river, then he led the way into the city and straight to a house in the Jewish quarter.

The city was Ecbatana, not Rages, and the house belonged to Sarah's father Raguel. He was overjoyed to see the man he took for Azarias, and even more delighted with Tobias. "Come in! Come in!" he said. "You're the image of your father, when he stayed here twenty, thirty years ago. Did you know he and I were cousins? Has he never spoken to you of Raguel? How time flies! Take off your boots, sit down, let the servants fetch cakes and wine." He hustled Tobias and Raphael inside, and servants pulled off their boots, fetched cushions and poured water for them to wash. Raguel's wife Edna brought wine, and behind her Sarah fetched biscuits on a silver tray. Raphael refused food and drink as he always did, but Tobias sipped wine and nibbled a biscuit for politeness' sake. Raguel was talking so much that he hardly noticed. "It's a miracle you've come," he said. "Only this morning, I said to

Edna – didn't I, Edna? – 'I wonder how cousin Tobit and his family are, after all these years'. I can't think what put that into my head. And there's another thing. No, Edna, don't shush me. It's our daughter, Sarah. She's a grown-up girl, and it's time she married. The trouble is, she's had seven husbands already, and not one has survived the wedding night. It's a mystery. But if she married you, Tobias – her own second cousin, the son of such a noble and God-fearing man as Tobit of Nineveh – surely God would bless the marriage, and both she and you would survive. Stay for a day or two; think it over. Then, if you agree, marry Sarah, spend your wedding-night here, and take her back with you to Nineveh."

As soon as he could, Tobias took Raphael aside and said, "Azarias, what can I do? I know my father would like me to marry his cousin's daughter. But I don't want to end up dead."

Raphael said, "Marry the girl. On the wedding night, send for a fire-basket and burn the fish's heart and liver."

"Why?"

"Just do as I say. You'll see."

That same day, Tobias told Raguel that he agreed to the marriage. Unlike Sarah's first seven weddings, it was a quiet affair: Raguel and Edna insisted on that. There were no witnesses but Raguel and Edna, and Raphael was the only guest. After the wedding-supper, servants took Sarah and Tobias to the marriage-room. They left a fire-basket as Tobias had instructed, then locked the door and went back to the kitchen, unsure whether to sing for Tobias' wedding or his funeral.

Raguel counted out the money for Sarah's dowry, in case Tobias survived the night, and dug a grave in the garden in case he didn't. Then he, Edna and Raphael knelt and prayed God to spare the young man's life.

As soon as Sarah and Tobias were alone in the marriage-room, Tobias made sure that the door was locked. Then he dragged the fire-basket beside the bed, and began fanning the flames and feeding them with sticks. "Don't bother," said Sarah. "It's a warm summer night. We don't need fire."

Tobias said nothing. He sat on the bed, watching the fire-shadows flicker on the walls. From time to time he jumped up and stoked the flames. The room grew as hot as an oven, and sweat poured down Tobias' face. But still he went on feeding the flames, while Sarah crouched in a corner of the room and watched. Then, in the darkest hour of night, when blackness cloaked the world, Asmodeus swooped into the room in a gust of wind, and the breath of his coming turned Tobias' sweat to ice. Tobias snatched the pots containing the heart and liver of the miraculous fish, and hurled them into the heart of the fire. The wax stoppers hissed and melted, the pots cracked open and the stench of burning offal filled the air. Black smoke billowed into every crevice of Asmodeus' being, swelling his emptiness like a living thing until he soared out of the house, shrieking and rattling the roof-tiles, and the room was still. Raphael, prince of light, soared after him, scooped him up and hurled him headlong into the gulf of space, while shooting-stars showered the earth like sparks and all creation cowered. Alone in the empty marriage-room, Tobias and Sarah held each other's hands, knelt, and thanked God for sparing them. Outside in the garden Raguel, too, praised his creator's mercy and filled in the grave. Next morning he sent for all his friends and neighbours, and celebrated the wedding-feast he'd never expected to see. The eating and dancing lasted for fourteen days, and in that time Raphael rode to Rages, found Gabael's house and fetched back Tobit's long-forgotten silver. As soon as the festivities were over, Raguel loaded Sarah's belongings on a string of camels, gave Tobias the leading-reins, and he and Edna waved tearfully at the city gate as Raphael led the young people along the desert road to Nineveh, with Tobias' dog frolicking at their heels.

What Happened in Nineveh

Tobias, Sarah and Raphael walked in the desert for weeks, and at last came in sight of Nineveh. When they were half an hour's journey from the city gate, Raphael said to Tobias, "Hurry ahead; leave Sarah here with me. Your mother and father are watching out for you. And as soon as you see your father, unstopper the fish-gall and smear it on his eyes."

Tobias put the gall-jar in his sleeve and quickened his steps, leaving Raphael and Sarah to follow at the camels' pace. In Nineveh, Anna ran down from the flat roof of her house by the city wall, shouting to Tobit, "I see him! I see Tobias at last, and his dog beside him. Praise be to God!"

Weeping with joy, she ran to the gate to hug Tobias, and Tobit followed as fast as he could behind her, feeling his way and stumbling in the sand. Tobias took him in his arms, and even as he hugged him he unstoppered the fish-gall and smeared it on his eyes. Tobit cried out in pain, and rubbed his eyes with his knuckles. The film of blindness peeled like grape-skin, and he could see again. He, Tobias and Anna fell on their knees, laughing with happiness, to give thanks to God, while the dog jumped and barked all round them. Then Tobias took his parents by the hand to meet Sarah, and the four of them hurried home, talking and laughing all together, while Raphael led the camels close behind.

Tobit and Anna gave their neighbours a week-long party to celebrate Tobias' wedding and his safe return. When it was over Tobit called Raphael aside and said, "Azarias, it's time to pay your wages, and to thank you again for bringing back my son. Take a drachma a day, as we agreed, and half of all I own as well, in gratitude."

Raphael said, "Give your gratitude to God, not me. God heard your prayer, and the prayer of Sarah your daughter-in-law. He knew that you were a good man, that you buried the dead and gave all you had to help the poor. He knew that Sarah was in Asmodeus' power. He sent me, Raphael, to help you. I was with you in all you did."

Tobit looked into his face and recognised an angel. He touched his forehead to the ground in awe. Raphael lifted a hand to bless him, and for a moment the house was filled with the radiance of the prince of light. Tobias, Anna, Sarah and the servants knelt beside Tobit and prayed to God. When they opened their eyes again, Raphael had disappeared and everything was as it had been before. They never saw an angel on earth again. But for the rest of their lives they praised and worshipped God*, and the powers of Heaven all smiled on them. Tobit and Anna lived to see six grandsons, and when the old people died Tobias, Sarah and their children went to live with Edna and Raguel, Sarah's aged parents in Ecbatana, where they enjoyed peace and happiness all the rest of their long lives.

13 · BETWEEN THE WOLVES AND THE WATCHDOG

It sometimes happens that when shepherds buy a watchdog to protect their fold against wolves, the dog itself turns wild. Fiercer and more dangerous than the beasts it was bought to drive away, it turns on its owners and savages them. So it was with the politics of the Promised Land in the second and first centuries BC. The shepherds were the Jews; the wolves were the Syrians; the watchdog, savage beyond control, was Rome.

The Abomination of Desolation

When Alexander the Great died, his generals divided his empire between them and made themselves kings. The most arrogant of all, Seleucus, founded a dynasty whose power extended from the Mediterranean coast to India, from the Black Sea shore to Egypt. Each of his descendants was more tyrannical than the last. They set a million slaves to building a new capital city, Antioch in Syria, and watered its foundations with human blood. They declared themselves divine, and cut the throats of anyone who refused to honour them equally with Zeus, Athene and the other great sky-gods. At first, busy with conquest, they let each of their subject peoples keep its own language, customs, dress and laws. But then Antiochus IV, a century after Seleucus, decreed that every subject in his empire was to wear Greek clothes as he did, speak Greek and worship the gods of Greece. He sent soldiers to read the decree in every town and village, to enforce sacrifice to their heathen gods, and to execute anyone who argued.

In the Promised Land, although many people were terrified of Antiochus' men and did everything they asked, others

resisted. The Jews had their own language, their own tradi-
tions of dress and food and their own code of laws. Above all
they worshipped the one true God and kept his commandments: no power on earth could change them. They watched
in horror as Antiochus' soldiers swarmed into Jerusalem,
looted the Temple, murdered priests, made bonfires of holy
books and stuffed age-old treasures in sacks to carry away to
Antioch. The soldiers patrolled the streets, arresting anyone
they found talking Hebrew or wearing Jewish dress. They
broke into people's houses, stripped their children and
hanged every circumcised boy before his parents' eyes. They
declared the Sabbath a working day like any other. They stole
cattle, sheep and goats to feed the army, and when the Jews
complained of starvation they forced them to eat the flesh of
creatures forbidden by God's law: pigs, dogs, donkeys, even
rats and snakes. In the end they built a statue of Zeus, king of
their idols, on God's altar in the Temple, and ordered the
Jews to worship it on pain of death. A few Jewish priests
preached against it, calling it the Abomination of Desolation –
and the soldiers flogged them to death before their own
people's eyes.

As the Syrians moved south through the Promised Land,
predatory as wolves, more and more true believers fled from
the cities to remote hill-towns. Antiochus' officers could
flood city streets with soldiers, overwhelming opposition.
But in the hills, where tracks were sparse and towns were
steep and small, only a handful of men could accompany each
official: the Jews could easily avoid them or outface them.
When half a dozen sweating soldiers clambered into Modin, a
village high in the hills beyond Jerusalem, and began gathering stones to build an altar in the market-place, they found
themselves outnumbered by a hostile, growling crowd. In the
front row of the crowd stood the village priest, Mattathias,
and a wall of warriors beside him, his sons Joanan, Simon,
Judas, Eleazar and Jonathan. All wore forbidden Jewish
dress; none had trimmed hair or beards in Greek style; none
moved or spoke. The Syrian officer nervously unrolled a
scroll and began to read Antiochus' decree, and the crowd
hissed to hear words in their conquerors' hated language. But

Mattathias gestured to them to let the officer speak, and for a while there was no sound in the sunlight but the clatter of stones as the soldiers worked on the altar, rooks cawing in the trees, and the oily sound of Greek. The officer finished, rolled up his scroll and waited. But Mattathias gave no sign; his sons neither moved nor spoke. The officer spoke over their heads to the crowd in Hebrew, his voice garbling the unfamiliar words. "You hear the king's orders. You see his altar. Sacrifice or die."

Mattathias said, "We're God's servants; we obey God's law. No mortal king will turn us one hair's-breadth from our religion. Do what you like to us."

Most of the crowd growled agreement. But one man darted out and cringed to the officer. "Not me, my lord!" he cried. "I've a wife and children! Spare us! We'll obey the king."

He threw himself on his knees at the half-built altar, and began babbling Zeus-prayers in broken Greek. Purple with fury, Mattathias brought his stick down on the man's head and killed him. The soldiers leapt for their weapons, and Mattathias' sons surged forward, beat them to death and tumbled the altar-stones round their ears. Only the officer escaped, running screaming down the hill to safety. "Let him go," said Mattathias. "It's time, now, to declare yourselves. Those who are for Antiochus, let them stay here and explain these deaths. Those who are for God, let them come to the hills with me."

He gathered his sons and marched out of the village without a backward glance. Several other villagers, mostly young men and boys, took scythes and cudgels and hurried after him. The older men, the women and the children went dejectedly home, leaving the bodies of Antiochus' men beside the ruined altar, and wailing to think of the retribution they knew was bound to come.

The Syrian revenge-party made no attempt to challenge Mattathias in the hills. Instead, for four days, while the terrified villagers peered down at them from their balconies high above, they massed in the valley and made no move. Then, on the Sabbath, the day of rest when Moses' law forbade devout Jews to cook, work, or even to stir outside their houses, the enemy swarmed up the hillside and attacked. They marched down the street, swords glinting, and their leader shouted, "Jews, where are you? Sacrifice and live – or fight and die." So they called – but not one man, woman or child in the village stirred. The Jews obeyed their Law: they sat quietly in their houses, praying to God, until Antiochus' soldiers broke down the doors and slit their throats. When Mattathias visited the town next morning, the air was greasy with death and a cloud of insects gorged on each gaping corpse*.

Judas

The massacre at Modin, and a thousand deaths at villages just like it, split the Jews. The weak and cowardly began fawning on the enemy, wearing Greek clothes, eating forbidden foods and praying to Zeus. The strong and pious, despising such collaboration, flocked to Mattathias in the hills. A network of resistance-fighters soon spread across the Promised Land. They lived in caves and forests, as David's outlaws had done centuries before when they fled from Saul. They raided the Syrians' supply-lines and command-posts. They smashed Zeus' altars, killed the heathen priests, and stripped and shaved the heads of villagers who refused to worship the one true God. Mattathias died, and under his sons, led by Judas Maccabee, "the Hammerer", the resistance-forces grew ever stronger: they were like a state within a state. Leader after leader tried to unite the Syrians against them, and died for it. If they could ever have enticed Judas down to pitched battle on the plains, they might have overwhelmed his army and killed him. But he stayed always in the hills: the Syrian generals were forced to take city-trained troops, lowlanders, along narrow mountain-passes where they were easily ambushed and no amount of battle-drill could save them.

Years before, when Antiochus took power in Syria, he had expected hostility from such giant neighbours as Persia and Egypt. He had thought no more about the Jews than a dog thinks of fleas. It had never occurred to him that they might prefer their own God and their own laws to his, or that they might pin down his finest generals and massacre his best-trained troops. The Jewish wars were like an open wound, draining the Syrian army of men and the treasury of cash. Years before, Antiochus had made an alliance with the Romans, the most warlike power on earth. They had promised to protect him against the Persians and Egyptians, and in return Antiochus had agreed to pay them two thousand silver talents every year. Now, in the time of Antiochus' successor Demetrius, all that money was needed to fight the Jews, and Demetrius knew that as soon as the Roman payments failed the alliance would come to a sudden, bloody end.

"My lord," said one of Demetrius' generals, Nicanor, "give me six months, and twenty thousand men. I'll blot Judas, and every Jew who follows him, from the face of the earth."

"It's impossible!" cried Demetrius. "Have you any idea what it would cost to finance twenty thousand men for a six-month war? I'd have nothing left for Rome."

"Leave it to me, my lord," said Nicanor. "Give me twenty thousand men, and in six months' time you'll have cash instead of Jews."

Demetrius gave the order, and Nicanor gathered his army. He set it to march on the Promised Land, and sent letters ahead of it to every merchant and slave-dealer in the kingdom. "In six month's time, the entire Jewish nation will be sold. One silver talent, paid in advance, will reserve you a batch of ninety adult males, ideal for hard labour, or twice that number of women and juveniles, suitable for light work or ornament." The advertisement worked. When Nicanor and his army reached the Promised Land, they found a thousand slave-dealers encamped on the plain, bargain-hunters, with wagon-loads of cash, whips, chains, and gangs of overseers, trainers and bodyguards. "What are you waiting for?" the dealers asked. "We're losing business, waiting here. Send your men into the hills to catch our slaves."

"No," said Nicanor. "In the hills, Judas always wins. We'll sit here on the plain, and wait for him to come to us."

From their hill-top watch-points, Judas' men looked down in dismay as the Syrians massed below. There were no more than seven thousand Jewish soldiers, plus women and children: they were outnumbered three to one. They were used to quick raids or ambushes, a few dozen men at a time: they had never fought a pitched battle in their lives. Judas reassured them. "The Syrians outnumber us," he said. "But what of that? Sparrows outnumber hawks. They've challenged not only us, but God. He stands on our side – and if God is for us, who can stand against us?"

The people took up the words like a battle-cry: "If God is for us, who can stand against us?" Then, when they had knelt and prayed, Judas divided them into companies of fifteen hundred men each, and told the officers his plan.

It was mid-morning. Judas' men let their enemies stand waiting on the plain, in the baking heat, all day. The Syrians sweated and muttered, shading their eyes and peering up at the hills for an attack that never came. Even when darkness fell, they had no chance to sleep: Nicanor knew Judas' guerrilla-tactics, and ordered his men to sit up fully-armed all night, and set double guards against a surprise attack. Dawn came, and the soldiers stretched their cramped limbs and dragged themselves back to their battle-lines, screwing up aching eyes against the sun. Once again Judas made them wait all day – and then, towards evening as their nerves were snapping, he gave the signal for attack. The first group of Jews poured down from the hills west of the Syrians. The setting sun hurled the Jews' shadows down the hill ahead of them. On the peaks women and children began shrieking, and trumpets blared from hill to hill. To the superstitious Syrians it was as if an army of giants and witches had taken arms against them. They turned in panic – and more groups of Jewish soldiers ran to attack them from each side and from behind. The Syrians began screaming that all the demons of the Underworld were attacking them. They threw down their weapons, broke their lines and ran, trampling their own comrades in their panic. They stumbled blindly into the slave-carts, drawn up on the edge of the plain, and tried to punch their way past the guards. The fighting bubbled and spurted like water in a pot, and the Jews fell on the struggling men and cut them to pieces. When darkness at last ended the massacre, the whole Syrian army was dead or stumbling blindly in the hills, and Nicanor's slave-dealers had long since fled, leaving their whips, their chains and their treasure abandoned on the plain. King Demetrius' cash was lost; the alliance with Rome was over.

The Romans

In five years of dazzling generalship*, inspired by God, Judas defeated every Syrian general, every army, sent against him. He drove the heathen from Jerusalem, and made it his head-quarters. He planned to create a second golden age, a Mac-cabee kingdom to rival those of David or Solomon centuries before*. But Jerusalem was tiny, and Syria was huge. To safeguard his kingdom against Syrian attack, he sent ambas-sadors to Rome offering friendship and alliance. But even while his ambassadors were still at sea, the Syrians sent a last, vast army against the Jews and Judas was killed in the fight-ing. There followed a century of war. In the Promised Land itself, there were constant power-battles, between members of Judas' own Maccabee dynasty and outsiders, jealous of their power*. While the Jews busied themselves with plots, political marriages, assassinations and imprisonments, outside their boundaries the Romans and Syrians, too, were at each other's throats. At last, a century after Judas' reign, the Roman general Pompey was sent to end Syrian power for good – and on his way north he marched on Jerusalem, conquered it, and scandalised the Jews by walking bareheaded into the Holy of Holies of the Temple – an unbeliever, a warlord in arms! – and defiled God's presence by handling the sacred vessels and unwrapping the sacred scrolls. The watchdog had turned on its owners. From that day on, the Chosen People were captives in their own country, the Prom-ised Land was renamed Judaea in Roman style, and the Jewish leaders were puppets whose strings were pulled from Rome.

14 · JESUS

Jesus' birth

The birth of Jesus Christ happened like this. In Nazareth, a town in the hills between the Mediterranean and the Sea of Galilee, a girl called Mary was due to be married to Joseph, a carpenter. Some time before the wedding God's angel appeared to her and said, "Hail, Mary. God has favoured you above all other women. You will conceive and bear a son, Jesus. God will give him David's throne; his reign will never end."

Mary was bewildered. "How can I conceive?" she asked. "I've never had a husband or a lover."

"God's holy spirit will be the father," answered the angel. "You'll be a mother and a virgin, both in one."*

At first, when Joseph discovered that his bride-to-be was pregnant, he wanted to cancel the wedding. But God's angel appeared to him in a dream and said, "Joseph, fear nothing. Mary's child will be Jesus, the Messiah, who will save the human race from sin."

Joseph married Mary, and they lived quietly in Nazareth. Then, in the ninth month of Mary's pregnancy, the Roman emperor Augustus passed a decree that everyone in his enormous empire was to register for tax. They were to travel to the city, town or village where they had been born, and Roman officials there would write their names on a census-list. For some people this involved a journey of months, vast distances over sea and land. For Mary and Joseph, however, who had both been born in the hill-village of Bethlehem near Jerusalem, it meant only two week's travelling, across the Samaritan Plain and by well-trodden passes through the hills.

Mary rode a donkey, and Joseph led it where the ground was smoothest, avoiding loose stones and potholes.

When they reached Bethlehem, they found the village crowded. Every room, every bed, was taken. It was late at night, and Mary was exhausted. The landlord of the inn said to Joseph, "Your wife's baby will soon be born. She needs a bed and a roof over her head. I can't offer you anywhere inside the house. But there's straw in the stable: she'll be well enough there, if she doesn't mind the animals." Joseph helped Mary down from the donkey and into the stable. There was very little room. The stable was crowded with the donkeys of visitors and with the landlord's own cows and goats. But Joseph settled Mary in a bed of straw, then sat down and cradled her in his arms. In the middle of the night her son was born, and she wrapped him and laid him in a manger (a wooden hay-trough for feeding animals).

That same night, in the fields near Bethlehem, shepherds were guarding their animals as usual. It was a still night, and they sat by the fire, talking quietly, while their sheep browsed and coughed all round them. Suddenly, in the middle of the night, the sky filled with light and they saw God's angel, towering from earth to sky. "Don't be afraid," the angel said. "I bring good news, to you and to every human being on earth. Your saviour has just been born. You'll find him in Bethlehem, lying in a manger."

Even as he spoke, a host of other angels appeared beside him, praising God and singing, "Glory be to God in heaven, and on earth be peace." The shepherds knelt on the ground, worshipping God, until the song ended and the angels disappeared. Then they hurried into Bethlehem, and found Mary and Joseph, and the baby in the manger as the angel had said. Without waiting for daylight, they began hammering on their neighbours' doors and windows, shouting that the Messiah*, the Saviour, had been born.

Mary and Joseph stayed quietly in Bethlehem for the next few weeks. It was too soon for Mary or the baby to travel, and Mary spent her days resting in the shade and her nights in the stable, nursing Jesus and wondering how such a tiny, helpless child could possibly be God's son. On the fortieth day after the baby's birth, she and Joseph went down into Jerusalem to make a thanksgiving sacrifice of two pigeons, as custom was. Among the other people in the Temple were an old, blind man, Simeon, and a woman, Anna. They spent their lives praying and meditating on Moses' law and the sayings of the prophets. As soon as the priest finished sacrifice, Simeon and Anna each took Jesus in their arms and blessed God for letting them live to see the day when the Messiah, the King of Kings, was born to save the world.* As Mary had with the shepherds, she said nothing now, but stored everything in her mind to think about in years to come.

So far, no one had recognised Jesus as the Messiah except shepherds and the two old people in the Temple. But the Roman empire was a police state: every part of it was filled with spies, alert for signs of revolution. The secret police began to hear gossip about Jesus' birth. They went to Herod, the Roman-backed king of Jerusalem, and told him that people were talking of a child, born in one of the mountain villages, who would grow up to be king of the Jews and save the human race. Herod, terrified of rivals, wanted to send soldiers at once to cut the baby's throat. But none of his spies knew which newborn baby was Jesus or the name of the village he lived in. Then three princes, wise men from the east, arrived in Jerusalem and bowed to Herod. "O king, live forever," they said. "We're scientists, trained observers of the sky. A new star, brighter than any ever seen before, has appeared, the sign that the King of Kings has been born. The star has guided us here, to your country. Tell us where the new king is, so that we can pay him homage."

Herod said slyly, "You follow your star, and look for him – and as soon as you find him, come and tell me where he is, so that I, too, can worship him."

That same night the star moved across the sky towards Bethlehem,* and the wise men followed its lead. They found Mary and Joseph in the stable, and Jesus lying in the manger. They knelt before the child; then, warned by angels not to go back to Herod or tell him where Jesus was, they hurried out of the country by a different route.*

As soon as Herod realised that he'd been cheated, he shouted to his guards, "Go into every town and village in Judaea. Kill every child under the age of two. Let none survive." Gangs of soldiers ran to obey. They beat out the brains of every child in the land. Only Jesus survived: angels warned Joseph in a dream, and he fled into Egypt, with Mary and Jesus on donkey-back beside him, long before the executioners reached Bethlehem. The holy family stayed in exile for four years, until word reached them that Herod himself was dead. Then Joseph, Mary and Jesus went home at last to Nazareth, and Joseph settled back to carpentry, his former trade.

John the Baptist

While Jesus was growing up in Nazareth,* his distant relative John was training to be a priest in Jerusalem. John was the son of a Temple priest, Zachariah,* and at first intended to follow in his father's footsteps. But when he was grown up he left the luxurious Temple service to become a wandering preacher in the hill-villages of Judaea. He lived wild, ignoring both rain and sun. He was naked except for a blanket and a loin-cloth. His hair straggled to his waist; he ate locusts and wild honey, and lapped puddle-water like an animal. At first people laughed at him, or picked up stones to drive him away. But as soon as he began to preach, his words blazed in their minds like fire. Eager crowds gathered everywhere he went, greedy for teaching. He told them that God would soon come to judge the human race. They were all sinners; they were like dead trees waiting for the axe, or corn-sheaves ready for the flail. He, John, would baptise them with water, sprinkling their heads or plunging them under the surface to show that they were sorry for their sins and promised true obedience in future. But someone else was coming, someone whose shoe-laces John was not fit to unloosen, and who would baptise his followers with fire, with the spirit of God himself.

At first the authorities treated John as a harmless joke. "Who cares about the Baptist?" they said. "The hills are full of lunatics. Let him preach. Let him baptise. He's doing no harm." But the crowds of John's followers grew ever larger, and soon there were so many that the Romans, and the Jewish leaders they supported, began to panic. "It may all be religious nonsense now," they said, "but what will happen if John takes up politics? Suppose he starts preaching revolution?" From that day on a group of secret policemen followed John wherever he went. They dressed as ordinary villagers, mingled with the crowds, and watched for evidence of treason.

One day John went to preach beside the river Jordan. He stood on a rock by a shallow pool, and his followers crowded round. They had come from all parts of the Holy Land: there were Judaean hill-villagers, plainsmen from Samaria, fishermen and their wives from the Sea of Galilee. John said, "I am the man spoken of by Elijah the prophet: 'the voice of a man crying in the wilderness, Prepare the way of the Lord'. I say to you: repent, now, for God's kingdom is at hand." He stepped down from the rock into the water, and people went forward one by one to be baptised. They prayed to God, admitting their sins and promising true obedience; then they bent their heads and John baptised them with river-water. It was as if God's power had descended into the river Jordan, to wash their sins away. The crowd was large, and the baptisms took many hours. Just before sunset a young man walked out of the crowd and down into the water. He was tall, neat-bearded and had long, flowing hair. To everyone's surprise, as soon as John saw him he knelt in the water before him and said, "Master, why have you come?"

"To be baptised."

"Lord, how can I baptise you? You should baptise me."

"Do it. It's what you were sent into the world to do."

John stood up, and for a moment he and the young man prayed silently together. Then John sprinkled the man's head with water – and at that exact moment the sky opened above them, God's spirit hovered like a dove over the young man's head, and a voice from heaven said, "This is my beloved son, in whom I am well-pleased." Though no one in the crowd knew his name, the young man was Jesus. His growing-up was over and his mission had begun.

Not long afterwards, John went to preach in Galilee – and gave the secret police exactly the evidence they were waiting for. The Jewish prince of Galilee was Herod Antipas, son of the Herod of Judaea who had ordered the baby-massacre years before. Herod Antipas had married Herodias, his sister-in-law, forcing her to divorce her previous husband, his own brother – and John the Baptist preached against the marriage, calling it a crime against God's law. At once the secret police arrested him for treason. Herodias heard him preaching and raving in the palace dungeons, and went down with her ladies to see the wild man from the hills. To her fury, as soon as John saw her he began to denounce her through the bars: she was an adulterer, a law-breaker; she was committing incest; she was no better than a prostitute. Herodias was determined to stop him repeating these insults in court, if his case ever came to trial. She had a beautiful daughter, Salome, Herod's step-daughter. Herodias knew that Herod was besotted with Salome and would refuse her nothing. She made Salome dance before Herod at a drunken banquet, and herself sat beside him, filling and refilling his wine-cup and asking him if Salome wasn't the most beautiful girl he'd ever seen. When Salome finished dancing Herod clapped his hands and said, "Ask any reward you like. Whatever you ask is yours, even to half my kingdom."

Salome replied in the words Herodias had told her. "Give me John the Baptist's head on a silver dish."

"I can't do that," shouted Herod. "He's a prisoner, waiting for trial. I can't just kill him: I have to find him guilty first."

"You promised," said Salome.

Herod sighed and gave the order. His guards ran to the dungeon, hacked off John's head and took it to Salome in a silver dish. Herodias smiled secretly to see it: John's scandalous tongue was stilled for good. She sent heralds to announce his death to the ragged group of his followers who crouched outside the prison. Except for a few brave souls, who stayed to gather the body for burial, they fled to the hills. Their leader was dead, and the young man he had proclaimed as the Messiah, the young man blessed by God himself, had disappeared as soon as he was baptised. They were at the mercy of Herod and his men. They hid in their homes, begging God to spare their lives.

Jesus' ministry begins

When Jesus was baptised by John, God's holy spirit poured into him. He went to meditate and pray in the high mountains, and lived there alone for forty days and nights. In that empty place, filled only with the howling of the wind, it was as if he could hear his own thoughts. The voice of the Devil, Satan, swirled in his mind saying, "Jesus, are you hungry? If you're the Son of God, turn one of those stones to bread."

Jesus answered with words from the Law of Moses: "A man shall not live by bread alone, but by the word of God."

Satan lifted him high above the earth, and showed him the teeming continents, seas and forests of the world below. "All this is mine," he said. "I can give it to anyone I choose. If you want it, kneel and worship me."

Jesus answered, "Get thee behind me, Satan. The Law says, 'Worship the Lord your God, and him alone.'"

Satan tried a third temptation. He carried Jesus to the highest, giddiest pinnacle of the Temple roof in Jerusalem and said, "If you're God's son, jump off. Your father will protect you – doesn't the Law say, 'His angels will keep you safe'?"

Jesus answered, "It also says, 'Thou shalt not tempt the Lord thy God.'" As soon as he spoke, Satan vanished like a dream, and Jesus found himself back in his own country, lying on a rocky beach beside the Sea of Galilee. He had been tempted by three kinds of greed: for food, power, and pride, and each time the power of God's spirit had protected him, had helped him not to yield.

Some time before Jesus' baptism in the river Jordan, his mortal father Joseph had died. Jesus himself, and Mary his mother, were the only people in the world who knew his true parentage, that he was the son of God. But he still felt that it was not yet time to reveal himself. Not long after his return from the wilderness, he went to a cousin's wedding in the village of Cana near Nazareth. The wedding was large, and at the banquet afterwards guests sat at tables all along the village street. They ate meat, bread, honey-cakes, figs, dates, grapes, and drank wine. But as toast followed toast throughout the day, Jesus' mother went to him and said, "They'll soon run out of wine. Think of the shame of it, at your own cousin's wedding!"

"Mother," answered Jesus, "You know it's still not time."

Mary took no notice. She said to the servants, "Whatever he tells you, do it. Don't ask questions."

After a while Jesus went inside, down to the storehouse. There, in a cool cellar, were six huge water-jars, each as high as a man. "Fill them up," he said.

The mystified servants did as they were told, pouring in water till the jars were full. Then an order came from the banquet outside: "Send up more wine!"

"Take it from the water-jars," Jesus said.

The servants dipped ladles into the jars – and found them full not of water, but of clear red wine. They filled jugs and skins and carried them to the banqueters. The senior guest tasted the wine, then clapped the bridegroom on the shoulder and said, "Well done! Most people serve their most expensive wine first – but you've kept the best till last!"

This was the first miracle Jesus performed on Earth; still no one but he and his mother knew who he was. But as the weeks passed, he began to feel that it was time to preach God's word, and went out into the villages of Galilee. Soon crowds were gathering to hear him as once they had for John. He spoke of God's law, of the writings of the prophets, and especially of the coming day of judgement, when God would decide the guilt or innocence of every person in creation.

One day Jesus went to the synagogue in Nazareth, his own village, and stood up to read. The priest gave him a scroll of the writings of the prophet Isaiah. Jesus unrolled it and read, "God's spirit is in me. He has sent me to preach to the poor, to comfort the broken-hearted, to talk of freedom to captives, of sight to the blind, of relief to those in pain. Above all, I am to speak of Judgement Day, God's chosen day." He rolled up the scroll and gave it back to the priest. Then he looked at the people and said simply, "Today this prophecy has come true – and your own eyes have seen it."

The people turned to each other, buzzing like wasps. "What's he talking about?" they asked. "Isn't this Jesus, the carpenter's son? What has he to do with prophecy?"

Jesus said, "No prophets are honoured in their own home-towns. Even Elijah, even Elisha, were respected first by strangers."

"Now he's comparing himself with Elijah and Elisha," the people shouted. "Who does he think he is?" They hustled Jesus out of the village, up to a rocky mountain-ridge. They wanted to throw him over, to teach him humility. But he slipped out of their grasp and escaped to the seashore. For days he walked along it, from village to village, town to town, until he reached Capernaum. Here he began preaching again, and at once crowds of people gathered, as eager to hear him as his own neighbours in Nazareth had been to drive him out.

One Sabbath day Jesus was in the synagogue of Caper-naum, speaking to the people, when a madman suddenly ran out and began writhing and rolling on the floor, making devil-signs at Jesus and shouting, "Leave us alone! Jesus of Nazareth – what business are we of yours? Have you come to destroy us? We know who you are: the Holy One of God!"

Jesus held the madman's shoulders to still his writhing. Then he looked into his eyes and said, "Be quiet. Come out of him. Leave him alone." The man stood rigid for a moment, then suddenly began bucking and tossing as if some invisible force were cracking him like a whip. Jesus kept firm hold of his shoulders, and after a while he and the man were picked up and thrown across the room like sacks. They stood up, dusted themselves down, and the madman walked to his place and sat down, as calm and clearheaded as if he'd just woken from a refreshing sleep.

"Look at that!" gasped the crowd. "Jesus drives out devils! He orders them out, and out they go." From that moment on, wherever Jesus went he was followed by coughing, limping, groaning people, stretching out their hands and begging him to cure them. Each day at evening, he laid hands on the sick and healed them. People began whispering that a miracle-worker had come to live in Capernaum, and that whenever devils felt his touch they flew out of their victims, shrieking with terror, and were never seen again.

The crowds of sick people and their relatives gave Jesus no peace. If he stayed indoors, they hammered on the shutters and pressed against the doors. If he tried to pray in the synagogue, they crowded after him, scrambling for seats near him and looking at him with pleading, eager eyes. Even if he left Capernaum before dawn to walk in the hills, the sun was hardly in the sky before he was surrounded by people as a shepherd is by sheep. When he told them gently, "I have to go to other places too, to preach God's kingdom," they fell on their knees, clutched his clothes and cried, "Stay, master! Stay and preach to us!"

One day Jesus was standing on the shore of the Sea of Galilee, waiting to preach. There were two fishing-boats hauled up on the sand, and the fishermen were washing their nets. Word had spread that Jesus was there. Crowds of eager people were thronging across the sand, jostling and chattering like children before a treat. There were so many of them that Jesus himself was pushed further and further down the shore, towards the water. At last, to make room and to let everyone see him equally, he climbed into one of the boats and asked the fisherman, Simon, to row him out to sea. Then, while Simon held the boat steady in shallow water, he sat down to preach. When he finished he said to Simon, "Sail further out, let down your nets and fish."

"It's no use, master," said Simon. "We've worked all night and caught nothing."

"Please do it," said Jesus.

Simon rowed out into deep water, and let down the net. At once the net filled with so many fish, floundering and struggling, that it began to tear. Simon shouted to James and John, his partners, to launch the second boat and come to help. They worked for two hours, until the boats were so full of fish that they were all but sinking, and water spilled in over the sides. Simon fell on his knees among the slippery, wriggling fish, held out his hands to Jesus and said, "Lord, leave me. I'm a sinner: I don't deserve your kindness. We could fish for months, and not catch as much as this."

Jesus answered, "Come with me, and fish for human souls."

Simon, James and John rowed the laden boats to land. Then they said goodbye to their families, shouldered their belongings, and ran to help Jesus without a backward glance.*

Capernaum

Jesus continued to preach in Galilee, and the crowds of his followers grew larger with every day that passed.* Many people thought of him as a kind of magician, and went out of curiosity to see who he would heal or what wonders he would work. Others, Pharisees, went to criticise his teaching. They believed that God's Law in the books of Moses was to be followed exactly, to the letter, and that anyone who thought or taught otherwise was a sinner, in Satan's power. But most of the people who followed Jesus were not interested in miracles or Law-books. They loved Jesus, and believed that he was the son of God. His presence on earth comforted them and gave them joy.

Even with the help of Simon, James and John, it was still hard for Jesus to control the crowds. Once, in Capernaum, people filled the house he was preaching in, standing shoulder to shoulder in the doorway and spilling into the street outside. Some men brought a paralysed friend on a stretcher to hear him, and could find no way through the throng. They would have taken the man home, but he was so desperate to see Jesus face to face, and to hear him with his own ears, that he persuaded his friends to haul him up to the house-roof, make a gap in the tiles and let him down on ropes, stretcher and all. The paralysed man lay at Jesus' feet, with tears of happiness running down his cheeks. He could move no part of his body except his arms, but he held them out to Jesus like a child asking to be hugged. Jesus held his hands for a moment, and then said gently, "Friend, your sins are forgiven."

At once the Pharisees, in the front of the crowd, began clicking their tongues and muttering, "Blasphemy! Only God can forgive sins – who does Jesus think he is?"

Jesus said, "Which is easier to say: 'Your sins are forgiven', or 'Stand up and walk'?" He took the paralysed man's hands once more and said, "Stand up, friend. Pick up your bed, and walk."

At once the paralysed man stood up, shaking his illness from him as a dog shakes water, and began leaping round the room, windmilling his arms and shouting, "Look, I can walk! Watch me! Watch me walk!" He kissed Jesus' hand in gratitude, picked up his stretcher and bounded out of the room. The crowd parted to let him pass; the Pharisees were left standing where they were, chewing their beards and muttering.

The Pharisees soon had another reason for annoyance. A tax-collector, Levi, invited Jesus and a crowd of his followers home to dinner. Levi's slaves served bread, meat and wine to the people outside, and Levi himself, Jesus and a few of Levi's friends, also tax-gatherers, sat at a long table in the courtyard, shaded by a vine-trellis. "Look at that!" sniffed the Pharisees. "Levi used to be a true believer, an honest Jew. Now he gathers taxes for the Romans. He's an enemy, a sinner – and Jesus treats him like a friend and eats with him!"

Jesus asked them, "Who needs me more, good people or sinners? Do doctors heal the healthy or the sick? I came to call sinners, not saints, to repentance."*

Jesus was happy to mix not just with friends of the Romans, but with the Romans themselves. Capernaum was a Roman garrison-town, headquarters of one of the legions which patrolled the Promised Land. The Roman headquarters were like a town inside a town. They had their own streets, houses, shops, inns and above all the temples and shrines of their outlandish gods. There was no reason for Romans to go out into Capernaum, except when they paraded on the Emperor's birthday or sent patrols for guard-duty at the customs-house. Few townspeople knew any Romans personally, and there was little friendship between them and the occupying force. But one day Jesus was wakened by knocking on his shutters, and found outside a messenger from the Capernaum town council. "Master, come quickly! One of the centurion's slaves is sick, near death. The council begs you to try and cure him. His owner's a good friend of Jews; he even gave us money to build our synagogue."

Jesus hurried after the man, and an inquisitive crowd began to follow them. But long before they reached the Roman barracks the centurion himself came out to meet Jesus. When the crowd saw his scarlet cloak and the glint of his armour they slunk back into the shadows, out of sight. But the centurion had eyes for no one but Jesus. He knelt at his feet and said, "Master, they had no right to bother you. Who am I that you should step under my roof? I'm a powerful man: when I say 'Come' men come, and when I say 'Do this' it's done. But I also know when to bow to higher authority. Lord, just say the word: I know my slave will live."

The listeners were astonished. Never in their lives had they seen a Roman kneel to a Jew, or speak so humbly. Jesus threw open his arms and said, "Even in Israel, I've never found such faith!" He smiled at the centurion, held out his hand to help him up and said, "Go home. Your slave's cured. Your own faith has healed him."*

As the months passed, the work of controlling the crowds, of making sure that Jesus had room to speak and that everyone could hear him and see him, grew too much for Simon, John and James. Jesus called nine more people to follow him, until he had a group of twelve "disciples", or pupils. They were all fishermen or farmers, except for two: Levi the tax-collector (who took a new name, Matthew, as a sign that he had begun a new life), and Judas, a businessman from the town of Kerioth near Jerusalem. The names of the twelve disciples were Simon, Andrew his brother, James and John the sons of Zebedee, James and Jude (Jesus' own brothers or half-brothers), Philip, Bartholomew, Thomas, Simon the Zealot and Judas. Jesus gave his disciples the power to cast out devils in God's name, and sent them into the towns and villages of Galilee to announce that the Messiah had come to Earth and that God's judgement-day was near. Their base was still Capernaum, on the shores of the Sea of Galilee. But from this time onwards they left it for weeks and months at a time, walking from village to village in the hills, preaching and healing in the countryside round about.

15 · JESUS IN GALILEE AND BETHANY

Gadara

Often, when Jesus finished preaching in a seaside town, he and his disciples escaped the crowds by rowing or sailing across the Sea of Galilee. One day Jesus, exhausted, was dozing in the boat's stern when a sudden storm blew up. They were in deep water. Wind tore at the sail and turned the boat beam-ends on against the sea. Water poured in round the disciples' feet. Andrew, James and John bent to the oars, shouting to the others to bail for their lives. But the waves snapped the oars like straws, and the boat wallowed and began to sink. The terrified disciples shook Jesus awake, crying that they were drowning – and he stood up, held out his arm above the sea and said, "Peace, be still." At once the wind dropped, the clouds disappeared and the sea grew calm. Jesus sat down and went back to sleep, leaving the disciples to set sail for land, asking each other in awed voices what sort of man they served, if even the waves and the wind obeyed him.

They landed on the eastern shore, not far from the hill-town of Gadara. Between them and the town was a steep, rocky slope filled with thorn-bushes. Part of it had been walled off with stones to make a cemetery, and the white-washed domes of the tombs gleamed in the sun. Further down, a herd of pigs was rooting among the bushes, with two small boys, pig-herds, dozing beside them in the shade. It was a still, hot day, with no sound but the chirping of cicadas and the pigs' snuffling as they fed. The disciples hauled their boat up the shore, and they and Jesus began to climb the hill. Suddenly, as they were picking their way past the wall of the cemetery, a man leapt out from among the tombs. He was naked; his hair reached to his knees; torn ropes hung round his wrists and ankles, as if they'd been ripped to pieces by some supernatural force. He capered round Jesus like a monkey, banging his knuckles on the ground; his shrieks bounced from tomb to tomb as if all the dead had leapt up to shout with him. "Jesus of Nazareth! Leave us! Leave us in peace!"

Jesus said, "What is your name?"

"Legion, because there are so many of us," the madman answered. He swung himself up on the cemetery wall and ran along it on all fours, leaving a trail of blood-drops where the sharp stones gashed him. He took no notice of the pain, chuckling to himself and repeating "Legion! Legion!" as if it were a magic chant.

Jesus held his arm to quieten him, and said sharply, "Come out of him. Leave him alone."

The man tried to writhe free. His face jerked, he howled like a dog and tears ran down his cheeks. He fell on his knees and clutched Jesus' legs. When he spoke, it was as if a whole crowd, a legion, were babbling and crying for mercy. "Spare us!" the voices cried. "Don't drown us! Send us into the pigs, but spare our lives!"

"As you ask," said Jesus, "so be it. Leave him now."

The madman screamed a long, thin shriek which bubbled among the tombs. There was a rushing sound, like a sudden whirlwind, and the pigs began running in circles, squealing, and jumping in the air like deer. The noise woke the pig-herds, and they jumped up shouting in alarm. At the sound of their voices the pigs whirled like a flock of sparrows, ran down the hill into the sea and drowned. The pig-herds fled to Gadara for help – and when their masters came running, they found the madman sitting at Jesus' feet in the shade of the cemetery wall, clothed, calm and in his right mind. The pig-masters were terrified. "Leave us, master!" they begged, clutching Jesus' knees. "Sail away from here! Leave us in peace!"

Jesus took the madman aside and said, "Go into the town. Tell everyone what happened. Show them that the devils have left you, that you're free of them." Eagerly the man ran up the hill into Gadara, and began shouting the good news to all the people. As soon as the Gadarenes realised that the devils were gone and that Jesus meant good, not harm, they sent a deputation to welcome him, and led him into the town through streets lined with smiling, cheering people.*

The ruler of the synagogue in Gadara was Jairus. His jobs were to arrange services, raise money and see to the cleaning and upkeep of the synagogue. He was an important man, a town elder. But now, when he saw Jesus walking through the streets, he ran and knelt at his feet, as humbly as a slave before his master. "Lord," he said, "my daughter's dying. Only you can save her. Please come to the house and help her."

Jesus answered, "Lead the way." Jairus led him through the streets towards his house, and the crowd jostled round them, eager to see what would happen. All at once Jesus stopped. "Who touched me?" he said. "Someone touched the hem of my coat."

"Master," said Simon Peter, "how can we tell? The crowd's pressing round on all sides. Dozens of people must have touched you."

"Someone needed help, and touched me," said Jesus. "I felt power go out of me. Show me who it was."

There was a sudden storm of weeping from the midst of the crowd, and a beggar-woman ran out and threw herself at Jesus' feet. Her clothes were sacks, caked stiff with blood. "Master," she said, "I touched you. I've suffered bleeding-sickness for eighteen years. Until you came I was a beggar, an outcast. I knew that if I could get near enough to touch you, even just a corner of your coat, you would answer my prayer and cure me."

She cringed back: she was used to kicks and sneers. But Jesus lifted her gently and said, "Daughter, be comforted. Your faith has cured you. Go in peace."

The cured woman burst into tears of joy, and the crowd buzzed with excited talk. Unnoticed by anyone except Jesus, one of Jairus' servants slipped through the crowd, took Jairus aside and said quietly, "Sir, trouble the Master no further. Your daughter's dead."

Jairus looked helplessly at Jesus, and Jesus said, "Don't be afraid. She'll be cured. Have faith." He hurried into Jairus' house, taking no one but Peter, James and John. Jairus' wife, his servants and his other children were tearing their clothes, weeping and comforting each other for the little girl's death. Jesus told them to dry their eyes. "She isn't dead," he said. "She's sleeping."

"She's dead!" wailed Jairus' wife. "Anyone can tell the difference! She's not asleep – she's dead!"

Leaving Jairus to comfort her, Jesus went alone into the child's room. The little girl was lying on the bed, corpse-still. Jesus took her cold hands and began calling gently, "Child, wake up." For a while she was a dead weight in his hands; but then she sneezed, sat up and blinked, as if freshly roused from sleep. Jesus supported her out of the room and into her mother's arms. "Give her something to eat," he said. "She's cured."*

The Son of God

Jesus knew that what he was telling people was hard to understand. For centuries prophets had spoken of the coming of a Messiah, a saviour who would rescue the Chosen People from their enemies. Now the Promised Land was ruled by Romans – and when Jewish people thought of the Messiah, they imagined not a healer or a preacher, but a warlord who would drive the legions into the sea and set all Israel free. When Jesus told them that he was the Messiah, and that he had come to save them not from flesh-and-blood enemies but from their own sinful selves, they found it hard to understand. He told them that every person was a blend of good and bad, and that God had given them free will, the power to choose. One day, God would call all human beings to give an account of themselves. He would be merciful to those who admitted their sins and begged to be forgiven; the others would be banished forever. He, Jesus, had come into the world to help people choose. Anyone at all – Jew, Roman, priest, beggar, queen, criminal, slave – could choose to follow him. If they believed in him, if they admitted the badness in their own natures and tried to live better lives, he would speak for them on Judgement Day and they would be saved.

To make this teaching easier to understand, Jesus turned it into stories. He told the people that he was like a shepherd, who protected his sheep and would never rest until he rescued all who strayed. He said that true understanding of God was like yeast in bread, like a priceless pearl, or like a tree which grows from a tiny seed to shelter everyone in the household. He told longer stories, too. He once said, "A farmer once went out to sow seed. Some fell by the wayside; people trod on it and birds ate it. Some fell on stony ground, and died for lack of moisture. Some fell among weeds, and was choked to death. But some fell in good soil, and grew so well that the farmer harvested one hundred grains for every one he'd planted." When people asked him to explain the story he said, "I am the sower, and the seed is God's word. Some people pay no attention to my teaching, as people trod on the grains by the wayside; or they peck it up like birds and then fly away to something else. Some people listen eagerly at first, as seeds begin well on stony ground; but then they lose interest, and their faith dies for lack of watering. Some believe, but their belief is choked by the cares and pleasures of ordinary living, as seeds are choked by weeds. But some people encourage and spread my teaching, as good ground feeds seeds." He added, "How lucky people are who feel hungry and thirsty for good – for they will be satisfied."

One day Jesus was preaching in the hills near Bethsaida, on the opposite shore of the Sea of Galilee from Capernaum. A large crowd had gathered: over five thousand men, women and children. Some of them had followed Jesus for days, walking round the coast or rowing across the sea. They sat on the hillside above him like people watching in a theatre. He began as he always did, by laying hands on sick people and healing them. Then he started preaching, telling the crowd about God's love and urging them to admit their sins and pray for forgiveness. The people listened all day, and when Jesus finished speaking they stood in excited groups, discussing what he'd said. The disciples took Jesus aside and said, "Master, it's nearly sunset. These people have had nothing to eat all day. Send them down to Bethsaida to buy food before it gets too dark."

Jesus said, "Let them stay. We'll feed them here."

"Master, it's an empty hillside. Where can we find the food?"

Andrew said, "There's a boy in the crowd with five barley loaves and two pickled fish. But that's all there is."

Jesus said, "Sit the people down, and bring me the loaves and fish."

The disciples organised the people into groups of about fifty, sat them down and told them that Jesus would feed them. Then they handed Jesus the loaves and fish. Jesus blessed the food and began breaking it in pieces for the disciples to distribute. The disciples ran backwards and forwards, up and down the hill, until the whole crowd was fed. Then they collected the scraps – and there was enough food left over to fill twelve large fish-baskets.*

The crowd clustered round Jesus, asking excitedly about the miracle. He said to his disciples, "Take a boat and sail home. When the people have gone home, I'll follow you." The disciples launched their boats and began rowing, and Jesus stood on a rock and lifted his arms to bless the crowd. People started moving away down the hill in groups in the darkness, and soon Jesus was left alone. The night was chilly, and the wind was gusting the sea to waves. When the disciples looked back, they could see no sign of him.

"Should we go back?" asked John.

"How can we?" Peter said. "The wind's against us. He'll probably stay in Bethsaida, or hire a donkey, or walk. He – "

"Look!" shouted Matthew, pointing back. There, in the midst of the storm, in the howling dark, Jesus was walking towards them across the sea. Wherever he trod, the waves stilled and the water gleamed calm in the moonlight.

The disciples thought that they were seeing the Devil, that Satan had taken Jesus' shape to trick them. They fell on their knees and begged for mercy. Jesus called, "Don't be afraid. Have faith."

Peter said, "Lord, if it really is you, let me walk to you across the water."

Jesus answered, "Come to me."

Trembling, Peter stepped out of the boat and began walking across the sea to Jesus. At first the water supported him.

But when he saw the size of the waves and heard the whine of the storm his courage drained away and he began to sink. He held out his arms to Jesus, calling piteously, "Master, save me!"

Jesus took hold of him and said, "Peter, why did you doubt me? Was your faith so small?" He supported Peter back to the boat and helped him in – and at once the wind dropped, the storm ceased and the sea grew calm.

In the weeks and months they were with Jesus, the disciples saw this kind of miracle every day, and heard Jesus' teaching – and even so they were still not sure of him. He tried, gently, to convince them that he was the son of God and to remind them that his time on earth was short. One day he asked, "Who do people say I am?"

"John the Baptist," said one of the disciples.

"Elijah," said another.

"The prophet Jeremiah," said a third.

"And who do you say I am?"

Peter ran to him, crying, "You're Jesus Christ, the Messiah, the son of God!"

Jesus said, "Simon Peter, you're the rock on which I shall build my church."*

Soon afterwards, Jesus took Peter, James and John to pray on a high mountain, as his custom was. The climb was steep, and the mountain was so high that although the sun blazed overhead drifts of snow still lay in the gullies and the water-pools were ice. Before they reached the summit Peter said, "Master, we're exhausted. Please let us rest."

"Rest," said Jesus. "Wait for me here, and rest."

He went on up the slope. The disciples watched him clambering through the mist till he was out of sight. Then they lay down, yawning. Tiredness seemed to pour into them as water fills a jug. They wrapped themselves in their cloaks, closed their eyes and slept. Then they woke with a start, all three together. The mist had vanished, and the mountain was shining with a clear, white light, brighter than any sun. High on the peak above them, Jesus was standing with two other men. Their faces shone, their hair and beards glowed, and their clothes gleamed like beacons, dazzling the disciples. The two men with Jesus were Elijah, the prophet who had foretold Jesus' coming eight centuries before, and Moses, who had been given the Ten Commandments by God himself. Humbly, the disciples knelt and prayed – and when they looked up again Elijah and Moses had disappeared, and Jesus was standing beside them. His face was like an angel's, serene and gentle. Peter whispered, "Master, it's good for us to be here. Let us build three shrines, one for Moses, one for Elijah and one for you."

Even as he spoke, a cloud came down and covered them. It was as if a whirlwind were raging through them, scouring them. They heard God's voice saying, "This is my beloved son, in whom I am well-pleased. Hear him!"

When the storm died and the cloud disappeared, Jesus was standing beside them in his ordinary clothes, smiling. He led the way down the mountain, and Peter, James and John were astonished to find a crowd waiting anxiously at the bottom. What they had taken for a morning's climb had actually lasted one whole day and night. The other disciples crowded round, asking them what had happened; but they could find no words to describe what they had seen and heard.

Jesus and the Pharisees

Jesus' disciples once asked him, "Master, how should human beings speak to God?"

Jesus answered, "When you pray, don't make a show of it as some people do, standing up and speaking in a loud voice to let everyone see how dutiful you are. Pray quietly, where only God can hear you. Say 'Our father in heaven, blessed be your name. May your kingdom come, on earth as in heaven. Give us enough to eat, today and every day. Forgive our mistakes, as we forgive other people's. Keep us from temptation. Save us from wickedness. Amen.'"*

Answers like this horrified the Pharisees. They believed that God had given Moses clear rules for prayer, as for everything else in life – and that Jesus should be teaching those instead of making up new ones of his own. Experts in

Moses' law travelled from Jerusalem to test him, to ask him questions and try to catch him out. "Teacher," they said, "Tell us about the Ten Commandments. Which is the most important?"

Jesus answered, "Only two commandments matter. The first is 'Love God with all your heart, soul and mind'. The second is 'Love others as much as you love yourself'."

This was not the answer the Pharisees expected. They argued about it for days – did it show that Jesus agreed or disagreed with the Ten Commandments? It was the same each time they challenged him: he gave them answers based not on the Law of Moses but on common sense, answers no one but a fool would disagree with. Once, he sat down to eat without washing his hands as the Law decreed, and when they reminded him he said, "It's not the dirt going into our mouths which poisons us, but the hatred which comes out of us, the cruel words we speak."

The worst thing the Pharisees could find against Jesus was that he took no notice of the Sabbath Laws. The Fourth Commandment said that just as God rested on the seventh day of creation, so human beings should work for six days and then rest. They should give the Sabbath day to God, praying, reading and thinking about the Law; they should not be distracted by work, or by such everyday activities as cooking or travelling. It seemed to the Pharisees that Jesus treated the Sabbath like any other day – but as usual, whenever they challenged him they found his replies unanswerable. Once, when he was walking with his disciples through a cornfield on the Sabbath day, some of the disciples picked ears of corn and rubbed off the husks to eat the grains. The Pharisees gleefully called this work. But when they asked Jesus why he let his disciples break the Sabbath laws, he answered, "Which matters more, human need or the Sabbath law?" On another Sabbath day, in the synagogue, a man with a withered arm begged Jesus to heal him, and the Pharisees said that healing counted as work and was unlawful. Jesus asked them, "If one of your sheep fell into a hole on the Sabbath, wouldn't you climb down to rescue it, work or no work? Are people less valuable than sheep?" He turned to the man and said, "Hold out your arm" – and when the man obeyed his arm was as healthy as the rest of his body.

One of the other people healed by Jesus on the Sabbath was a man inhabited by a devil which made him blind, deaf and dumb. Jesus drove the devil shrieking out of him, and instead of rejoicing that the man was cured the Pharisees muttered to each other, "How can this fellow order devils about, unless his power comes from Satan, prince of devils?"

Jesus asked them, "Why should Satan drive out devils? Why should he fight his own kind? I drive out devils by the power of God. God's power is here, among you, if only you choose to see it."

Jesus often seemed to challenge another belief of the Pharisees. They thought that keeping God's Law was all that mattered for a mortal, and therefore that anyone who followed it exactly was a good person, and anyone who broke it was an outcast, barred from God. But Jesus seemed to have no time for people who kept the Law. He ate with taxgatherers, held beggars in his arms, cured mad people and told criminals that their sins were forgiven. Once, a woman's husband caught her making love with another man, and the Pharisees dragged her before Jesus and said, "Teacher, this woman is guilty of adultery. Moses' Law says that adulterers are to be stoned to death. Tell us – should we obey the Law or not?" The question was a catch. If Jesus said that Moses' Law should be obeyed, the Romans would arrest him: the laws of Rome said that only the Roman authorities had power to order executions. On the other hand, if he said that the woman should be set free, the Pharisees could claim that he had defied Moses' Law. Once again, however, Jesus gave them a different answer from any they expected. He sat silently for a time, drawing in the sand with a stick. Then he looked at the woman's accusers and said, "She's guilty of adultery, under Moses' Law. But which of you, which man here, is so free from guilt of any kind that he'll throw the first stone at her?"

On another occasion, when the Pharisees objected to Jesus spending time with sinners, he answered with a story. "There is more joy in heaven over one sinner who repents than over ninety-nine good people who need no repentance," he said. "A man once had two sons. The younger son went to him and said, 'Father, I know that when you die your property will be divided equally between my brother and me. Please give me my share now.' The father gave his son half of everything he owned – and instead of spending the money wisely the son went to live in a distant town and wasted every penny on parties, wine and women. Soon everything was spent and he was penniless. He took the only work he could find, as a pigherd, and he was often so hungry that he grubbed on the ground for acorns beside the pigs. He thought, 'If I stay here, I'll starve. I'll go back to father: even his most worthless servants have enough to eat.' He went home, threw himself at his father's feet and said, 'Father, I've sinned. I don't deserve to be called your son. Make me one of your servants; let me earn the food I eat.' To his surprise, instead of punishing him the old man shouted eagerly to his slaves, 'Dress him in new clothes! Put rings on his hands and shoes on his feet. Kill the fatted calf for a feast – my son that was lost is found again!' The feast began, and the elder son, who had stayed loyally with his father all those years, heard the noise of it from the fields, ran home and asked his father crossly, 'Why, when I do everything a loyal son should, when I stay with you and obey you in every way, do you never make feasts for me? My brother has wasted every penny you gave him – why do you kill the fatted calf for him? Why do you make such a fuss for a sinner, and none for a good man?' His father answered, 'Son, you're always with me. Everything I have is yours. But your brother was lost and is found; he was dead and is alive. Isn't it right that we should make a feast to show our joy?'"*

Bethany

It was spring. Jesus had been preaching for three years in Galilee. He began telling his followers that it was time to go to Jerusalem for the Passover festival. He said, "The Messiah will be betrayed. He will be accused by priests and Pharisees. He will be killed, and will rise again on the third day."

Jesus' followers found these words hard to understand. Some wept to think that Jesus must be killed, and begged him not to go to Jerusalem. Others thought that God's Judgement Day must be near at hand, and began anxiously wondering if they would be taken with the good people into heaven, or condemned with the wicked to hell. A rich young man asked Jesus, "Sir, what must I do to be saved?"

"Love God and keep the commandments."

"I've kept the commandments since I was a child. What else can I do?"

"Sell all you have and give the money to the poor. Let your wealth be in heaven, not on earth."

"Sir, I can't do that!"

The young man turned sadly away, and Jesus said to the disciples, "How can people be saved if their minds are burdened with thoughts of treasure? It's easier for a camel to go through the eye of a needle, than for a rich person to enter Heaven."

Another man, a Pharisee, asked, "Master, what should I do to deserve everlasting life?"

"What do the commandments say?"

Instead of quoting Moses' Law, the Pharisee replied with Jesus' own commandments. "Love God with all your heart, soul and mind. Love other people as you do yourself."

"Do this," said Jesus, "And you'll have eternal life."

"Master, I still don't understand. What other people? Who must I love?"

Jesus answered with a story. "A man once left Jerusalem to walk to Jericho. On the way thieves took everything he had, stripped him naked, beat him and left him half dead beside the road. The next two people who passed that way were holy men, a priest and a Levite. They prided themselves on being honest, God-fearing people, but each of them, when he saw the body, crossed the road, pretended not to notice and passed by on the other side. Finally came an idolator, one of the despised people of the Samaritan Plain. He had no reason to love true believers or their God, but as soon as he saw the injured man he ran to help him, washed his wounds, put him on his own donkey and took him to an inn. He gave the landlord some money and said, 'Look after him. If it costs more than this, I'll pay the rest tomorrow when I come back this way.' Now, out of those three people, which truly loved the man who was attacked by thieves?"

"The Good Samaritan, who helped him."

"You've answered your own question. We should all help other people, whoever they are, in just that way."

As always, this kind of teaching made Jesus as many enemies as friends. As he and the disciples travelled towards Jerusalem, they were welcomed in some villages, and driven from others with showers of stones. When they were about one morning's walk from Jerusalem, they spent the night in the village of Bethany, at the house of Lazarus, Mary and Martha, a brother and two sisters Jesus had long ago converted in Galilee, and who had gone to Bethany to preach his message there.* It was three weeks to Passover. Jesus said to Lazarus, "I'll spend a few days preaching in the villages round about, then pass one more night here before I ride into Jerusalem."

Jesus and his disciples spent the next nine days preaching. They travelled as far as Jericho* in the Jordan valley and back again, making many converts.* At evening on the tenth day, as they were walking back along the hill-track to Bethany, Martha came to meet them with a crowd of weeping people. Her clothes were torn and her hair was sprinkled with ash as a sign of mourning. "Master," she said to Jesus, "soon after you went away, Lazarus fell sick and died. If only you'd stayed, he might have lived!"

Jesus said, "Your brother will live again."

Martha said, "I know he will: at the resurrection, on Judgement Day."

Jesus said, "I am the resurrection and the life. Anyone who has faith in me will be given everlasting life. Do you believe this?"

"Lord, I believe it," said Martha. "You're the son of God, the Saviour."

"Fetch Mary," said Jesus. "Tell her I need her."

Martha ran into the village to fetch her sister. The two women took Jesus to Lazarus' tomb, a cave with a stone rolled across the entrance. In the crowd that followed, some people were muttering, "What's wrong with Jesus? He makes the blind see, the lame walk, the deaf hear – why couldn't he save his own friend from death?"

Jesus stood outside the tomb and said, "Move the stone away."

"No, master!" sobbed Martha. "He's been dead four days!"

"Move the stone away," repeated Jesus. Unwillingly, holding cloths over their noses to hide the corpse-smell, servants rolled the stone away. Jesus looked up at the sky and prayed. Then he turned back towards the tomb and called, "Lazarus, come out!" For a moment, while the echoes of his voice rolled round the cave, nothing happened. But then Lazarus appeared, wrapped in white grave-clothes, walking with firm steps out of his own tomb. The crowd fell on its knees and worshipped God, and Jesus said to the disciples, "Take him home."

The disciples led Mary, Martha and Lazarus back into Bethany, and groups of awe-struck villagers walked after them. Jesus stayed by the empty tomb to pray. Some Pharisees who had seen the miracle saddled horses and galloped into Jerusalem to tell Caiaphas, the high priest, and the other Temple authorities. "What are we to do?" they asked. "If people keep calling him the Messiah, and the Romans get to hear that a leader has come to free the Jews, they'll kill us all."

Caiaphas said, "Perhaps just one man should die, so that everyone else may live."

While the priests and Pharisees were meeting in Jerusalem, in Bethany Martha and Mary were holding a joyful, excited feast. Overcome by the miracle of Lazarus' return to life, and at Jesus' presence in her house, Mary fetched a jar of expensive perfume, olive oil scented with spikenard, poured it over Jesus' feet and wiped them with her own hair.* The scent of spikenard filled the house, and everyone there was filled with joy. Only Judas Iscariot, Jesus' twelfth disciple, was displeased. "What a waste!" he muttered. "We could have sold that perfume, and used the money to help the poor."

Jesus looked at him and said, "The poor are with you always, but I shall soon be gone. She has anointed me as priests of old anointed kings, and as people anoint the dead for burial."

No one else understood Jesus' words. Only Judas knew that they foretold Jesus' death. He said nothing, but watched and waited: his moment had not yet come.

16 · JESUS IN JERUSALEM

Jesus in the Temple

Every year in spring, thousands of people went to celebrate the Passover festival in Jerusalem. The streets were crowded and the inns were full. Detachments of Roman soldiers patrolled the city, alert for trouble. Every nearby town and village teemed with strangers, using the festival as an excuse to see the Temple and to visit their relations. All day the road between Jericho and Jerusalem bustled with travellers, their feet and their horses' hooves raising dust-clouds in the still, hot air. The road climbed steeply to the top of the Mount of Olives, about an hour's walk from the Jerusalem gate, then sloped down to the city past groves of date-palms, fig-trees and the olive-trees which gave the Mount its name.

Six days before Passover, Jesus and his disciples set out for Jerusalem. They walked along the crowded road to a small village, Bethphage, at the top of the Mount of Olives. The Jerusalem road was the main village street, and most travellers passed through Bethphage without stopping, or sat outside one of the village inns to catch their breath after the climb. Jesus took two of his disciples, pointed down a side-alley and said, "Down there, you'll find a donkey tethered, with her foal beside her. Unfasten them and bring them here. If their owner asks questions, just say 'The Lord needs them', and he'll let them go."

The disciples did as they were told. They brought the donkey, laid cloaks on her back for a saddle and sat Jesus on top. Then they took the reins and set off through the crowds towards Jerusalem, shouting, "Make way for the son of David!" When they came over the brow of the hill and started down the road through the olive-groves, people from the crowd began pulling off leafy palm-branches and scattering them at Jesus' feet. They shouted and sang, "Hosanna to the Son of David! Blessings! He comes in God's name! Hosanna!" Soon the whole road was a mass of singing, dancing people, with Jesus in the middle of it, riding his donkey over a palm-leaf carpet. When bystanders asked curiously, "Who is this son of David?", the disciples answered, "Jesus of Nazareth, the prophet, the holy one of God."

The noisy procession passed through the Jerusalem gate and along the narrow streets to the Temple. Here, as usual at Passover time, the main courtyard had become a marketplace, full of stalls selling food, drink, pigeons for sacrifice and lambs, wine and herbs for the Passover meal. There were money-lenders' booths and stands for fortune-tellers and letter-writers. Jugglers, fire-eaters and acrobats performed wherever there was space to draw spectators. Jesus dismounted from the donkey and strode into the courtyard. His followers thought that he was going into the Temple to pray, or perhaps meant to buy food or drink. They were astonished when he knotted three cords together and began scattering the stall-holders, driving them out of the courtyard and shouting, "My house is a house of prayer, and you have made it a den of thieves!" His rage was so great, his power so unanswerable, that the merchants and money-lenders moved one by one, grumbling, out of the Temple and set up their businesses in the street outside. Jesus stood in a corner of the courtyard to pray, and gradually people plucked up courage to approach him, until he was surrounded by an enormous crowd. As always, blind, sick and crippled people were led to the front, and he laid hands on them and healed them. He began to preach, telling the people that God's kingdom was near and that if they repented their sins they would be given eternal life.* He said that God's blessing was for everyone, not just for those who kept strictly to Moses' Law. In fact, unless people truly repented, truly believed, obedience to Moses' Law would not be enough to guarantee eternal life.*

Every morning for the next four days, Jesus walked from Bethany into Jerusalem, followed by joyful crowds, and spent the day preaching and healing in the Temple courtyard. The

Temple authorities were furious. They would gladly have arrested him and kept him in prison till the festival was over. But they were afraid of his popularity with the crowds. There seemed to be no way to trap him. They demanded to know who gave him authority for what he preached, and he replied by asking them what authority John the Baptist had had – a question they could not answer "None" without antagonising the crowd. In front of a patrol of Roman soldiers, they asked him whether Jews should pay tax to Rome or not, hoping that he would declare God's kingdom more important than any mortal state – and he showed them Augustus Caesar's portrait on a coin and said, "Pay Caesar what belongs to Caesar; pay God what belongs to God". There was nothing they could do. They had to listen while he preached against Pharisees, scribes and anyone else who preferred love of the Law to love of God.* They had to watch him healing on the Sabbath, against Moses' Law.* They had to hear him prophesying the destruction of Jerusalem and the downfall of the Temple* – and still they could think of no way to silence him. They set spies on him; they wrote down every word he said in case he uttered treason; they plotted to arrest him as soon as they could get him on his own, away from the protecting crowds.

The Last Supper

On the first day of Passover Jesus said to the two disciples who had found the donkey for him in Bethphage, "Go into the city. Look for a man carrying a water-jar, and follow him. When he goes into a house say to the owner, 'Please show us the guest-room, where the Master can eat the Passover with his disciples.' He'll show you a large upstairs room, with table and couches ready. Make the Passover supper there."

The two disciples hurried into Jerusalem. On their way they bought bread, wine, herbs and a Passover lamb. They found the room, exactly as Jesus had described, and made everything ready. Jesus spent the day preaching in the Temple, and at evening went to the house with his disciples. Bread and wine were already on the table, and while two of the disciples fetched the dish of roast lamb, the others stood in groups, talking quietly about the day's events. To their surprise, Jesus took off his outer clothes, wrapped a towel round his waist and fetched a basin and a water-jar. Then he went round the disciples one by one, kneeling like a slave to wash their feet, and drying them on the towel. Most of the disciples were embarrassed, but none except Peter dared to argue. He said angrily, "Master, you're not my slave. I won't let you wash me."

Jesus answered, "Only those I wash are with me."

At once Peter cried, "In that case, Master, wash my feet, hands, head – wash all of me!"*

Jesus finished the washing and put his clothes back on. Then they all moved to the table to begin the meal. The disciples had eaten Passover suppers every year of their lives. They knew the customs. Wine would be poured and blessed. Prayers would be said. The story of the first Passover would be told. There would be hymns and more prayers, and then everyone would eat. But this time Jesus did nothing as they expected it. He took bread, blessed it and gave it to the disciples saying, "Take, eat. This is my body." Then he took a cup of wine, gave thanks and handed it to them saying, "Drink, all of you. This is my blood, shed for many for the remission of sins. I will not drink again of the fruit of the vine until I drink it new with you in my Father's kingdom." Finally he said, "Tonight one of you will betray me to the authorities."

The disciples looked at each other in horror. One by one they asked Jesus fearfully, "Lord, who is it? Am I the one?"

Jesus said, "One of you sitting at this table, eating from this dish, will betray me." He took a piece of bread, dipped it in wine and gave it to Judas Iscariot, saying, "The time has come. Go, quickly. Do what you have to do."

Judas hurried out of the room. The others thought nothing of it. Judas looked after the disciples' money, and often disappeared to buy things or to make arrangements. Perhaps now he was going to pay for the hire of the room, or to give money to charity. The disciples made no connection between

his going and Jesus' words. But Judas went straight to the
palace of the high priest, Caiaphas. He burst in on him in the
middle of the Passover meal and said in a low voice, "Give me
thirty pieces of silver,* and I'll take your men to a quiet place
where they can arrest Jesus without antagonising the crowd."

"As you say," said Caiaphas, "So be it."*

When Jesus and the disciples had finished eating, they sang
a hymn, as custom was at the end of the Passover meal. Then
they went into the cool evening air, out of the city and along
the Jericho road towards the Mount of Olives. As they
walked Jesus said, "Every one of you will desert me tonight.
The shepherd will be struck down, and the sheep will all be
scattered."

Peter said hotly, "Master, I'll never desert you."

"I tell you, Peter," said Jesus, "that before the cock crows
tomorrow morning, you'll deny me three times."

There was a bridge at the bottom of the valley, and to one
side was a quiet place, the Garden of Gethsemane. Jesus said
to his disciples, "Wait here, while I go inside to pray." He left
the others on the bridge, and took Peter, James and John
down into the garden. At the gate he told them, "Watch here,
and wait." He went alone into the garden, knelt down and
prayed to God. "O Father, if it's possible, take this cup from
me. Nevertheless, not my will be done, but yours." He
walked back to the three disciples at the gate. They were all
asleep. He woke them, and asked Peter sorrowfully,
"Couldn't you stay awake one hour with me? Watch – and
pray: the spirit is willing, even if the flesh is weak." He went
back into the garden, and prayed a second time, "Father, if I
must drink from this cup, if it can not be taken away, your
will be done." Once again he went to the gate, and found the
three disciples asleep. He prayed a third time, using the same
words, and then said to the disciples, "While you sleep, the
Son of Man is betrayed into the hands of sinners. Wake up:
my betrayer is here."

Even as he spoke Judas ran into the garden, and behind him
a gang of Caiaphas' servants armed with sticks and swords.
They had crept through the city, hiding their weapons from
Roman patrols. Now Judas whispered to them, "The one I

kiss is Jesus. Hold him fast!" He went up to Jesus, kissed him and said, "Hail, master!" – and at once Caiaphas' servants ran up and took Jesus prisoner. Startled out of sleep, Peter, James and John rushed to defend Jesus – and Peter swung his sword wildly and sliced off the ear of one of Caiaphas' men.

"Peter, sheathe your sword," said Jesus. "Those who use force will die by force." He touched the servant's head with his hand and healed the wound. Then the others picked him up and hustled him into Jerusalem, to Caiaphas' palace, before Jesus' disciples could gather their wits to rescue him.* Peter trailed miserably after Jesus, slipped into the courtyard of Caiaphas' palace and sat in the shadows beside a fire, waiting to see what would happen. Jesus' other disciples, terrified, hurried to the safety of Lazarus' house in Bethany.

Jesus on Trial

It was the middle of the night. Surrounded by Temple guards, Jesus stood in a large room of Caiaphas' house. The High Priest's servants hurried through the streets, calling Caiaphas' advisers to council. Others rounded up anyone they thought would give evidence against Jesus. Speed was essential: Jesus had to be tried, convicted and taken to the Romans for punishment before crowds of believers could gather and demand his freedom. Caiaphas and his advisers sat on thrones, yawning, dressed in their priestly robes and holding their staffs of office. Beside them stood secretaries, Law-experts and other officials. The room filled with a sleepy, sullen crowd, the men and women dragged from their beds to accuse Jesus.

Most of the people had only one thought in their minds: to get back to bed. They began charging Jesus with every crime they could think of, hoping that he would be quickly condemned and they would be allowed to go. They spoke of murder, robbery, tax-evasion, even kidnapping. Then one man said, "He threatened to tear the Temple down with his own bare hands."

"He said he'd build it again, by magic, in three days."

Caiaphas shouted at Jesus, "Do you hear these charges? Answer them!" Jesus said nothing. Caiaphas lost his temper. He pointed his staff at Jesus and asked, in a voice trembling with hatred, "Are you the Messiah?"

"Would you believe me if I told you?" said Jesus. "The Son of Man will sit at God's right hand."

"What does that mean?" asked Caiaphas. "Are you or aren't you the son of God?"

"You say so."

Caiaphas threw down his staff with a clatter. Purple with rage, he took the skirt of his robe and tore it, slowly and deliberately, from knee to waist. "Blasphemy!" he shouted to the council. "You heard him. Out of his own mouth, he's condemned himself."

The crowd began making the sign of the evil eye at Jesus and hissing, "Blasphemy!" The guard captain punched Jesus in the face and said, "How dare you say such words to my lord High Priest?" The other guards blindfolded Jesus with a napkin and began pushing and jostling him from one to another. "Come on, son of God," they jeered. "If you're so clever, tell us which of us is hitting you."

Outside in the courtyard, Peter sat in the shadows, waiting for dawn. He heard the jeering and the sound of blows from inside, and shivered. A girl, one of Caiaphas' kitchen-slaves, found him there and said, "I've seen you before. You were in the Temple. You're one of Jesus' men."

"I don't know what you mean," said Peter defiantly.

He moved out of the courtyard into the porch, into deeper shadow, and pulled his cloak round his face. But people were already moving in and out, slaves beginning their day's work – and one of them said, "I know that man. He was with Jesus."

"I've never heard of him!" said Peter.

"Of course you have. You're from Galilee – I can tell by your accent."

"Leave me alone," snarled Peter. "In God's name, I swear I don't know the man."

No sooner had he spoken than a cock began crowing. Peter remembered Jesus' words on the way to the Garden of Gethsemane, 'Before the cock crows tomorrow morning, you'll deny me three times'. He covered his face with his hands and stumbled into the street, weeping bitterly, while Caiaphas' slaves stared curiously after him.

As soon as it was daylight, Caiaphas' counsellors hurried to the headquarters of Pontius Pilate, the Roman governor of Jerusalem. Temple servants hustled Jesus along behind them, bruised, stumbling, and surrounded by the hostile crowd. There was no sound but the slap of the people's footsteps and their hoarse, eager breathing. They were intent on Jesus' death; they had no need of words.

It was Pilate's custom, every morning during the Passover season, to try any suspects arrested the night before. Most were drunks or tramps, picked up by Roman patrols in the city streets. He followed the same procedure in each case. He listened to the charges, asked the prisoner to admit them or deny them, and ordered immediate release or punishment. When Caiaphas' counsellors pushed their way through the crowd, important men, Pilate immediately brushed lesser business aside and invited them to speak. The Temple servants flung Jesus to the ground in front of him, and Caiaphas' secretary announced the charges against him: that he had broken the Law of Moses, and that he claimed to be the Messiah, the king who would save the Jews.

The first charge hardly interested Pilate. It was up to the Jews to look after their own religious laws. But if the second accusation meant that Jesus was a political agitator, a threat to Rome, it was serious. He said sharply to Jesus, "Get up. Answer. Are you the king of the Jews or not?"

Jesus said, "Do you believe it?"

"Your own people, your own priests, declare it."

"My kingdom is not of this world. If it were, my subjects would be fighting to rescue me. My kingdom is still to come."

"Does that mean you're a king or not?"

"I was born into the world to witness to the truth. Everyone who understands the truth hears my voice."

Pilate spread his hands and said, "What is truth?" Then he turned to Caiaphas' counsellors. "I find no fault in him," he said. "But I'm happy to do as I always do at Passover. I'll set one Jewish prisoner free. The choice is yours. You can have

Barabbas the murderer, or this man, the King of the Jews. Which will it be?"

Pilate thought that he was giving them no real choice. Barabbas was a criminal, a notorious murderer; Jesus was an innocent preacher. He was astounded when Caiaphas' counsellors answered "Barabbas" as one man, and the whole crowd joined in, stamping their feet and shouting, "Barabbas! Free Barabbas!"

Pilate called the counsellors aside, out of earshot of the crowd. "Jesus is innocent," he repeated. "I find no fault in him."

"He claims to be God's son, the Messiah. Under Jewish law, that means that he should die."

"Jewish law! *You* kill him."

"Only you, a Roman, have the authority to kill. Crucify him!"

"He's innocent."

"He claims to be King of the Jews. He challenges Tiberius Caesar. If you let him go, you challenge Caesar too."

Pilate said, "You want me to crucify your king?"

"We have no king but Caesar."

Pilate called for a bowl of water. He ceremonially washed his hands in front of them and said, "I leave it to you. He's innocent. I won't take the blame. His blood will be on your heads."

"Let it be! On ours and our children's heads!"

Pilate said, "As you say, so be it. Let him be crucified."*

The King of the Jews

Pilate's soldiers stripped Jesus and beat him, as they did all condemned criminals. Then one of them fetched a purple cloak from the guard-house, and hung it round his shoulders. Another twisted thorn-twigs into a crown and rammed it on his head. A third stuck a reed into his right hand and cuffed him till he held it. Then they all knelt mockingly at his feet, shouting, "Hail, king of the Jews!", and began parading him round the room while the crowd spat, kicked and punched.

Finally they dressed him in his own clothes again and led him out to crucifixion.*

The execution-ground was a sloping, stony field nick-named Golgotha or "skull-place". It lay outside the city wall, next to the Roman amphitheatre where gladiator-fights were staged. Jesus had to carry his execution-pole all the way across the city, from Pilate's official residence on the other side. The pole was to form the arms of his cross. It was as tall as a man and about as thick as a human thigh. It was all Jesus could do to lift it, let alone carry it. The soldiers tried pushing him, flogging him and dragging him by the clothes. In the end they lost patience, picked the strongest man they could find in the crowd (his name was Simon; he was visiting Jerusalem from Cyrene in north Africa, to celebrate Passover), and made him carry the pole to Golgotha.

There were two other criminals already in Golgotha, wait-ing for execution. Their poles lay beside them, and next to them were three much longer poles, and three deep holes in the stony soil. The executioners – four young soldiers from the Roman barracks, led by a centurion – offered each pris-oner wine mixed with myrrh, to dull the pain, and then laid the poles on the ground, short nailed across long, to form three crosses. They stripped the prisoners, forced each of them to lie on one of the crosses, and nailed his hands and feet in place. Then they hammered a board above each man's head, with the name of his crime scribbled on it. The first man was a thief, the second a murderer – and on Jesus' board, because the soldiers could think of nothing else, their cen-turion wrote "I.N.R.I.", the first letters of the Latin words for "Jesus of Nazareth, King of the Jews". Finally, they wedged the crosses upright in the ground so that the prisoners dangled as if from trees. As the soldiers raised his cross, Jesus said quietly, "Father, forgive them, for they know not what they do."

The soldiers ignored him. They were already sharing out the prisoners' clothes at the foot of the cross: after each execution, they were allowed to sell the belongings and keep the money. They came to Jesus' cloak, and the first soldier said, "If we rip this into four, it'll be worthless. Let's throw dice for it: highest wins."

While the soldiers diced, their centurion tried to disperse the crowd which had gathered to watch the execution. "Go home," he said. "What's the point of staying? They'll take days to die."

Some of the people moved away. Others looked up at Jesus and began jeering, "Son of God, come down! Never mind others – save yourself! If you're the Messiah, jump down from the cross. We'll believe you then!" The thief on Jesus' left also snarled at him, "Come on, Messiah! Save yourself – and save us too!" But the other criminal shouted, "Don't be such a fool. We deserve to die, but this man's innocent." Then he turned his head and said humbly to Jesus, "Lord, remember me when you come to your kingdom."

Jesus answered, "I tell you: today you will be with me in paradise."

It was four hours after dawn. As Jesus and the criminals hung in agony, they could hear behind them, from the other side of the city wall, the shouts of people hurrying to work, the rumble of carts and the crying of animals. Many of the spectators in Golgotha, too, had jobs to go to. Pausing only to spit one last time at Jesus, or to make the sign of the evil eye against him, they left the execution-ground and hurried about their business. Soon only the centurion and soldiers were left, and a huddle of four people, cloaked and sobbing at the foot of Jesus' cross. Jesus looked down and recognised them: his own mother Mary, her sister Mary the mother of James, Mary Magdalene, whom he had healed of devils years before*, and his disciple John. He called gently down to his mother, "Woman, behold your son," and to John, "Behold your mother!" – and John, knowing that this was a sign that he was to look after Mary in the days to come, took her in his arms like a dutiful son to comfort her.

For the rest of the morning the only sounds were the cawing of crows, bursts of laughter from the soldiers dicing in the shade of the wall, and grunts of pain as the men on the crosses tried to shift themselves and ease their agony. The sun blistered the hanging men's faces and seared their eyes. Then, at midday, without warning, the sky was plunged into darkness, as abruptly as if the sun had been blotted out, and the soldiers heard Jesus groaning on his cross and crying out words in a language they didn't understand: "Eli, eli, lama sabachthani."

The soldiers drew their swords and ran over. "What are you saying?" they growled. "Are you calling your friends to rescue you? Is this a code?"

"He said 'Eli, eli'," jeered one of them. "He wants Elijah. Well, let's just see see if Elijah comes."

"It's Aramaic," said the centurion. "He's saying, 'My God, my God, why hast thou forsaken me?'"

The soldiers shrugged and went back to their game, feeling for their dice in the darkness. A few minutes later Jesus cried out again, this time in Latin: "I thirst, I thirst." Grumbling, one of the men stuck a wine-soaked sponge on a spear-butt and held it up to him.

At first the soldiers thought nothing of the darkness. It was the beginning of an electrical storm; it was common; it would be quickly over. But by the time three hours had passed with no sign of light, they were beginning to peer round nervously, gripping their daggers and muttering prayers to their barbarian gods. Then, without warning, Jesus suddenly shouted in a loud voice, "It is finished! Father, into thy hands I commend my spirit" – and at once thunder split the sky and the earth of Golgotha shuddered apart, throwing up bones, skulls and grave-sheets from the burial-pit beneath.* The soldiers jumped to their feet, shouting in panic. They ran to break the legs of the crucified men, to make them sag down on the crosses and choke to death. They wanted to bury the bodies and hurry back to the barracks where there was noise and light. They broke the two criminals' legs, but when they reached Jesus they found him already hanging limp and still.

"This one's finished," the first soldier said. He stabbed his spear into Jesus' side, just below the ribs, and a stream of watery blood ran out. The soldier caught it in a basin, turned to the centurion and said, "He's dead, sir. Permission to take him down?"

At first the centurion made no answer. He was staring up at Jesus like a man transfixed. Then he whispered, "Truly this man was the son of God", and to his soldiers' astonishment fell on his knees beside John, Mary and the other two women and began to pray.

The Resurrection

Most of the criminals executed at Golgotha had no relatives to claim the bodies. Their corpses were buried in a common pit, covered in quicklime to make them rot faster. Pilate was surprised, therefore, when Joseph of Arimathea, a rich Jewish counsellor, went to him and begged Jesus' body for burial.

"Why should you bury him? Your council sentenced him to death. What is he to you?"

"Sir, I was not one of those who sentenced him. I believed in him. I still believe."

"Where will you bury him?"

"In the cemetery beside Golgotha. I bought a rock-tomb years ago, to lie in when I died. It was fresh-cut: no one has ever lain there."

"Take the body. Do what you like with it."

Joseph hurried to Golgotha with a friend and fellow-believer, Nicodemus.* Joseph carried a grave-cloth, a roll of brand-new white linen. Nicodemus took myrrh and aloes to anoint the body. It was still pitch-dark, and the streets were empty. In the execution-ground, Joseph handed the centurion the scroll with Pilate's order, and he and Nicodemus helped the soldiers to take down Jesus' cross and unfasten the body. They anointed it with myrrh and aloes and wrapped it in the grave-cloth. Then they carried it to the cemetery, laid it in Joseph's tomb (a cave cut in a wall of solid rock) and blocked the entrance with a boulder. From a distance, Mary Jesus' mother, John and the two other Maries watched the burial. When it was over Joseph and Nicodemus knelt with them to pray, and they all went sadly home.**

On the next day, the Sabbath, no one visited the tomb. But at dawn on the third morning, Mary Magdalene went alone to the garden to pray. She found that the boulder had been rolled from the tomb-entrance and the tomb was empty. She ran for Peter and John, crying hysterically, "The Lord's gone!

They've stolen him! We don't know where he lies!" Peter and John hurried back with her to the tomb, and found nothing but the grave-cloth lying on the ground, and folded beside it the napkin which had fastened Jesus' jaw. In their distress their first thoughts were that tomb-robbers had stolen him, or that the Romans had thrown him into the common pit; they forgot his teaching that the Son of God would be crucified, buried and would rise again. They ran to tell the other disciples, leaving Mary weeping in the garden.

After a while Mary plucked up her courage to look into the tomb. She saw two angels, dressed in white, sitting where Jesus' body had lain, one at the head and one at the feet. They asked her, "Woman, why are you weeping?"

"Because they've taken away my Lord, and I don't know where he lies."

She was suddenly aware of a man standing in the garden beside her. He was dressed in workman's clothes, and she took him for the gardener. He held out his hand without touching her, and said gently, "Woman, who are you looking for?"

"Sir, if you took my Lord away, tell me where he is: I'll look after him."

The man said simply, "Mary." At once Mary realised that he was Jesus. She gasped with joy and opened her arms to hug him. "Don't touch me," Jesus said. "I am not yet ascended to my father. Go to my brothers and say these words to them: 'I ascend to my father and your father, and to my God and your God.'"*

Mary found his words hard to understand. But she ran, weeping with happiness, to tell the disciples. They were terrified. They were already hiding from the authorities, afraid of being charged with stealing Jesus' body – and now Mary was babbling of angels and the risen Lord. They barricaded themselves in the upper room where they had eaten the Last Supper two days before, sent Thomas (the least-known of the disciples) to Bethany to tell Lazarus and Martha what was happening, and spent the day in wide-eyed, anxious prayer.

In the evening, at dusk before the lamps were lit, the disciples suddenly realised that Jesus was standing in the midst of them, in the centre of the room. At first they shrank back, afraid that it might be a vision sent by Satan. But as soon as he raised his hands to bless them and said, "Peace be unto you", they knew that he was really Jesus and fell on their knees to welcome him. Jesus said, "Give me something to eat." They gave him a piece of fish and some honey, and watched him eat. Then he breathed on them and said, "This is my spirit, breathed into you. As my father sent me, so I send you." He blessed them once more and disappeared, leaving them trembling with excitement. Soon afterwards, Thomas came back from Bethany, and they ran to meet him on the stairs, shouting that Jesus had risen from the dead.

"I don't believe it," Thomas said. "Show me proof."

"He stood here, in the room beside us. He blessed us. He ate before our eyes. He breathed his spirit into us."

"I'll believe it when I see him with my own eyes, touch him with my own hands."

For a week the disciples tried to persuade Thomas, and he refused to believe their story. Then, on the evening of the eighth day, Jesus appeared again and said, "Peace be unto you," exactly as he had before. The other disciples knelt, but Thomas cringed back, convinced as they had once been that he was seeing devil's work. Jesus said, "Thomas, reach out. Touch the nail-wounds in my palms. Feel the spear-thrust in my side. Believe."

Thomas touched Jesus and found him flesh and blood like other men. He fell on his knees, crying, "My Lord, my God," and Jesus said, "Thomas, you believed because you saw me. How blessed are people who have never seen me, and still believe!" He turned to the other disciples and said, "It is for you, now, to tell the world this story, to give every human being the chance to believe in me. I am the way, the truth and the light; everyone who believes in me will not perish, but will have everlasting life. Go out, now, and teach this to all the world."*

17 · THE FIRST CHRISTIANS

Speaking with Tongues

For forty days after his resurrection, Jesus stayed with his disciples, preparing them for what they had to do. He told them to preach to everyone that the end of the world was coming. The whole human race would be called before God for judgement. The disciples should baptise all who believed in Jesus and repented their sins: those people would be given everlasting life. At first, the disciples misunderstood this teaching. They thought that when Jesus said "the end of the world is coming" he meant in a few days or weeks, and that when he said "baptise all who believe in me" he was thinking only of Jewish people. It never occurred to them that he might also mean Greeks, Romans, Africans and people from far-distant corners of the world.

A few days before Pentecost, the Jewish celebration of the beginning of harvest, Jesus and his disciples were sitting in the shade of a grove of trees on the Mount of Olives. The disciples leaned back against the tree-trunks, their ears filled with the buzz of insects and the braying of distant donkeys, and listened to Jesus' words. He said, "Stay in Jerusalem for the next few days. God's promise will come true. Just as John baptised with water, so you will soon be baptised with the Holy Ghost."

The disciples began asking, fearfully and eagerly, "Lord, is it the end of the world? Are you coming to save all Israel?"

"It's not for you to know God's times or seasons. The Holy Ghost will inspire you, and you'll preach and baptise in

Jerusalem, Samaria, Galilee and the furthest corners of the world."

He had no sooner spoken when a dark, dense cloud swirled from a clear sky and covered the mountain. The blood pounded in the disciples' ears. Their eyes were darkened and their voices withered in their throats. They fell on their knees to pray, and it was not till the cloud lifted and daylight returned that they dared to look up again, and saw that Jesus had disappeared. Two angels in shining white robes were standing in his place. "Galileans, what are you staring at?" the angels said. "Jesus has been taken from earth into Heaven – and in just the same way, he will come again from Heaven to earth."

The angels disappeared. The disciples, convinced that Judgement Day was near, ran to fetch Mary Jesus' mother, Martha, Lazarus and the others, and hurried to Jerusalem. They sent word to every Christian in the city, everyone who believed in Jesus, and told them to get ready for salvation. Led by the disciples, and keeping well clear of the authorities, the Christians began to meet each day in halls and private houses, to pray, sing hymns and prepare themselves for Judgement Day.

Peter said, "We should choose a twelfth disciple, to take Judas' place. He should be someone who's believed in Jesus from the beginning, from the time when he was baptised in the river Jordan."

Two names were suggested: Joseph Barsabas and Matthias. While the people prayed to Jesus to choose between them, Peter cast lots, and the lot fell on Matthias. From that day on he was counted as the twelfth disciple, equal with all the others.

The Feast of Pentecost was fifty days after Passover. Priests sacrificed spring lambs and loaves baked with early grain, and prayed to God to bless the coming harvest. It was a smaller festival than Passover, but still thousands of visitors thronged into Jerusalem to celebrate. On the morning of the feast-day, the Christians met as usual for hymns and prayers. But before they could begin, the sound of rushing wind filled the house. Serpent-tongues of fire flickered over the disciples' heads, and the twelve began calling out like men entranced. The noise drew people from the street outside, and the hall was soon jostling with strangers. "Who are those people – drunks?" they asked the Christians in amazement.

"They're Jesus' disciples: Galileans."

"Nonsense! They're Greeks. I come from Athens, and I can understand every word they say."

"They're not Greeks, they're Persians. How else could I understand them?"

"They're talking Syrian."

"Latin."

"Ethiopian."

So everyone in the crowd heard the disciples in his or her own language. Once, God had cursed mortals with different languages, and made them build the Tower of Babel. Now it was as if that curse had been lifted, and everyone joined together to sing Jesus' praise.* When the singing was finished, Peter stood on a table to preach – and once again, although he spoke in his own language, Aramaic, everyone understood him perfectly. "We're not drunk," he said. "Remember what the prophet Joel said would happen in the world's last days. 'God will pour out his Holy Spirit on mortals. The young will see visions, and the old will prophesy. There will be wonders in Heaven and on earth. The sun will be darkened; the moon will turn to blood. The Day of Judgement will come, and anyone who repents, who begs God for mercy, will be saved.' So Joel said. God sent you Jesus of Nazareth, and despite the miracles he worked and the wonders he showed you, you crucified him. God raised him from the dead and took him into Heaven – and when Judgement Day comes, as surely as Jesus rose from the dead, so all who believe in him will have everlasting life."

These words terrified the strangers. They asked the Christians anxiously, "Brothers, what shall we do?"

Peter answered, "Repent. Be baptised in Jesus' name. Then you, too, will be given the gift of the Holy Ghost."

The people crowded to be baptised – and when word spread, many more hurried in from the street to join them. The disciples spent the whole day baptising in Jesus' name, and by dusk more than three thousand men, women and children had accepted Christianity. They went to their homes all over the city, to praise Jesus' name, pray for mercy, and wait quietly for Judgement Day.

Miracles

At first, the authorities took little notice of the Christians. "Let them baptise," they said. "Their leader's dead; they won't last long." That was their opinion, until miracles began happening and changed their minds. It was Peter's custom to pray in the Temple every day, at the exact hour when Jesus died on the cross. He went alone, or with one or two others; he never preached, never did anything to draw a crowd. The porches and courtyards of the Temple were filled with beggars, and usually Peter gave them each a coin and promised to pray for them. But on the day after Pentecost, when he and John were going into the Temple by the Beautiful Gate (so-called because of the coloured tiles which decorated it), a man plucked at his coat and cried, "Alms, master! Alms for the lame!"

"Come here," said Peter. The man shuffled forward on his haunches and gazed up like a dog hoping for a titbit. "Tell me what's wrong with you," Peter said.

"Master, I've been crippled since the day I was born. My legs are twigs. I've been a beggar for forty years."

Peter said, "I've no money. But what I have, I give you. In the name of Jesus of Nazareth, stand up and walk."

He took the cripple's hand and lifted him. Strength flowed into the man's legs and ankles, and he stood by himself, shakily at first like a newborn calf, then more and more confidently until he ran into the Temple in front of the disciples, leaping and praising God. People crowded round to ask about the miracle – and Peter began to preach, telling them about Jesus and urging them to repent and be baptised. They were in a covered walkway called Solomon's Porch, and soon the crowd was so dense that the authorities had to send guards to break it up. But the next day, and for many days afterwards, whenever Peter left home for the Temple crowds lined the streets, praying as he passed and trying to touch him. They brought sick people for him to cure, or laid their beds in the street so that his shadow would fall on them as he passed. People from the villages flocked into Jerusalem, bringing friends and relatives who were blind, sick, deaf or afflicted by devils. They took them to Solomon's Porch, and Peter and the other disciples healed them in Jesus' name. Thousands of people listened to the disciples' preaching, and many – including even Temple guards and priests – were baptised each day.

Caiaphas, the high priest, sent furiously for his soldiers. "These Christians must be stopped," he said. "Their madness is worse than plague. Forbid them to preach – and if they refuse, arrest them."

Late that evening, as soon as the crowds dispersed, Temple guards broke down the door of the Christians' house, arrested all twelve disciples and locked them in the common prison. The prison was part of the old fortress of Jerusalem. Its walls were as thick as barrels and its windows were barred and high. The last thing the guards saw was the disciples kneeling on the prison floor, surrounded by prostitutes, drunks and thieves; the last thing they heard was Peter's voice, praying. But next morning, when they unlocked the door to drag the disciples to trial, they found the dungeon empty. No bolts had been forced, no stones dislodged, but the disciples and all the other prisoners had disappeared. Frantic, the guards began searching all Jerusalem – and soon found Peter and the other disciples preaching in Solomon's Porch as usual, and the thieves, prostitutes and other ex-prisoners standing in the crowd and singing Jesus' praise. The guards were afraid to rearrest the prisoners at once, in case the crowd turned on them. But as soon as it was dark they rounded them up, threw the criminals back in jail, and took Peter and the other disciples to Caiaphas for questioning.

Caiaphas said, "You were ordered not to preach in Jesus' name. You disobeyed. Day after day you remind all Jerusalem that this court ordered his execution. Why are you stirring the people against us?"

Peter answered, "We take orders not from mortals but from God. You killed Jesus; God raised him from the dead. The stone the builders rejected has become the keystone that supports the arch. We are God's witnesses, filled with the Holy Ghost."

"Take them away! Execute them!" shouted Caiaphas.

"There's no need," said Gamaliel, one of Caiaphas' counsellors. "These movements never last. Don't you remember Theudas? He called himself the Messiah, and went about with four hundred followers – and soon after he was executed, the whole movement collapsed. The same thing happened with John the Baptist. Now people think they believe in Jesus of Nazareth. Either he's another false leader, and his followers will disappear of their own accord, or he truly is the Son of God, and if we fight his followers we'll be fighting God. Give these men a thrashing and let them go. They're fools, not criminals."

Caiaphas turned to the disciples. "This time, you can go," he said. "But forget Jesus, stop preaching, go back to honest work. Guards! Thrash them and release them."

The disciples were hustled out, defiantly shouting Jesus' name. When they were gone Caiaphas told the guards, "Watch them carefully. As soon as they utter one word of blasphemy against Moses' Law, the Temple or God's true religion, arrest them. They seem glad enough to be beaten for Jesus' sake – what will they think of death?"

Stephen

The people converted to Christianity were of every kind: shopkeepers, beggars, priests, workmen, aristocrats, counsellors, slaves. They all believed Jesus' teaching that everyone was equal in God's sight and that treasure in heaven was more valuable than treasure on earth. To show this belief, everyone sold his or her possessions and gave the money to the disciples; then, every morning, the disciples handed each person back enough for food, clothes and any other needs. The more people who were converted, the longer this distribution took

– and the disciples also found themselves having to settle squabbles, to judge between people who claimed to be getting more, or less, than they deserved. In the end the twelve disciples called the Christians together and said, "We need a better way. We're preachers, not bankers. Choose stewards to look after the money; leave us free to teach God's word." The people elected seven stewards, and the disciples laid hands on them and blessed them in Jesus' name. From that day on the stewards, inspired by the Holy Ghost, not only looked after the money but also helped the disciples to teach, preach and heal the sick.

The number of Christians in Jerusalem was doubling every day. The authorities could do nothing to stop it. Their spies mingled with the crowds, listening for treason – and heard none. The disciples taught, baptised and healed; the authorities might disapprove, but they could find no harm in them. In the end Caiaphas' counsellors appointed a special group of men to make trouble for the Christians. They were trained in Moses' law, loyal to the Temple and fanatically anti-Christ. Their instructions were to break up Christian meetings and scatter the worshippers. One morning they burst into the hall where Stephen was distributing money to the people. They pushed the crowd aside, knocked over the tables, and marched Stephen to a dungeon in Caiaphas' palace. That same afternoon, they dragged him for trial before the council.

"What charge?" the senior counsellor asked.

"Blasphemy. He says that Jesus of Nazareth came to destroy the Temple and sweep away Moses' Law."

The counsellors looked at Stephen. He was standing like a man in a trance, ignoring the trial, paying no attention to the guards. His face was as radiant as an angel's. "Answer the charge," the chief counsellor snapped. "Will Jesus sweep away Moses' Law, or not?"

Stephen said calmly, "Jesus will fulfil Moses' Law, not sweep it away. God gave Moses orders for the people – and the people disobeyed. God sent prophets to turn the people from idolatry – and the people ignored them. God sent Jesus, his only-begotten Son, and you condemned him to death. How have you honoured Moses' Law?"

The counsellors ground their teeth with rage. They shouted at Stephen to apologise. But Stephen was gazing upwards, as if the ceiling and roof were as clear as glass. He was enrapturd by a vision none of the others shared. "I see clearly into Heaven," he said. "I see Jesus, enthroned at God's right hand."

The counsellors covered their ears to drown such blasphemy. They hustled Stephen out of the room, through the streets to a deserted, stony space. They laid their robes at the feet of a young man named Saul. Then they picked up stones and pelted Stephen to death. He made no move to defend himself. He stood gazing up at the sky, radiant; he showed no pain as the blood ran down his face and soaked his clothes. Then, slowly and calmly, he knelt down, said, "Lord Jesus, lay not this sin to their charge", and fell dead, as easily as a person slips into sleep. The counsellors dusted their hands, collected their clothes from Saul and went home, leaving Stephen's Christian friends to creep out of hiding and gather his body for burial.

Saul

Stephen's death began a time of pitiless persecution for the Christians. Temple guards broke into their houses, rounded up hundreds of men, women and children and threw them into prison. There were no executions – the Romans were already asking questions about Stephen's illegal death – but many Christians died in their dungeons from sickness or starvation, and those who were set free found their houses looted, burned or wrecked. The chief persecutor was Saul, the young man who had guarded the clothes of the people who stoned Stephen. He was a student from Tarsus, a Roman citizen who had come to Jerusalem to finish his education. He hated the Christians with fanatical ferocity. He often led raiding-gangs in person, splintering doors in the night, driving terrified people into the street and confiscating their property. He broke into prayer-halls, scattering the worshippers and smashing the furniture. He presided at blasphemy-trials, shouting wildly at the Christians that they despised God and spat on Moses' Law. He was possessed: even his own men were afraid of him.

Some Christians accepted persecution unflinchingly, as Stephen had done, praying serenely to Jesus to forgive their tormentors. Others screamed and wailed, convinced that what was happening was the beginning of Judgement Day. Many fled from Jerusalem, north, south, east and west – and wherever they settled, in capital cities like Damascus in Syria or country villages like those on the Samaritan Plain,* they held prayer-meetings and preached and healed in Jesus' name.

After six months Saul went to Caiaphas and said, "The more we root out Christianity in Jerusalem, the more it springs up elsewhere. Give me letters to the authorities in Damascus. I'll hunt for Christians there: I'll close their meetings and arrest their preachers."

"How many guards do you need?"

"One patrol only. It's a week's ride to Damascus. A large party would alarm the Romans. Give me six men; I'll go at once."

Saul and his men rode by easy stages: to Jericho, down the Jordan Valley to the Sea of Galilee, then north-east along the Damascus road. The sun blazed down. The desert was empty. It was as if Saul and his soldiers were the only beings in creation. Then, in the empty heart of the wilderness, where sand stretched flat as a tray to each horizon, it seemed suddenly to Saul as if God opened a window in paradise, as if a pillar of light fell from Heaven, imprisoning him. He slid from his horse and fell on his knees. His soldiers reined in, astonished. Their master had wrapped his head in his cloak and was whimpering like a dog attacked by bees. Saul felt as if all the angels in heaven had fixed their eyes on him. His eyes were seared. The blood thundered in his ears. He was like a man floundering in a tunnel. Then, abruptly, silence fell: deep, breathing stillness, as if the whole universe were a living thing, concentrating its gaze on him alone. He flattened himself on the ground and covered his ears. A voice seemed to swell and billow inside him, as if he were hearing it not only with his ears but with his flesh, blood and bones. It was part of him: it pulsed in his brain and filled his soul.

"Saul, Saul, why do you persecute me?"

"Lord, who are you?"

"I am Jesus, whom you persecute. Why do you reject me? You're like an animal kicking against the goad. You're making your own life hard."

"Lord, tell me what to do."

"Get up. Go to Damascus. There you'll be told."

The voice stilled, the light faded and Saul's blood stopped pounding. He felt as if his brain had been wiped clean, as people smooth paper before they write. He lay motionless on the sand. His soldiers ran to pick him up – and found that he was stone blind. He sat on his horse, tears running down his cheeks, docile as a child, while his soldiers led him to Damascus. They took him to the house of a synagogue-elder called Judas, and he lay there for three days without food, drink or sleep.

On the fourth day, Jesus appeared in a vision to a Christian convert called Ananias. "Go to Judas' house in Straight Street. Ask for Saul of Tarsus. Touch him and restore his sight."

"Lord, how can I? This is the man who tortured and imprisoned your worshippers in Jerusalem. He has letters from Caiaphas, to kill us here."

"He's my chosen vessel. He'll carry my name to every corner of the world. Do as I say."

Trembling, Ananias went to Straight Street, to Judas' house. The soldiers thought him a spy, and took him straight to Saul. Saul was kneeling on the bare floor, staring ahead with sightless eyes. He was trying to pray, but his brain was as blank as straw: he could find no words. Ananias touched his shoulder with a shaking hand and said, "Brother Saul, Lord Jesus has sent me. Your sight will return; you'll be filled with the Holy Ghost."

It was as if scales fell from Saul's eyes. He jumped to his feet, and Ananias started back, afraid for his life. But Saul ran to hug him, whooping like a criminal reprieved from death. "Baptise me!" he said. "O Ananias, baptise me in Jesus' name!"

Saul and Ananias hurried out of the house – and the soldiers, thinking that they were going to meet other traitors, made no attempt to stop them. But by the middle of next day, when there was no sign of Saul, they began to be alarmed. They searched the Christian area of Damascus – and to their amazement found Saul in an open space, preaching and baptising in Jesus' name. "What shall we do?" they asked each other. "How can we arrest our own leader?"

They decided to ride to report to Caiaphas in Jerusalem. At first he refused to believe them. "How can Saul be a Christian?" he said. "It's a trick. He's gaining their confidence. In a day or two, he'll arrest them all."

"Sir, he was baptising. We saw him heal people in Jesus' name."

"Go back. Wait and watch. As soon as you're certain, kill him. Then round up the rest for trial."

The soldiers galloped back to Damascus. But before they were halfway there the Holy Spirit whispered a warning to the Christians. The city gates were guarded: there was no escape that way. But Ananias took Saul up on to the city wall at night, and let him down in a basket in the darkness. By the time Caiaphas' men reached Damascus, Saul was safely gone. The Christians in Jerusalem, warned by the Holy Ghost, hid him till the hue and cry died down, and then smuggled him to Caesarea on the coast.* From there he took ship home to Tarsus, far from Jerusalem, and at once began preaching and baptising in Jesus' name.

Peter and Cornelius

Cornelius was a Roman centurion in Caesarea. He and his men supervised the movements of trading-ships to and from the Promised Land. Although he was not a Jewish convert, he attended the synagogue and had married a Jewish wife. He kept Jewish feasts and holy days, prayed three times a day, and kept a wing of his house always open for the poor and homeless. One afternoon, when he was sitting in his office at the customs-house, he heard God's angel calling his name. He fell on his knees, his centurion's staff clattering to the floor, and asked timidly, "What is it, Lord?"

"God has heard your prayers and seen your kindness to other people. Send men to Simon's house by the fish-dock in Joppa. Tell them to ask for Peter, who lodges there. He'll tell you what to do."

Joppa was the next town along the coast from Caesarea. When Peter moved out of Jerusalem during the persecution of the Christians, the Holy Spirit had guided him there.* Now God sent a vision to warn him of Cornelius' coming and to tell him what to do. It was early morning, and while servants prepared breakfast Peter went up to the flat roof of the house, faced out to sea and knelt to pray as he always did. He was hungry, and had to wrench his mind from the smell of bread and the clatter of dishes from below. As he prayed, the sky seemed to open like a curtain in front of him, and he saw a gigantic sheet tied at each corner and filled with pigs, cats, cows, locusts, chickens, butterflies, ducks, ants, goats, pigeons, lambs and wolves. A voice said, "Peter, choose and eat."

"Lord," said Peter, "You know I keep the Law.* Not all these creatures are fit to eat."

The voice answered, "What God calls fit, let no mortal call unfit."

The vision appeared twice more, and the same words were said. Then the sheet and the animals disappeared. Peter felt like a man waking from sleep; the sun's reflection glittered from the sea and dazzled him. He went down to breakfast – just as a patrol of Romans hammered on the door and asked if Peter the preacher lodged there. "Go with them, Peter," said the angel's voice. "Fear nothing. They were sent by Jesus."

Peter and a group of Christian elders walked with the soldiers from Joppa towards Caesarea. People darted into their houses as they passed, snatching their children from playing in the street. They were terrified of Romans. They thought that the Christians were being led to death. But when the party reached Caesarea, Cornelius himself hurried out to meet them. Ignoring his men, ignoring the stares of passers-by, he knelt at Peter's feet, kissed his hands and said, "Welcome, master."

"Sir, get up," said Peter, embarrassed. "I'm a man like any other."

"Please, master, come home with me. Tonight, I've hired a hall in town. Dozens of people will be there: Roman officers, soldiers and their wives. Teach us! Baptise us in Jesus' name!"

Some of the Joppa elders frowned. Cornelius and his troops were pagans, outsiders. It was unheard-of for Christians to mix with such people, let alone to baptise them. Until now, no Gentile (that is, someone not of the Jewish faith) had ever been baptised a Christian. Peter knew this too. But he remembered the angel's words in the vision: "What God calls fit, let no mortal think unfit". He went gladly with Cornelius, and stood up that evening to preach in a room crowded with Gentiles. "Brothers and sisters, welcome," he said. "God is no respecter of persons. He accepts anyone, from any race or faith, who believes in Jesus and who does good works. Jesus came to save the whole human race, and everyone who believes in him will have everlasting life."

The Joppa elders tried to pluck his sleeve, to catch his eye. Was he really promising Gentiles everlasting life? But before they could speak, the sound of rushing wind filled the room, and tongues of fire flickered above the crowd. Everyone, Jews and Gentiles alike, began calling out, speaking with tongues as the disciples had done in Jerusalem at Pentecost. Convinced by the miracle, the Joppa elders fell on their knees to pray – and Peter called for water and began baptising the people, welcoming every one of them in Jesus' name.

Converting the Gentiles

At first, news of Cornelius' baptism horrified the Christians in Jerusalem. Even Jesus' disciples found it hard to accept that a Gentile had been promised everlasting life. But when Peter described his vision of the fit and unfit creatures, and the Joppa elders told them about the coming of the Holy Ghost, the Jerusalem Christians were convinced. They decided to send missionaries beyond the boundaries of the Promised Land, to carry word of Jesus to Jews and non-Jews alike. One of their leaders, Barnabas, set out for Antioch, the old Syrian city on the banks of the river Orontes. On his way, he travelled to Tarsus to visit Saul (who had now changed his name to Paulus, in Roman style, or Paul), and invited him to share the missionary work. They rode together to Antioch, rented a house and began to teach.

After a year in Antioch,* Paul and Barnabas went to preach in the Greek towns of Cyprus and Asia Minor. Word quickly spread, and they were surrounded by excited crowds, greedy for miracles. In Paphos a Greek prophet, Elymas, preached against them, and Paul called down blindness on him until he opened his eyes to Jesus, as Paul himself had done. In Lystra Paul healed a man crippled from birth – and the Greeks took him for Zeus, king of their gods, and Barnabas for Hermes. They showered them with flowers and brought white bulls for sacrifice. Paul said, "Give up this superstition. We're human beings, not gods. Worship the living God who made you; fill your souls with Jesus Christ." The people fell on their knees and prayed: it was as if God's word were seed, and they were fertile ground.

After fifteen months' travelling, Paul went home to Antioch to rest and to prepare a second journey. This time his companion was Silas, and the journey lasted three years and took them as far as Athens, the heart of Greece. At Philippi Paul drove out a devil of prophecy which was tormenting a slave-girl, and her owners, furious at losing the income she brought them from fortune-telling, threw Paul and Silas into jail. Paul and Silas spent the night singing hymns and preaching to their fellow-prisoners. Just before dawn an earthquake rocked the town, crumbling the prison-walls like cheese. The jailer snatched a sword and ran to stop the prisoners escaping, only to find them kneeling beside Paul and Silas in the ruins, praying to Jesus. That day he, his servants and many of the prisoners were baptised, and the authorities freed Paul and Barnabas and sent them on their way. In Athens, Paul preached on the Areopagus, the hillside where Athenians had gathered for public meetings since ancient times. "On your Acropolis," he said, "I see temples and shrines to all kinds of deities – and on one small altar is written 'To the unknown god'. He is the God I serve. He created the world and everything in it, and he sent his son Jesus so that everyone who believes in him will have everlasting life." When the Athenians heard this teaching, they begged to be baptised – and the same happened in Corinth, where many Jews, including synagogue elders, were also converted. Paul spent eighteen months in Corinth, and then sailed home to Antioch.

Paul's third, five-year journey took him to the eastern coast of the Aegean Sea. His most important stopping-place was Ephesus, centre of the worship of the moon-goddess Diana. Centuries before, a woman-shaped stone had fallen out of the sky, and the Ephesians identified it as Diana and built a temple to it which was hailed as one of the wonders of the world. Hundreds of thousands of tourists visited Ephesus every year, to worship the goddess, marvel at the temple and buy souvenirs. Most of the city's inhabitants worked in the tourist trade, as innkeepers, guides, souvenir-sellers, priests, entertainers and fortune-tellers. In such a whirlpool of pagan religion, the Jews were no more than single water-drops; nevertheless Paul settled in Ephesus and began to preach. For three months he spoke in the Jewish synagogue, but when the crowds grew too large for the building he moved outside, baptising and healing in a large city square. At first people took him for just another tourist attraction. But the power of his preaching, and the cures he worked in Jesus' name, soon won converts, and one afternoon a group of prosperous Greek soothsayers and fortune-tellers all accepted baptism and celebrated it with a bonfire of their magic books.* Spectacular events like this made Paul the most famous man in Ephesus, and wherever he went crowds followed him, trying to catch a glimpse of him, to hear him preach, or to beg one of his handkerchieves or a strip of his clothing to bandage sick relatives and heal them. His fame began to alarm the souvenir-sellers at Diana's Temple. "He'll ruin us," cried a silversmith called Demetrius. "If he goes on converting people to Jesus, who'll visit the Temple and buy our souvenirs?" The souvenir-sellers marched through the city, shouting "Great is Diana of the Ephesians" and hunting Paul, and a huge holiday throng collected behind them, excited as children, with no idea where they were going or who was leading them. They crowded into an open-air theatre outside the city, and spent

the afternoon there chanting "Great is Diana of the Ephesians" while Demetrius tried to persuade the authorities to
arrest or banish Paul. The town counsellors, however, refused
to take sides. They said that everyone knew that Ephesus was
sacred to Diana and not to Christ. If Demetrius had any
quarrel with Paul he should take him to court in the normal
way. As darkness fell, the crowd began to melt away, looking
for other entertainment, and Demetrius' men went muttering
and grumbling home.

After leaving Ephesus, Paul travelled to Troas* in northern
Greece, and then through many Greek towns, both on the
mainland and in the islands, before sailing back to the Holy
Land and visiting the Christians in Caesarea. While he was
there, a Jewish prophet called Agabus tied his own hands and
feet with the belt of Paul's robe and said, "This is how the
Jews in Jerusalem will bind the owner of this belt, before they
hand him to Gentiles for punishment." Alarmed by the
prophecy, the Christians begged Paul to stay with them in
Caesarea and not to risk going to Jerusalem. But Paul
answered calmly, "God's will be done", and went – and
almost at once was surrounded by a murderous mob, shouting that he had taken a Gentile into the holiest part of the
Temple, despite notices warning instant death for anyone but
Jews. A platoon of Roman soldiers broke up the riot and
arrested Paul as a trouble-maker. He would have been beaten
and imprisoned that same morning, if the guard commander
had not discovered that he was a Roman citizen, with the
right to a proper trial. He sent Paul under escort* to Caesarea,
with a request for the Roman governor to hear the case. Paul
seized his chance to travel to Rome, and appealed for justice –
as all Roman citizens had the right to do – to the emperor in
person. This meant that although it was autumn and the sea
was stormy, he had to be sent to Rome for trial.* He lived
under house-arrest there for two years, preaching, baptising
and writing letters* to Christians all over the Roman empire.
By accepting God's will, by travelling to the hub of the then-
known world, he had ensured that Jesus' promise of everlasting life would spread far beyond the borders of the Promised
Land. Whatever happened to Paul or to the other disciples,*

the religion they preached was unstoppable: it would grow
and thrive in every corner of the world.

Notes

ADAM AND EVE *(page 3)*

In one Bible account, Eve was not made from Adam's rib, but from the dust of the earth in the same way and at the same time as Adam. The name Adam means "human being". The name Eve means "mother of life". In one version of the story, from times when women were regarded as inferior to men, it was not God but Adam who gave Eve her name, thus exercising authority over her in the same way (by naming) as over every other creature in the world.

CHERUBIM *(page 5)*

Nowadays the word cherub (plural cherubim) has come to mean a plump, naked little boy, often with wings. Cherubs flit or hover in paintings of religious and mythical scenes, and are decorative rather than frightening. But the real meaning of cherub is "storm wind". Cherubim were God's soldiers, his anger personified. They swept across the sky in gales and swollen clouds, and released God's fury on the earth in the form of typhoons, hurricanes and tidal waves. In some ancient art (for example stone-carvings made 3000 years ago in Babylon) they are shown as monsters: gigantic bulls with human faces and eagles' wings.

THE MARK OF CAIN (page 5)

Later legend gave the name "mark of Cain" to the blood-coloured birthmark, or "port-wine stain", which appears on some people's faces. Such people were regarded as Cain's descendants, and were treated, quite unjustly, as criminals and outcasts like their mythical ancestor.

CAIN'S LIFE (page 6)

In the Bible account, Cain fled from God's presence to the "Land of Nod" east of Eden, where he settled and founded a dynasty which included Jubal the first musician, Tubalcain the first blacksmith, and Lamech who repeated his ancestor's crime and killed a man, so becoming the second murderer in human history. No one has exactly identified the "Land of Nod", but some scholars say that "Nod" means "wandering", and that Cain and his family never truly settled anywhere, but became nomads. Every time they pitched their tents and tried to grow crops the earth, polluted by Abel's blood, refused to support them and they had to move on somewhere else.

Later legends extended this idea, saying that Cain wandered restlessly about the world until the day he died. He devoted himself to crime, and in particular coupled with living creatures of all kinds: whales, cows, eagles, lionesses, snakes. His monstrous offspring, half human half animal, have lurked ever afterwards in the world's holes and crevices, hiding from God.

NOAH'S MOUNTAIN (page 8)

Some scholars say that the place where Noah's ark came to rest was Mount Ararat (modern Agri Dargh), in what is now the Armenian region of Turkey. The mountain in 5230 metres (17,000 feet) high. For centuries, local legends told of pieces of pitch-covered timber strewn across the hillside. There was even said to be a pile of fire-blackened stones, the altar on which Noah in the story sacrificed to God.

BABEL AND BABYLON (page 10)

Scholars explain the myth of the tower of Babel by saying that Shinar was the fertile country between the rivers Tigris and Euphrates (part of modern Iran), one of the earliest inhabited places in the world. Babel was Babylon, a city on the banks of the Euphrates. It was the hub of a huge trading-empire, and would have been filled with merchants from many nations – hence, perhaps, the babble of languages and religions which filled its streets. Its chief building was a ziggurat, a mud-brick pyramid whose base was a rectangle of 93 x 93 metres (300 x 300 feet). The ziggurat was seven storeys high, each storey slightly smaller then the one below. The first six storeys were solid platforms; the seventh was a temple to the god Marduk (or Baal), the Babylonian king of Heaven. Anthropologists (people who study how human communities develop) say that Babylon and the ziggurat came first and that the myth of the tower of Babel was invented to explain them. The Old Testament writers, by contrast, believed that the order of events was exactly the other way about, and that the myth is true.

HAGAR AND ISHMAEL (page 14)

Throughout Abraham's and Sarah's lives, childlessness had been their bitterest grief. Thirteen years before, in the hope of ending it, of producing an heir who would enable Abraham's descendants to "fill the land", Sarah had invited him to take a concubine or secondary wife: Hagar, a beautiful young slave she had brought from Egypt. Sarah's idea was that Hagar's child would be Abraham's legitimate heir, so long as she (Sarah, his chief wife) produced no children of her own. But when Hagar became pregnant, Sarah was filled, to her surprise, not with joy but with furious jealousy. She sent Hagar into the desert, to live or die as God decided. Hagar sat by a water-spring, and wept. An angel appeared to comfort her. The angel said that she should go back and throw herself on Sarah's mercy. She would give birth to a son, and would call him Ishmael ("wild one") because he was destined to be an outlaw, with every man's hand against him.

Hagar went back to Abraham and Sarah, and God persuaded Sarah to accept both her and the newborn child. Ishmael grew up as Abraham's son and heir. But when Sarah's own son Isaac was miraculously born (see page 15), Ishmael (by this time a boy of thirteen) laughed at the baby's puniness, and Sarah's fury erupted. She banished Hagar and Ishmael into the desert once again, and once again God sent an angel to save their lives. But Abraham now had Isaac for his son and heir: there was no place for Ishmael. Hagar took her son to Egypt, and found him an Egyptian wife. Later, Ishmael's descendants settled in the country east of the river Jordan, between the places now known as the Dead Sea and the Gulf of Aqaba (part of present-day Jordan). Moslems say that Ishmael was one of the ancestors of the prophet Mohammed, and that Ishmael and Hagar are buried in the Ka'aba, the shrine at Mecca.

HONESTY *(page 14)*

When God sent his angels to Sodom, Abraham was horrified to think of the impending destruction of the cities of the plain. He asked God nervously, "Do you mean to destroy good people as well as bad? What if fifty honest people live in Sodom?"

God said, "If fifty honest people live in Sodom, I'll spare it."

"What if the number falls just short of fifty?" asked Abraham. "What if only forty-five honest people can be found?"

"For forty-five honest people," said God, "I'll leave the cities standing."

"What if there are only forty?"

"Forty will be enough."

"Thirty?"

"Thirty."

"Twenty?"

"Twenty."

"Lord, don't be angry. What if there are only ten?"

"For the sake of ten honest people, I'll spare them all."

So Abraham pleaded, and so God promised. In the event, however, only one honest person – Lot – lived in Sodom, and the cities were destroyed.

CITIES OF THE PLAIN (page 15)

The five towns known as the "cities of the plain" were Sodom, Gomorrah, Admah, Zeboiim and Zoar. No trace of them survives. Archaeologists believe that the story of their destruction is connected with a real geological event, the formation of the Dead Sea. Originally, the place where the Dead Sea now lies was a bowl of fertile land, watered by the river Jordan, temperate and fruitful. But the land, and the towns built on it, lay over a volcanic fault, and in about 1900 BC there was a huge earthquake. The towns were engulfed, and the land sank to produce a landlocked lake, 400 metres below sea level. This lake is now known as the Dead Sea. Because the sea has no exit for its waters other than evaporation, they are choked with mineral salts which extinguish all life; salts have also polluted the surrounding countryside, turning it to desert. The salt-laden pumice-stone on the banks of the Dead Sea has been weathered into needle-tipped standing stones, some of which are eerily like statues, as if real people had been turned (like Lot's wife in the story) into pillars of rock and salt.

ISAAC AND REBEKAH (page 18)

Rebekah was Isaac's second cousin, the daughter of his Syrian cousin Bethuel. When Abraham set out, long before, from Haran on his long journey south to Egypt (see page 11), Bethuel stayed behind. He and his family were shepherds, and over the years they prospered until they needed a whole town to live in, and their flocks filled the fields for a day's journey on every side. From the moment when Abraham set out for Egypt, he was anxious one day to reunite the two branches of the family, and he determined, as soon as Isaac was old enough, to find him a wife in Haran. He sent his most trusted servant, Eliezer, north to Haran, leading ten camels loaded with gold and jewels. Eliezer's orders were to travel on until he came to a well, and to wait there for a sign.

Eliezer led the loaded camels north. He came at last to a town on the edge of a desert, and sat in the shade beside a well. It was evening, and women and girls from the town were gathering to fetch water. Eliezer prayed to God to send a sign. At once, one of the girls came forward. She was Bethuel's daughter Rebekah, and she smilingly offered Eliezer and his camels water from the well. Recognising this as God's sign at last, Eliezer gave Rebekah gold earrings and a bracelet. She took them home, and as soon as her father Bethuel saw them he recognised them, and welcomed Eliezer eagerly as Abraham's messenger. Eliezer repeated Abraham's wish that Rebekah should go back with him as Isaac's future wife, and to everyone's joy Rebekah agreed of her own free will. Leaving eight camels, and all the treasure, as the bride-price, Eliezer led Rebekah south through the desert to Abraham's lands beside the river Jordan. They were still an hour's walk from the camp when Rebekah saw a young man nearby, walking alone in the cool evening air. God filled her heart with sudden love for him, and she asked Eliezer his name. "That's Isaac," Eliezer answered, "Abraham's son, your future husband." Rebekah modestly veiled her her head and hid her face. Isaac took the reins of her camel and led her to camp, where Abraham and Sarah welcomed her as their dear son's wife.

RACHEL'S TRICK (page 23)

Although Jacob knew nothing about it, Laban was searching the camp for actual stolen goods. Before Rachel left her father's house, she took the statues of his household gods and hid them in a high wooden camel-saddle, which now stood like a throne on the ground beside her tent. All the time

Laban was searching the camp, she sat on the saddle, spread her skirts wide and watched him. When he came up to her she excused herself for not standing up to kiss him by saying that her period had started. It was the custom that no man touched a woman during her period; so Laban left her where she sat, and never found his gods. It was partly because he was demoralised at losing them – he thought that they had vanished into thin air and left him at the mercy of Jacob's God – that he so readily proposed the truce between his people and Jacob's (see page 24).

JOSEPH ENSLAVED (page 26)

There are different versions of this story. In one, Joseph was not sold into slavery at all. The brothers planned to take him out of the cistern and cut his throat; but Reuben, the eldest, persuaded them to spare him, saying that it would be better to set him free in the morning after a terrifying night underground. Then, while the brothers slept, a group of passing traders traders heard Joseph shouting for help, unstoppered the cistern and stole him into slavery. The brothers made up the lion story to account for his disappearance. In another version, it was not Reuben but Judah who persuaded the brothers not to kill Joseph. Instead he suggested selling him as a slave and telling Jacob the lie about the lions. He negotiated with the traders, and was so unused to bargaining that he accepted only twenty silver pieces for Joseph, the price of a child: the traders claimed that Joseph, being only seventeen and unused to hard labour, was not worth the price of a full-grown man.

THE MONEY IN THE SACKS (page 31)

In the Bible, two accounts of this story were mixed together. The result is that Joseph's men were said to have hidden coins twice in the brother's sacks. The first time was when the brothers were sent from Egypt to fetch Benjamin. They

found the hidden coins, but instead of awakening guilt-feel-
ings the discovery merely mystified them. It was only on the
second occasion, when the discovery of Joseph's drinking-
cup threatened Benjamin, that they realised that the cause of
what was happening was their own mistreatment of Joseph
years before, and God's purpose was fulfilled.

THE INHERITORS *(page 32)*

Jacob's twelve sons, as God prophesised here, became ances-
tors of the twelve tribes of Israel, and in later years (under
king Solomon: see page 107), each tribe was given its own
area of the Promised Land (the country bordered by the
mediterranean coast, the Dead Sea and the Sea of Galillee).
The twelve sons, each of whom gave his name to a tribe, were
Leah's children Reuben, Simeon, Levi, Judah, Issachar and
Zebulun, Bilhah's (a concubine's) children Dan and Naphtali,
Zilpha's (another concubine's) children Gad and Asher, and
Rachel's children Joseph and Benjamin. (Joseph's inheritance
in the Promised Land was divided among his sons Ephraim
and Manasseh.)

MOSES *(page 35)*

The Egyptian spelling of Moses' name, Mose or Mese, is often
found on the end of longer words, for example the names Ra-
mese ("son of Ra") or Tut-mose ("son of Tut"). Some
scholars say that the name was not Egyptian but Coptic – the
language spoken in the Nile delta – and that it means "saved
from the water". This is close to the explanation suggested in
the Bible itself, that "Moses" comes from the Hebrew word
mashah, "to draw out". Ever since Moses' time, the Hebrew
form of his name, Moise or Moishe, has been a popular boy's
name.

THE NAME OF GOD *(page 37)*

"I am that I am" is an English equivalent of the Hebrew word Jahweh (or Yahweh). The Jewish people avoided speaking or reading God's holy name. Instead of Jahweh they substituted the word Adonai, "Lord", commonly used by servants to their employers. The modern name "Jehovah" is a mixture of the two words, the Hebrew vowel-sounds of Adonai (sounding E-O-A) interspersed with the consonants of Jahweh (J-H-V).

THE SECOND AND THIRD PROOFS *(page 37)*

God gave Moses two more proofs that he was God's chosen messenger. He told him to put his hand inside the bosom of his tunic. It came out leprous and white, and when Moses put it back again, it came out healed. The third proof was that whenever Moses chose, he would be able to turn Nile-water into blood.

BRICKS WITHOUT STRAW *(page 38)*

This Bible account of the story makes better sense than the later, more usual, one, that the Pharaoh ordered the Israelites to make bricks without any straw at all. (The phrase "to make bricks without straw" has become a proverb, meaning to work hard at something without all the necessary equipment or evidence.) Mud-bricks were certainly made without straw in ancient times; but bricks including chopped straw not only lasted longer, but would – as the Pharaoh well knew – give the Israelites double the amount of work, if they had to gather and chop all the straw themselves.

THE PLAGUES (page 41)

Many Bible readers take this story as literally true: God sent
the plagues to demonstrate his power to the Egyptians and
Israelites alike, and hardened the Pharaoh's heart to make the
lesson even sharper. Some people, however, have explained
the plagues as natural events, as follows. Blood in the Nile: in
years when the Nile floods were unusually high, extra mud
was washed down, colouring the river red and choking life.
Frogs: the spawn, trapped in the red mud, was released when
fresh water flowed, and grew into millions of tadpoles. Since
no fish survived to eat them, the tadpoles thrived, but there
was not enough water to support such a huge colony of frogs,
and after a day of two hopping desperately across the land,
searching for moisture, they died. Lice and flies: these bred in
the dead frogs' carcasses. Ulcers and boils: the insect-bites
infected animals and humans alike, causing festering skin-
infections. Hail and thunder: these were a natural outcome of
the hot, close weeks beforehand. Fierce elecrical storms are
still common both in Egypt and in other north African states.
Locusts: locusts were (and are) a common pest in north
Africa, and all that was needed to blow them into Egypt was a
strong east wind. Darkness: this, one of the most terrifying
plagues of all to the Egyptians – because it meant that the
power of Ra, the sun, their greatest god, was blotted out –
was probably a freak sand-storm, of the kind still often expe-
rienced in desert countries and called khamsin in Arabic.
Death of the first-born: this has been explained as a lingering
sickness caused by the insect-bites and worsened by malnutrition and the unseasonable weather. No one has ever
explained, however, why it should have only affected the
first-born. To those who believe that the plagues were all sent
by God, this is a clinching argument.

NUMBERS (page 42)

No one knows exactly how many Israelites escaped from
Egypt. The Bible talks of 600,000 "men" (that is grown

adults), plus children, perhaps a million or more – but Bible figures are notoriously inaccurate, sometimes as many as ten times too big. Scholars have reckoned that there were about 1200 people in each of the twelve tribes of Israel at this time. This gives a total for the whole nation of about 14,400, a far more likely number of people to uproot themselves and cross dangerous deserts into unknown and probably hostile lands.

CROSSING THE SEA (page 44)

Until recently, people had been sure that the area crossed by the Israelites was the north-westernmost finger of the Red Sea, the part now known as the Gulf of Suez. But some scholars have put the crossing further north, either over the Great Bitter Lakes or across the narrow Mediterranean sea-inlet which lies west of modern Port Said. Modern scholars also say that the explanation of the crossing is natural, not miraculous. The Israelites crossed reed-marshes, which bore the weight of people on foot but sank under chariots, so drowning the Pharaoh's army. This account fits the part of the Bible story which refers to choking mud. But the rest of the Old Testament account (the parting of the sea; the walls of water on each side), unless it is writer's imagination – a rare thing in these stories – seems more easily explainable as supernatural, the work of God.

MANNA (page 45)

Manna is real: it is secreted by insects which feed on the tamarisk tree. They exude a liquid which evaporates into white, sticky dust like frost. In normal desert conditions there would never be enough of it to feed human beings. The miracle here, the Bible claims, is that God provided enough for each Israelite to gather one omer (a medium-sized modern cupful) every day, to be eaten raw, ground into flour and baked or (if there was enough water) boiled into a kind of porridge. The Old Testament also says that the supply was unfailing for forty years, and that the Israelites were sick of both it and the quail-meat long before they reached the Promised Land,

THE AMALEKITES (page 46)

None of the Israelites knew that every painful step of their way across the Wilderness of Sin had been watched. A warrior-tribe, the Amalekites, lived there, and preyed on travellers. They had been waiting to pounce until the Israelites were weak from thirst and hunger; they had stood amazed at the quail-clouds each evening and the manna each morning; now, with the Israelites trapped between the desert and the cliffs, they thought it time to strike before their prey moved into the uplands and out of their territory. They galloped to the attack, their swords drawn and their war-cries echoing from the hills. The startled Israelites defended themselves with sticks, stones, pots, pans and whatever else came to hand. But they were no match for well-armed men on horseback, until at last Moses lifted his arms and prayed to God. To his amazement, as soon as his hands were high in the air the Amalekite horses reared and swerved, snorting in panic. He lowered his hands, and the Amalekites renewed their charge; he raised them, and the horses fled again. For the rest of that day, Moses sat on a rock with his hands in the air, and when his arms grew heavy Aaron and Hur stood beside him to support them. A young man called Joshua rallied the Israelites, and gradually they beat the Amalekites back, pulling them from their horses and disarming them. At last, as the sun began to set, the Amalekites turned and fled, and Moses was able to drop his aching arms at last. God had given his people victory.

THE TABERNACLE (page 47)

The tabernacle was a portable sanctuary, a home for God's spirit as the Israelites' tents were homes for human beings.

The Bible says that God gave exact instructions for making it, specifying materials, measurements and every detail of its decoration. It was a large tent with pillared, boarded walls and a curtained entrance. It was surrounded by an enclosure of wooden posts hung with animal skins. Inside the tabernacle, in a curtained-off Holy of Holies, was the Ark, a chest containing the stone tablets which God gave to Moses, and on its lid the Mercy Seat where God's presence dwelled. During the Israelites' desert wanderings, the Levites looked after the tabernacle, dismantling it, carrying it and re-erecting it in each camp. In the wars after the Israelites' arrival in the Promised Land (see page 51), the tabernacle and ark were fought over, lost and recaptured many times. Finally, when Solomon built the temple in Jerusalem (see page 108), its heart was a replica of the tabernacle, built more permanently in stone, wood and precious metals.

AARON *(page 49)*

Apart from innocent children, the only Israelites spared from punishment were Joshua (who had been with Moses on the mountain), the Levites (who had taken no part in worship of the golden calf) and Aaron. In some ways Aaron was the guiltiest man of them all. The calf was his idea, he made it and he encouraged the Israelites to worship it. But God thought him weak-willed rather then wicked, and spared his life. He made Aaron (a Levite) chief priest of Israel, and when the elders of the other tribes objected that the Levites were being specially favoured, he confirmed Aaron's authority with a miracle. Each elder left his rod of office overnight in the tabernacle, and next day, although no other rod had changed, Aaron's was covered in buds and blossom, like a branch from a living tree.

Although Aaron was chosen in this way for special honour, despite his guilt, he also shared the fate of all the other adult Israelites: he was barred from setting foot in the Promised Land. He was chief priest of the people for forty years, throughout their wandering in the desert; he died, aged 123, on the slopes of Mount Hor overlooking the Promised Land.

GIANTS *(page 51)*

The Israelites believed that when God sent the Flood to cleanse the world (see page 6), a few creatures had escaped destruction as well as the species rescued by Noah in his Ark. Among these creatures were giants: enormous, brainless monsters who had avoided drowning by burying themselves in air-pockets deep underground. The giants hated God, and planned to revenge themselves on him for the Flood by murdering and eating anyone who worshipped him. They skulked in the dark places of the world, and occasionally came out of hiding to fight human beings and feast on their flesh. The Promised Land, the Israelites thought, was infested by several tribes of giants, who would fight to keep their territory.

One explanation for giant-legends is that the Israelites were, quite simply, shorter than the people who lived in the Promised Land, as Celts in medieval Britain were shorter than Angles or Saxons. Over the years this difference (a few centimetres) was exaggerated in stories until the idea grew up that everyone the Israelites fought was gigantic. (An example of this belief is the story of David and Goliath: see page 85.) A second explanation is suggested by the story of Og, king of Bashan. Og ruled one of the tribes conquered by the Israelites, and after his death the story grew up that he was a giant, who slept in an iron bed over four metres (13 feet) long. Modern archaeologists suggest that the story of Og's size arose because of the bed, and that the bed was really a sarcophagus or coffin: kings and queens, of quite ordinary size, were often buried in enormous coffins of this kind. The sarcophagus was not even made of iron, but of basalt, a smooth black rock easily mistakable for metal.

BAD BLOOD *(page 62)*

Like most stories of the Israelites' early years in the Promised Land, this one ended badly: human nature soon turned triumph sour. Apart from the farmers who cut the Midianite soldiers to pieces, most Israelite villagers were jealous of Gideon's three hundred men and refused to help them track the surviving enemies down, or even to give them food and shelter. As soon as the Midianites were driven out of Israel, therefore, Gideon rounded on the villagers and took revenge. He killed some of their leaders and humiliated the others by throwing them into the nearest briar patch. This show of strength terrified the rest of the Israelites into accepting him as leader in peace as well as in war. At once, although he refused the title of king, he took other symbols of royal power. He built a glittering royal palace, filled it with wives and concubines, and fathered over seventy children. He stuffed his treasury with the dead Midianites' gold and silver, and later melted the metal down and made it into an image, a statue of himself – and his power and arrogance were so great that no one dared to point out that he was breaking the second of the Ten Commandments. When he died, his son Abimelech seized royal power by force, and ruled as a tyrant until his cruelty provoked civil war; he was killed at the siege of the town of Thebez, by a woman who dropped a millstone on his head.

WATER FROM THE JAWBONE *(page 64)*

When Israelite priests told this story, they wanted to show that Samson was God's chosen servant and that God approved of his slaughter of the Philistines. Accordingly, they said that Samson, thirsty after this battle, prayed to God for a drink – and God answered the prayer by making water gush from the jawbone to slake Samson's thirst.

SAMSON AND THE GAZA GATE *(page 65)*

Whatever traps the Philistines laid for Samson, God always helped him to escape. Once, when he was visiting a woman in the Philistine town of Gaza, soldiers closed and barred the town gates. "He'll never get out now," they said. "Let him rage till morning: we'll take a dozen men and arrest him then." But at midnight, when Samson got up to go home and found the way barred, he wasted no time looking for guards or gatekeepers: he simply prayed to God for strength, picked up the gates in his hands and ripped them from their hinges. Then he carried them out of the town – some say for as much as 34 miles, nearly 50 km –and threw them away on the hillside beside the road.

GOD'S MESSENGER (page 76)

In fact Eli was not surprised by Samuel's words. Some time before, God's angel had appeared to him disguised as a holy man. The angel had accused Eli's sons of blasphemy, of stealing for themselves the parts of the sacrifice reserved for God. Although God had long ago chosen Eli and his family as priests and leaders of Israel, the sons' blasphemy meant that they would lose both their office and their lives. The angel said that God would send a new priest, pure and faithful, to replace them, and that he would lead the people back to true worship. As soon as Samuel was brought to Shiloh, Eli suspected that the child was this chosen priest – and now God spoke to Samuel in the shrine, and proved it true.

GOLDEN IMAGES (page 78)

The images beside the Ark were rats and plague-sores, modelled in gold. The Philistines thought that God, like their own idols, loved gold, and that if they dazzled his eyes with golden images of what was plaguing the Philistine towns, he would start hoarding all rats and plague-sores, like a miser, and so the Philistines' own misery would end.

THE ARK IN BETHSHEMESH (page 78)

Not everyone in Bethshemesh was anxious to sacrifice to God. Some wanted to keep the Ark and its treasure for themselves. They picked up the Ark, and the plague which had devastated the Philistines transferred itself to them. Many villagers died, and the survivors, even more convinced that the Ark belonged to God, gladly let the priests take it away and set it up in God's honour somewhere else. Some accounts say that this other place was the town of Kiriath-jearim, and that when David set up his capital in Jerusalem (see page 93) he transferred the Ark from there and had it carried into the city in procession. Other legends say that the Ark disappeared soon after it reached Bethshemesh, and that all later Arks were copies. The original Ark, with its power to bless or blight, has been carried secretly from place to place about the world, and is still, today, one of the oldest and most sought-after treasures from the ancient past.

THE PHILISTINES (page 83)

The reason for Philistine superiority was simple. While every other nation in the area was armed with bronze, they had iron weapons, harder and sharper. They jealously guarded the secret of smelting iron: the Bible even says that when Israelite farmers wanted to sharpen their iron sickles, scythes or knives, they had to take them to Philistine blacksmiths, in unknown territory often several days' journey away from home.

DAVID AND GOLIATH (page 87)

In another version of this story, David did not become Saul's lyre-player before he met Goliath. He was still a shepherd-boy, too young to follow his brothers and join the army. When the Philistines invaded, David's father Jesse sent him with food for his soldier-brothers, and David arrived just in time to hear Goliath's challenge to the Israelite army. He announced that he would fight Goliath, and his elder brother Eliab told him to mind his own business and go back to their father's sheep. But David insisted on fighting, and killed

Goliath with the stone and sling. After the battle Saul (who until that day had no idea of David's existence) took him as his servant – and it was after that that David's musical skill was revealed, and he began to play and sing to calm Saul's moods.

DAVID AND JONATHAN (page 88)

Before he fled to Nob, David tried once more to end the quarrel with Saul. He went secretly to Jonathan, Saul's son and his own best friend, and asked him to make peace between them. Jonathan agreed. He said that there was a feast next day, and that if Saul were in his right mind he could be grieved to see David's place empty. Then he, Jonathan, would beg Saul to spare David's life, and would send a message to fetch David back. If Saul still demanded David's life, Jonathan would warn David to stay away.

On the day of the feast, Saul missed David, exactly as the two young men had hoped. But when Jonathan asked his father to pardon David, Saul turned furiously on him, accusing him of preferring an outlaw and a traitor to his own father. Jonathan stormed away, and instead of sending David a message met him and told him the bad news personally. The two friends embraced for the last time, with tears in their eyes, and then David ran into exile, making for the town of Nob, while Jonathan went home to face his father.

DAVID IN GATH (page 88)

At first, David was so bewildered by exile that he took no heed of where he was. He stumbled by chance into the streets of Gath, the Philistine town where Goliath had been champion. Recognising Goliath's sword, the townspeople surrounded David and picked up stones to kill him. He escaped by falling on the ground, foaming and gibbering like a madman. The superstitious townspeople fell back, as if from a rabid animal, and the town guards drove David away with sticks and spears.

THE DEATH OF AHIMELECH *(page 89)*

Ahimelech thought that no one had seen his kindness to David. But a herdsman, Doeg, was visiting the shrine, and watched everything from the shadows. Doeg went straight to Saul, and Saul sent for Ahimelech, his wives, children, servants and followers. Soldiers gathered the people in the palace yard. Saul walked up and down in front of Ahimelech, raging that he was a traitor and a friend of the king's enemies. Ahimelech quietly denied it, saying that no one was more loyal to Saul than David. Saul shouted to the guards to kill Ahimelech, and when the men held back, reluctant to harm a priest, Doeg was suddenly filled with the same murderous rage as his master Saul. He snatched a sword, hacked Ahimelech to pieces, and then fell on the unarmed people in the yard, butchering men, women and children until 85 corpses lay on the bloodsoaked ground.

NABAL AND ABIGAIL *(page 89)*

During the years of David's exile, many people in Israel were only too pleased to provide him and his followers with food and to hide them from pursuing soldiers. But other people were more reluctant, either because they were afraid of Saul or for reasons of their own. When David and his followers left Ramah after visiting Samuel's grave, they passed through the lands of a rich farmer called Nabal. David sent Nabal a polite message, asking food for the outlaws, and Nabal angrily asked why he should take food from the mouths of his own servants to feed runaways and exiles. But Nabal's wife Abigail loaded asses with bread, wine, raisins, figs and mutton, and took the food to David. She begged him to take it in God's name, and to ignore her husband's rudeness. Soon afterwards, Nabal got drunk at a banquet, had a stroke and died – and everyone took it as God's punishment for refusing to help the man anointed king of Israel in God's name. Abigail joined David's followers, and in due course he married her.

DAVID AND SAUL'S SPEAR (page 89)

Not long after stealing the spear, David asked for a safe-conduct and went to see Saul. He asked why Saul was angry with him, why the king of Israel should spend time pursuing anyone as insignificant as a flea or a partridge on the mountains. He showed Saul the spear and pointed out that he could have used it to kill the king. He asked Saul, in God's name, to spare his life in turn. Saul burst into tears. He said that David was a fine man, blessed by God, and would live to do great things. But he neither thanked David for sparing his life nor offered to call off his soldiers, and David sadly left him and went back into exile.

THE WITCH OF ENDOR (page 89)

Before this battle began, Saul was anxious to know how it might end. He went to the village of Endor to consult a witch. Some years before he had forbidden witchcraft in Israel, on pain of death, and even though he went in disguise the witch at first hesitated to use her skills. But Saul persuaded her, and asked her to conjure up the ghost of Samuel from the dead. The witch put herself in a trance and summoned Samuel, showing him to Saul as an old man with his head hooded in a cloak. Saul knelt before Samuel, who asked him irritably what he wanted. Saul begged Samuel to forecast the outcome of the battle, and Samuel bleakly replied that God had given Saul's power to David, and that Saul and his three sons would die that day, fighting the Philistines. The vision faded, leaving Saul sobbing on the ground, and the witch took pity on him, helped him to his feet and made him eat and drink. It was the first disinterested kindness anyone had shown Saul since his fits of craziness began. But for all her kindness, the witch had no power to prevent Saul's destiny, and he had no choice but to leave at last for the battle he knew meant certain death.

DAVID'S LAMENT FOR SAUL AND JONATHAN (page 90)

A soldier from Saul's defeated army took the news of Saul's death to David, who was celebrating the end of the siege at Ziklag. The man knew that David was the new king of Israel, and hoped to make his fortune by claiming that he had found Saul helpless on the ground after his attempted suicide, and had granted the king's last request and killed him. But David, appalled that anyone should boast about killing God's anointed king, ordered the soldier's execution. Then, the Bible continues, he made up a song of lamentation for the deaths of Saul and Jonathan. The words of this lament still survive, and are among the oldest and most beautiful writings in the Bible. They include these verses:

> The beauty of Israel is slain upon thy high places. How are the mighty fallen! Tell it not in Gath, publish it not in the streets of Askelon, lest the daughters of the Philistines rejoice. Ye mountains, let there be no dew, neither let there be rain upon you nor fields of offerings; for there the shield of the mighty is vilely cast away, the shield of Saul, as though he had not been anointed with oil.
>
> Saul and Jonathan were lovely in their lives, and in their death they were not divided. They were swifter than eagles, they were stronger than lions. Ye daughters of Israel, weep over Saul. How are the mighty fallen in the midst of the battle! O Jonathan, I am distressed for thee, my brother Jonathan. Very pleasant hast thou been unto me: thy love to me was wonderful, passing the love of women. How are the mighty fallen, and the weapons of war perished!

MEPHIBOSHETH (page 93)

Many people expected that one of David's first acts when he was accepted king over all twelve tribes would be to persecute the surviving members of Saul's family. He did exactly the opposite: he sought them out, treated them kindly and welcomed them among his followers. An example is Mephibosheth, the son of David's friend Jonathan.

Mephibosheth was a baby when news came of his father's and grandfather's deaths in battle (see page 90), and his nurse was so startled by the news that she dropped the child, breaking his pelvis and crippling him for life. All through the civil war Mephibosheth lived in hiding, terrified of David's anger. But when David became king he sent for the young man, gave him servants, land and a place of honour in the royal household.

Mephibosheth's chief servant was a man called Ziba. He was jealous of his master, and looked for a chance to enrich himself at Mephibosheth's expense. During Absalom's revolt (see page 102), Ziba hurried to take David food and weapons, and told him that Mephibosheth had deserted to the enemy. David rewarded him with all Mephibosheth's lands. But later, when David went back to Jerusalem, Mephibosheth explained that he had been too lame to ride out in David's support, and claimed to be one of David's most loyal followers. Unable to decide who was telling the truth, Mephibosheth or Ziba, David divided Mephibosheth's property between them.

UZZAH, OBEDEDOM AND THE ARK
(page 94)

Two brothers travelled with the ox-cart carrying the Ark from Kiriath-jearim. Uzzah rode on the cart, driving the oxen with a goad; Ahio walked beside the animals, leading them. Ahio thought he had the lesser honour of the two, but in the end his lowly position saved his life. When the cart came down from the hills into the valley below Zion, it rocked on the uneven ground and Uzzah put his hand on the Ark to steady it. This was blasphemy – no one was allowed to touch the Ark but God's anointed priests – and Uzzah was struck dead on the spot. After this disaster, the story continues, David halted the Ark for three months on the land of a farmer called Obededom, before ordering it to be carried into Zion in procession. Ever afterwards, Obededom's land was among the richest in the kingdom.

THE PROCESSION *(page 94)*

Some experts say that Bible still contains the song of procession which was used when the Ark was carried into Jerusalem. It is Psalm 24, and is believed to have been written by David himself. The psalm includes these words, meant to be sung, as question and answer, by two separate choirs:

> (Both) Lift up your heads, O ye gates, and be ye lift up, ye everlasting doors, and the King of Glory shall come in.
> (A) Who is this king of glory?
> (B) The Lord strong and mighty, the Lord mighty in battle.
> (Both) Lift up your heads, O ye gates, even lift them up, ye everlasting doors, and the King of Glory shall come in.
> (A) Who is this king of glory?
> (B) The lord of Hosts: he is the king of Glory.

MICHAL (page 94)

The only person who failed to welcome the Ark into Zion was Michal, Saul's daughter whom David had married long before after paying a bride-price of two hundred Philistine foreskins (see page 87). When Saul went mad he took Michal from David and married her to another man, with whom she was well content. But after Saul's death David demanded that she return to him, and forced her to join his large harem of wives and concubines. Michal hated him for this – and now, when she looked out of the harem window in Zion and saw David leading the procession of the Ark, she shouted, "What a wonderful sight! Our lord and master, the king of Israel, stripped to his shirt, dancing half-naked before his own giggling maidservants! Aren't you ashamed?" David answered gently, pointing out that no God-fearing maidservant would giggle to see her master honouring God. But although David forgave Michal's sharp tongue, the story ends by saying that God punished her with barrenness: from that day onwards she could never conceive a child.

DAVID REALISES HIS GUILT (page 97)

As soon as Bathsheba's child was born, David fell on his knees and began to weep and pray. For seven days he refused food and drink; he refused to sleep on his bed, but instead lay couched on the ground; he begged God unceasingly to spare the baby's life. But as soon as the child died, he stood up from his prayers, washed himself, changed his clothes and called briskly for food and drink.

"Sir," asked one of the courtiers, "Why fast and weep for the child when it was alive, and not now when it's dead?"

"While the child was alive," answered David bleakly, "I fasted and wept in case God would be gracious to me and spare the baby's life. But now it's dead, what use are tears and prayers? Can I give the child back its life? I've sinned, and must suffer for it. God's will be done."

SHIMEI (page 101)

When David and his party first walked into Bahurim, they were attacked by a man called Shimei, whose family had supported Saul years before. Shimei threw stones as they passed, showered David with dust and jeered that he was now suffering exactly the same disgrace as he had caused Saul's true heirs when he stole the throne. One of David's fiercer followers, Abishai, wanted to cut off Shimei's head for these insults, but David stopped him. He said despondently that nothing Shimei did or said could hurt him. If Absalom, his own son, wanted him dead, why should one of Saul's old followers not do the same? The matter was for God to judge, and if Shimei was to be punished, God would see to it.

DAVID'S POETRY (page 106)

David's legacy to his own people, power, has faded with the centuries. But his legacy to the world survives: his poems. Over 70 Psalms, and several other pieces of poetry in the

Bible Old Testament, are thought to be by David himself, or to have been written to please him. They include songs of despair from the time of David's exile (eg Psalm 38) or from his flight from Absalom (eg Psalm 3), songs of worship (eg Psalm 15), of praise (eg Psalm 19), and three of the best-loved passages in the Bible, Psalm 23 ("The lord is my shepherd . . ."), David's lament for Saul and Jonathan ("How are the mighty fallen!": see page 255), and David's heartbroken lament for Absalom ("O my son Absalom, my son": see page 104).

SOLOMON'S WISDOM (page 107)

Several surviving books of the Bible are said to be by Solomon, and to contain his wisdom. The books of Proverbs and Ecclesiastes in the Old Testament, and The Wisdom of Solomon in the Apocrypha, are full of opinions on religion, politics and ordinary life. Many were collected in Solomon's own time; some may be the king's own words. Several are still heard today, 3000 years after Solomon's time: "The fear of the lord is the beginning of wisdom"; "A soft answer turns away wrath"; "Pride goes before destruction, and a haughty spirit before a fall"; "He that spares his rod hates his son" (the origin of "Spare the rod and spoil the child"). In addition, some people say that Solomon wrote or inspired the Song of Songs, a poem about the love of a king, a farmer's daughter and a shepherd, one of the oldest and best-known pieces of all Bible verse.

REHOBOAM (page 111)

In the last years of Solomon's reign, many local clan-chiefs had begun to challenge his power. They stirred up their people, claiming that for forty years Solomon had impoverished the villages and kept the farmers docile by taking each generation of young men away and putting them to forced labour on building-work or in the army. They were determined to increase their own power after Solomon died. Before his son Rehoboam was crowned, therefore, their spokesmen put questions to him in front of all the people, and demanded answers.

"Your father's yoke was heavy. If we make you king, will you lighten it?"

"I'll double it," said Rehoboam arrogantly.

"Your father beat us with whips – will you?"

"I'll beat you with scorpions."

These answers convinced the people of ten tribes that Rehoboam was no king for them. They sent for Jeroboam, a revolutionary exiled in Egypt, and crowned him king. Only two tribes, Benjamin and Judah, stayed loyal to Rehoboam. The country was split between Israel (or Samaria: Jeroboam's lowland followers) and Judah (Rehoboam's highland followers, centred on Jerusalem).

ELIJAH (page 112)

Although Jezebel pretended to let Elijah go, she secretly sent soldiers to hunt him down. God hid Elijah in a cave by the brook Cherith, a tributary of the Jordan. Elijah drank water from the brook, and God's ravens flew down to him with food each day. But as the drought continued, the brook diminished to a trickle, dried up and disappeared. God sent Elijah to the hill-village of Zarephath, and told him to sit down beside the gate. In the evening, a woman came out to gather firewood. "Please," said Elijah, "give me some water and a piece of bread."

"Sir," said the woman, "I've nothing left but one handful of flour in a barrel and one finger of oil in a jar. I'm gathering sticks for a fire, so that I can bake a loaf for my sick son and me – our last meal on earth."

"Let me share it," said Elijah. The woman took him home, and to her surprise the flour in the barrel never ran out however much she used, and the oil-jar filled as often as she emptied it. Food was guaranteed to the woman and her son as long as Elijah stayed with them. But food was no help to the child: he had suffered malnutrition for too long, and died. Elijah carried the body up to the attic where he slept, and laid it on the bed. Then he knelt and prayed to God. "Oh Lord, what has this poor woman done? Will you reward her kindness to me by killing her only son?" He stretched himself out three times on the child's body, and blew into the child's mouth – and God filled the boy's lungs with air and gave back his life. Elijah lived with the woman and her son until the drought had lasted for three full years, and it was time for him to go to Ahab's court and confront the idolators once more.

ELIJAH IN THE DESERT *(page 116)*

As he had before (see page 260), God took pity on Elijah. He sent angels to feed him, and to guide his steps. Elijah wandered in the desert for forty days and nights, and came at last to Mount Sinai, to the place where Moses had heard God's commandments centuries before (see page 47). Elijah was exhausted. He hid in a cave, as terrified of God's presence on the mountain as he was of Jezebel's pursuing soldiers. He lay on the ground, shaking with sobs. "Oh Lord," he cried, "what hope is left? Ahab and Jezebel still rule. The people were convinced by your miracle of holy fire, and worshipped you – but they'll soon turn back to Baal. Only I am left, your one true worshipper in Israel – and when the idolators find me, they'll kill me."

"Elijah, go up the mountain. Stand before God."

Trembling, Elijah did as he was told. Gales blew round his head, driving storm-clouds before them and battering the rocks. The storm crashed and roared all round him, and he listened for God's voice. But God was not in the storm. There followed an earthquake, and the ground opened its jaws to gulp the rocks; but God was not in the earthquake. Fire blazed, and lava spewed from the shattered mountainside; but God was not in the fire. Then the storm died, the earth shuddered itself still and the fire died. Elijah heard a still, small voice, so quiet that it was almost as if there were no sound at all, as if the words had formed inside his own head.

"Elijah, God will triumph over idolatry, though you will not
be on earth to see it. Go to Syria; crown Hazael king. He will
invade Israel and kill those who scorn my name. Make Elisha
a prophet, your successor. He will guide the people in my
name, and will anoint Jehu king, to kill the idolators left by
Hazael and bring all Israel back to God."

The sound ceased, clouds parted like curtains and the sun
shone as if nothing had happened. Elijah hurried down to the
plain, and set off across the desert to Israel, to confront Ahab
and Jezebel and carry out God's commands.

ELIJAH AND ELISHA (page 117)

Elisha was a farmer near the town of Tishbe, east of the river
Jordan. Elijah passed on his way to Damascus, and found
Elisha and his servants ploughing with twelve pairs of oxen.
Elijah walked across the field, laid his cloak on Elisha's back
and then continued on his way without a word. Elisha, filled
with God's spirit, ran after him and said, "Master, let me kiss
goodbye to my mother and father, and follow you." He took
a pair of oxen, sacrificed them to God and gave all his farm-
hands a share of the sacrificial feast. Then he put on a travelling cloak, took a knapsack on his back and a stick in his
hand, and ran to join Elijah.

ELIJAH TAKEN INTO HEAVEN (page 117)

When it was time for Elijah's earthly life to end, he and Elisha
went alone to the river Jordan. Elijah struck the river with his
cloak, and the water parted to let them cross. They climbed
the hill on the far bank, and Elijah said, "Ask any gift. What
shall I give you before I leave the earth?"

Elisha answered, "I pray God to give me twice your prophetic spirit."

"If your eyes see me carried into heaven," said Elijah,
"you'll know your prayer is granted."

They walked on up the hill. All at once the clouds parted
above their heads and a fiery chariot swept between them,

riding on the wings of the whirlwind. It carried Elijah far beyond Elisha's reach, and Elisha watched till it was out of sight among the clouds. Then, on the rock beside him, he noticed Elijah's cloak: the mantle of the prophet. He picked it up, walked down the hill and struck the Jordan, and at once the water parted for him, just as it had for Elijah. He shouldered the cloak, crossed the river and went back to his followers. They saw the light of God in his eyes and bowed to the ground to honour him.

ELISHA'S MIRACLES (page 117)

The people of Jericho asked Elisha to end a drought. The ground was parched, and the water from the only spring was too foul to drink. Elisha asked for a double handful of salt and dropped it into the spring – and instead of polluting the water the salt purified it and redoubled its force, so that it gushed out to fill the people's jars and irrigate the land. On another occasion, also in Jericho, Elisha helped a poor woman who was being pressed to pay a debt. He made her oil-jar flow with unceasing oil, until every basin and bowl in the house was full and she could sell the oil and pay her debt ten times over. He fed a hundred people on twenty barley loaves, and there was bread to spare. He lodged with a childless couple in the village of Shunem, and soon after his arrival the woman conceived and bore a son. The child grew strong and healthy until his fourth or fifth year, when he caught a sudden chill and died. Elisha laid the body on a bed, and prayed to God. Then he lay down beside the corpse, put his mouth on the child's mouth, his eyes on his eyes and his hands on his hands. God gave the boy back his life; his body warmed and stirred; he sneezed seven times and opened his eyes, and Elisha sent Gehazi his servant to tell the parents that their son was cured.

JONAH'S HYMN (page 126)

The book of Jonah in the Old Testament of the Bible gives the words it says Jonah sang inside the fish. They include these verses:

> I cried . . . to the Lord, and he heard me; out of the belly of hell cried I, and you heard my voice. For you had cast me into the deep, in the midst of the seas. . . The waters compassed me about, even to the soul; the depth closed round about me, the weeds were wrapped about my head. I went down to the bottom of the mountains; the earth with her bars was about me forever; yet . . .when my soul fainted within me I remembered the Lord . . . I will sacrifice to you with the voice of thanksgiving; I will pray what I have vowed. Salvation is of the Lord.

THE END OF THE ASSYRIAN ARMY
(page 132)

The Old Testament says that the Assyrian soldiers were struck down by God's angel, gives an exact number (185,000 men), and pithily concludes "When they arose early in the morning, behold, they were all dead corpses". The terrified survivors left the bodies where they lay and galloped home – and soon afterwards their leader was assassinated by his own sons as he prayed before the idol of Nisroch, his god.

JOSIAH (page 133)

Josiah, son of Manasseh, was the only royal prince who escaped child-sacrifice. In the fifty-five years of his father's reign, the Temple had grown filthy and deserted. The wood panels of the walls were black with smoke and greasy with the fat of sacrifice from the Baal-altars in the courtyard; the rooms were empty and the corridors were dark and deserted. The superstitious people thought that a monster lived in the Holy of Holies, a demon who drank human blood like wine. Only God's priests ever visited the sanctuary, and they were gaunt and terrified, living forever in the shadow of arrest and supported only by their belief in God and by the offerings of the few faithful worshippers left in Jerusalem.

Manasseh died when Josiah was eight years old, and the little boy became king. For ten years courtiers ruled Jerusalem in his name, and he had no power. But on his eighteenth birthday God appeared in a vision and told him to restore the Temple and lead the people back to true worship. Josiah was terrified. He had lived all his life as an idolator: he had no idea what true worship was, or how to teach it. He decided to begin by ordering the cleaning and restoration of the Temple. The workmen had hardly begun when they found, stuffed in a dusty cupboard, a scroll of the law of Moses. They gave it to Shaphan, Josiah's court historian, and he showed it to Josiah, saying that it was the word of God. Josiah said, "Take the book, and teach the people God's commandments. And ask a prophet if this book will save us from destruction." Shaphan went to the prophetess Huldah, one of the few true believers left in Jerusalem. She had no comfort to offer. "Whether the people repent or not," she said, "they are so sunk in idolatry, and will sink so far again, that God's anger against them will not be quenched."

Undeterred by this prophecy, Josiah ordered work to continue on the Temple. The heathen altars were removed, the walls cleaned, the floors scrubbed; the shrine was dusted and the priests were brought out of hiding and dressed in new, rich robes. When the work was done, Josiah declared a public celebration of Passover, the feast in remembrance of the time when God had sent plagues on the Egyptians but spared all true believers (see page 42). Musicians played; priests sacrificed; the people prayed; orators read aloud from the holy scroll. But Josiah's eagerness to please God then drove him to defile the feast. He murdered every heathen priest and prophet in the kingdom, and burned their bones on their own altars. The stench of burnt flesh rose to heaven, and God's anger was redoubled, not assuaged. He sent the Egyptians to invade Josiah's kingdom, and when Josiah led his troops out to fight at the battle of Megiddo, an archer shot him dead. The Egyptians made Josiah's son Jehoiakin puppet-king of Jerusalem, and ordered an immediate return to idolatry, to the worship of Horus, Isis, Osiris and the rest of the Egyptian gods. Josiah's return to true religion had lasted little more than a dozen years, and after his death, just as Huldah had prophesied, the Chosen People sank even deeper in idolatry than before.

THE HOST OF HEAVEN (page 133)

The gods whose altars thronged the Temple were the Host of Heaven. Many ancient peoples (for example Greeks, Persians and Egyptians) believed that the whole sky was peopled by gods, and that each god or goddess had a palace in one of the heavenly bodies. The king or queen of the gods ruled the sun, the spirit of night ruled the moon; every planet, star, comet and asteroid had its own governing deity. To keep the sky-powers friendly, to ensure good weather and avoid earth-quakes, storms and plagues, it was essential to sacrifice regu-larly to each one of them. In case any gods lived on stars invisible to human eyes, and of whose existence human beings therefore had no idea, people usually put up an altar "to the unknown god", and sacrificed there most frequently and anxiously of all.

JUDITH (page 134)

Nebuchadnezzar had other reasons than greed for attacking the Promised Land. As Babylon's power grew, it had begun to challenge the huge Median empire, and Nebuchadnezzar had sent requests to every small independent state between Egypt and Syria, asking for recruits to help him fight the Medes. Most states sent soldiers; but the Jewish towns of the Promised Land had all refused. This was the first time Nebuchadnezzar had even heard of most of them, but he made his secretaries write down their names, marking them for punishment as soon as the Median war was won. Jerusalem's name therefore appeared on two separate lists; without God to protect them, its people stood no chance.

To other, more devout towns, God sent help. When Nebuchadnezzar's general, Holofernes, besieged Bethuliah with a hundred thousand men, the inhabitants first defied him, trusting in God. Then, when the Babylonians blocked the streams and let the cisterns run dry, they begged their counsellors to forget God and surrender before the entire town died of thirst. The counsellors went to Judith, a wise and pious woman, to ask advice. She told them to wait five days, and that if God had not helped them in that time, they should surrender. Then she walked down into the Babylonian camp, accompanied by a single servant with a bag of food. She told Holofernes that the people of Bethuliah were so near starvation that they were ready to commit blasphemy, to eat the sacred bread and drink the holy water from the Temple. She herself, she went on, was a devout worshipper – and to punish the blasphemers she would lead Holofernes' army, four days hence, by a secret path into Bethuliah. They would capture the town without losing a single man.

Holofernes was as smitten by her beauty as by her plan. He begged her to eat, drink and spend the night with him. Judith refused. She said that she had her own Jewish food with her: to eat foreign food was a sin against her God. That night, and for two more days and nights, she stayed in camp, living in a tent Holofernes' guard had pitched for her, eating her own food and praying to God night and morning – and the longer she stayed, the more Holofernes lusted after her.

On the fourth night Judith pretended at last to agree to let Holofernes make love with her. She told him to send away all his guards, and wait alone in his tent for her. As darkness fell, Holofernes feasted, licking his lips and drinking toasts to Judith's charms. At last he staggered to his feet, sent away his guards and collapsed on his bed in a drunken sleep. Judith crept in, unsheathed his sword and cut off his head. She stuffed it into her empty food-bag and she and her servant hurried back to Bethuliah in the darkness. None of Holofernes' soldiers dared to disturb their master until daybreak – and when they discovered his murder the whole army took it as a warning from the Jewish God and fled to the hills, where guerrilla warriors slaughtered them like goats.

WEEPING FOR JERUSALEM (see page 136)

The words of Psalm 137 are about the Jews' longing for Jerusalem, and may have been made up by Jewish exiles in Babylon. Using Zion as another name for Jerusalem, the Psalm begins:

> By the rivers of Babylon, there we sat down. Yea, we wept when we remembered Zion. We hanged our harps upon the willows in the midst thereof. For there they that carried us away captive required of us a song; and they that wasted us required of us mirth, saying, "Sing us one of the songs of Zion".
>
> How shall we sing the Lord's song in a strange land? If I forget thee, O Jerusalem, let my right hand forget her cunning. If I do not remember thee, let my tongue cleave to the roof of my mouth, if I prefer not Jerusalem above my chief joy.

DANIEL AND SUSANNA (page 137)

The Apocrypha tells a story of Daniel's boyhood, showing that God gave him commonsense far beyond his years. A beautiful woman called Susanna lived with her husband Joachim in a house with a high-walled garden. Every day she went into the garden, locked the gates and bathed – until two lascivious city counsellors saw her by accident and were so smitten with her beauty that they determined to hide in the garden and rape her. Next day, therefore, as soon as Susanna locked the gates, the two men jumped out of hiding and demanded that she make love. Susanna refused, and the men ran to Joachim and shouted that they'd found her making love with a young man who'd scrambled into his clothes and run away.

The accusation was serious. If it were true – and who could argue with the word of two counsellors? – Susanna's crime would be adultery and her punishment death by stoning. Joachim called a gathering of friends and neighbours to hear the evidence, and the two wicked counsellors gleefully told their story, supporting it with all kinds of detail about the mysterious young man's appearance. Their words were so persuasive that no one believed Susanna's tearful denials, and Joachim sighed and said, "Neighbours, if we all agree, let her be taken away and stoned."

"No!" shouted a voice from the crowd. "I don't agree."

It was Daniel. The crowd recognised the uniform of the royal school, and bowed as low as if to the King himself. "Are you such fools," he said, "that you condemn someone to death after hearing only half the evidence?" He took the first counsellor out of earshot of the other, and asked, "When you saw them making love, where was it?"

"Under a gum-tree. If I'm lying, may I be cut in two."

"As you say, so be it," said Daniel. He took the second counsellor aside and asked, "When you saw them making love, where was it?"

"Under a laurel bush. If I'm lying, may I be cut in two."

Daniel told the people the two men's answers. "Out of their own mouths, they've condemned themselves – and they've named their own punishment," he said. "Praise God, who reveals the guilty and protects the innocent." Soldiers dragged the counsellors away, Susanna went back to her husband, and the whole crowd fell on its knees and thanked God for blessing Daniel with wisdom.

THE SONG OF SHADRACH, MESHACH AND ABEDNEGO (page 141)

In the Apocrypha, the Bible gives the words it says Shadrach, Meshach and Abednego sang in the burning fiery furnace. Some of the words were made into a praise-song for Christian churches: it is called Benedicite, and is still used today. Some of its verses are;

> O all ye works of the Lord, bless the Lord. Praise and exalt him above all forever. O ye heavens, bless ye the Lord. Praise and exalt him above all forever. O ye angels of the Lord, bless ye the Lord. Praise and exalt him above all forever . . . O ye sun and moon, bless ye the Lord. Praise and exalt him above all forever. O ye stars of heaven, bless ye the Lord. Praise and exalt him above all forever . . . O give thanks unto the Lord, because he is gracious, for his mercy endureth forever. O all ye

that worship the Lord, bless the God of gods, praise him and give him thanks, for his mercy endureth forever.

NEBUCHADNEZZAR'S GARDENS (page 142)

The gardens of Nebuchadnezzar's palace – the Hanging Gardens of Babylon – were one of the wonders of the ancient world. They were a wedding present for one of his wives, a Median princess called Amytis. The Medes were a mountain people to the north of Babylon, the only race in the world too powerful for the Babylonians to defeat in war. Instead of fighting them, therefore, Nebuchadnezzar made peace – and marked it by marrying Amytis and taking her back to Babylon.

Babylon was a country of plains and deserts: flat land as far as the eye could see. Amytis, a mountain-princess, felt homesick for the tree-covered slopes and flowery meadows of her native hills. To please her, Nebuchadnezzar ordered his slaves to build an artificial hill in front of her palace window, and to plant it with trees and flowers. The slaves made a foundation of brick arches, as high as the city walls, and laid stone terraces on them, lined with lead (to make them waterproof) and covered with earth. The terraces were like an enormous flight of steps, and Nebuchadnezzar's gardeners planted them with trees, flowers and shrubs imported from Amytis' native land. When the queen looked out of her window, it must have seemed as though a whole city park, green with vegetation, had risen in the air and was floating where once there had been nothing but a flat, bare yard.

In Nebuchadnezzar's and Amytis' time, the gardens were private, reserved for the royal family and a few favoured courtiers. But in later years they were opened to the public, and they were still a tourist attraction in the time of Alexander the Great, 350 years after Nebuchadnazzar's death.

NEBUCHADNEZZAR'S SONG (page 142)

The Book of Daniel in the Bible ends this story by quoting Nebuchadnezzar's song, making it the triumphant end to his conversion. These are the words it says he sang:

> I lifted up mine eyes unto heaven, and mine understanding returned unto me . . . I blessed the Most High, and I praised and honoured him that liveth forever, whose dominion is an everlasting dominion, and his kingdom is from generation to generation . . .
>
> At the same time my reason returned unto me . . . mine honour and brightness returned unto me, and my counsellors and lords sought unto me, and I was established in my kingdom, and excellent majesty was added unto me. Now I Nebuchadnezzar praise and extol and honour the King of Heaven, all whose works are truth and his ways judgement; and those that walk in pride he is able to abase.

THE WRITING ON THE WALL (page 144)

The words MENE, MENE, TEKEL, UPHARSIN are the names of weights; they mean "fifty shekels, fifty shekels, one shekel, two half-shekels". No one can really explain how they got the extra meaning Daniel gave them, that God had weighed Belshazzar (in the "balance" or scale) and found him unsatisfactory ("wanting"). Some scholars say that a similar phrase was written on the walls in Egyptian tombs, referring to the dead; they suggest that "Mene, mene, tekel, upharsin" may have been a proverb meaning something like "You're dead, and that's all there is to it".

DANIEL'S MAGIC POWERS (page 145)

Two stories (from the book Bel and the Dragon in the Apocrypha) show what the people probably regarded as Daniel's "magic" powers – and they involve common-sense, not wizardry. In the first, Daniel refused to worship a statue of Baal because it was not a real god but an idol of clay and bronze.

The Baal-priests said that they could prove that their god was alive: when food was left for him in the Baal-house overnight, it was gone by morning. The King ordered a test. Food and wine would be left in the Baal-house, and the doors would be sealed to keep out thieves. If the food was gone by morning, Daniel would die; if it was still there, the Baal-priests would be executed and the Baal-house destroyed. Daniel said nothing, but before the Baal-house was sealed he sprinkled ashes all over the floor. Next morning, when the doors were unsealed, all the food and drink had disappeared – and a line of footprints in the ash led to a secret door in the foot of Baal's statue, through which the priests, their wives and children crept in the night to eat the offerings.

In the second story, the Great King told Daniel of a fire-breathing dragon worshipped in a distant province, and said, "Can you deny that this is real? It eats and drinks: it's a living god. Worship it!"

Daniel said, "If I kill the dragon without sword or spear, will you believe in the living God I serve?"

"As you say," said the king, "So shall it be."

Daniel sent his servants to the slaughterhouse to collect hides, fat and fleeces. He fastened the skins round lumps of pitch, and shaped them to look like sheep and cattle. Then he laid the bait in the dragon's grove, in place of the usual offerings. The dragon smelt the animal-fat, gulped down the offerings – and the heat of its breath sent pitch trickling into its lungs and choked it to death.

DANIEL IN THE LIONS' DEN (page 146)

In another version of this story (told in the book Bel and the Dragon in the Apocrypha), the Great King threw Daniel into the lions' den to quell an uprising by people infuriated that Daniel had killed the dragon they worshipped (see above). In this account, Daniel was to be left with the lions for seven days: even if the lions spared him he would die of starvation. But on the first night of his imprisonment, God sent an angel to the Promised Land, to a farmer called Habbakuk. It was harvest-time, and Habbakuk had just packed a basket of food for the reapers in his fields. The angel told Habbakuk to pick up the basket, then carried him through the air to Babylon and the lions' den. "Daniel! Here's your dinner! Take it, quickly!" said the terrified Habbakuk – and he had no sooner spoken than the angel carried him back through the air to his own farmyard. So Daniel had food to keep him alive among the lions, and emerged as healthy as when he'd been condemned.

ESTHER'S DATES (page 151)

Unlike many Bible stories, this one is thought to be fiction: a story made up to explain the Jewish festival of Purim (celebrated on the 14th and 15th of March each year). The author sets the story during the reign of the Persian king Ahasuerus (Xerxes), probably in 473 BC. But the exact dates of the Jewish exile in Babylon are not clearly known. Most scholars say that Nebuchadnezzar sacked and enslaved the Jews in 586 BC, and that Zerubbabel led the first group of exiles home (see page 153) about fifty years later, after the Persian king Cyrus captured Babylon. If these dates are all correct, then the story of Esther concerns not Jewish slaves during the Babylonian exile but settlers who stayed in Babylon long after their fellow-countrymen had returned to the Promised Land.

ZERUBBABEL (see page 152)

The Bible says nothing about the names of the first two young men. But the third, Zerubbabel, was the grandson of Jehoiachin, the king of Jerusalem taken into exile by Nebuchadnezzar (see page 134). The name Zerubbabel means "shoot of Babylon". The Babylonians (who changed the names of all their foreign slaves) called Zerubbabel Sheshbazzar, which means "may the moon-goddess protect his father"; this name appears in several Bible accounts.

SACRED VESSELS (page 153)

The sacred vessels are listed in the Book of Ezra in the Old Testament of the Bible. 5400 items survived from the Temple treasure looted by Nebuchadnezzar: they included 30 large gold dishes, 1000 large silver dishes, 30 gold bowls, 410 silver bowls, 29 knives and 1000 "other vessels" (cups, trays, ladles, incense-burners, spoons).

EZRA AND NEHEMIAH (page 153)

The Jews' triumphant return to Jerusalem was not the end of their suffering. The hills round the city were already tenanted, by the descendants of people who had escaped the exile. They resented the newcomers' outlandish clothes and Babylonian ways, and were afraid of the power a newly-built Jerusalem might have. Zerubbabel's followers had time only to rebuild the foundations of the Temple before they were attacked. At first they tried to defend themselves, but then most of them threw down their weapons and promised to abandon the building-work if only they were left in peace. For two generations they made the ruins of Jerusalem a shanty-town of tents and huts; some so far forgot their vows as to marry idolators and worship heathen gods. In the reign of the Great King Artaxerxes, therefore, God sent two further waves of settlers. Ezra led the first group: priests, prophets and teachers of the Law. He called the people back to God, and set up courts to try those who had married idolators and to divorce any who repented. Nehemiah led the second group, with soldiers. He organised the people into building-teams, and set them working to rebuild the shattered walls and to finish the Temple. When the work was done, Ezra and Nehemiah declared a solemn religious festival. Priests read aloud from the law of Moses, and the people went forward one by one to renew their vows to God.

JOB (page 154)

Unlike such people as Gideon, Samson or Jezebel, Job is not a real individual, a person from history. He is a made-up character, and the Old Testament Book of Job is fiction. It is a poem in the style of a play, and gives its characters long philosophical speeches like those in Greek tragedy or in some of Shakespeare's plays. The writer was interested in two ideas above all: how human beings cope with a God whose power they can never equal and never understand, and the age-old question "If God is fair, why does he let innocent people suffer?" The Book of Job has a prologue to set up the story and an epilogue to end it. In between is the poem, the heart of the book. It consists of speeches made by Job, by his friends Eliphaz, Bildad and Zophar, and by the young man Elihu. In each of the first three sections, Job's friends speak in turn and Job answers each one of them; in the fourth section, Elihu speaks. There is no action, as in a modern play: the speeches, the pattern of thought, and above all the poetry, are what matter.

This chapter gives only the book's skeleton, the basic ebb and flow of argument. The note below gives a brief sample of its poetry.

GOD'S POETRY (page 159)

The speech in which God describes his power contains some of the most sonorous of all ancient Hebrew poetry, and the English translation in the Authorized Version of the Bible (made in Shakespeare's time) is almost equally magnificent. In the section where God asks Job to compare his own power with his creator's, for example, these lines occur:

> Gavest thou . . . wings unto the peacocks, or wings and feathers unto the ostrich? . . . Hast thou given the horse strength? Hast thou clothed his neck with thunder? Canst thou make him afraid as a grasshopper? The glory of his nostrils is terrible. He paweth in the valley, and rejoiceth in his strength . . . He is not affrighted, neither turneth he back from the sword . . . He

swalloweth the ground with fierceness and rage . . . He saith among the trumpets Ha, Ha, and he smelleth the battle afar off, the thunder of the captains and the shouting.

Doth the hawk fly by thy wisdom, and stretch her wings towards the south? Doth the eagle mount up at thy command, and make her nest on high? She dwelleth and abideth on the rock, upon the crag of the rock and the strong place. From hence she seeketh the prey, and her eyes behold afar off. Her young ones also suck up blood, and where the slain are, there is she.

TOBIT'S HYMN OF PRAISE *(page 166)*

The Apocrypha of the Bible gives the words of a hymn of praise which it says Tobit sang to God. The hymn tells of God's goodness and mercy, and of Jerusalem, the holy city from which Tobit and his family, like most of the Jews in Nineveh, Ecbatana and other foreign towns, were exiles. The hymn includes these verses:

I will extol my God, and my soul shall praise the King of heaven, and shall rejoice in his greatness. Let all men speak, and let all praise him for his righteousness. O Jerusalem, the holy city, he will scourge thee for thy children's work, and will have mercy again on the sons of the righteous. Give praise to the Lord, for he is good: and praise the everlasting king . . . O blessed are they which love thee, for they shall rejoice in thy peace . . . they shall rejoice for thee, when they have seen all thy glory, and shall be glad forever. Let my soul bless God the great King. For Jerusalem shall be built up with sapphires and emeralds and precious stone: thy walls and towers and battlements with pure gold. And the streets of Jerusalem shall be paved with beryl and carbuncle and stones of Ophir. And all her streets shall say Alleluia, and they shall praise him saying, "Blessed be God, which hath extolled it forever."

FIGHTING ON THE SABBATH *(page 171)*

In another account, this Sabbath massacre took place not at Modin but in Jerusalem, and thousands of Jews were killed.

But wherever it happened, it resulted in Mattathias and his followers taking to the hills – and they also prayed to God to be allowed to defend themselves on the Sabbath. Ever since then, to this day, fighting in self-defence is one of the few exceptions orthodox Jews allow themselves to the Sabbath-laws.

GORGIAS (page 174)

Judas' victories against the Syrians continued to depend partly on God's guidance, partly on the bravery of his men, and partly on the same kind of cunning as he had used against Nicanor, when he demoralised the Syrians by keeping them sweating in the sun for two long days (see page 173). On another occasion, his army was once again outnumbered by Syrian troops, this time under general Gorgias. Gorgias' men pitched tents, lit cooking-fires and settled for the night, announcing that they would wait till morning to fight the Jews. But as soon as it was dark they crept silently out of camp to take Judas' army by surprise. Gorgias hoped to trap Judas with his own kind of trickery, but when his men crawled into Judas' camp they found it deserted: the Jews had disappeared. Gorgias' soldiers spent the whole night searching the hills, gully by gully, cave by cave, terrified of surprise attack – and when dawn came they saw that Judas had led his men down to the plain behind them and sacked their camp. The sight of their own burning tents convinced the Syrians that Judas had summoned demons from the Underworld to fight them. They fled for their lives, leaving the Jews to collect a vast hoard of treasure: the Bible lists "gold, and silver, and blue silk, and purple of the sea, and great riches."

CLEANSING THE TEMPLE (page 174)

As a start to his glorious new reign, Judas cleared Jerusalem of every trace of heathen occupation. In particular, he purified and rebuilt the Temple. The Syrians had turned its courtyard into a bazaar in heathen style, filling it with market-stalls and using it to buy and sell bread, vegetables, pots and pans, chickens, pigs and sheep. They had polluted God's altar with unlawful sacrifice, and had topped it with a huge Zeus-statue. They had looted the inner rooms, stripping the gold from the walls, melting down the sacred vessels, prising tiles from the floor and smashing the sacred furniture for firewood. Judas' men prayed to God to take vengeance not on them but on their enemies. They then set about cleansing and restoring the Temple. They toppled Zeus' statue, and stripped the top layer of altar-stones, defiled with pig-fat. They dug up the weed-strewn floors and laid new tiles; they repaired the scrolls of the Law, where the Syrians had torn them or scribbled idol-faces in the margins; they filled the cupboards with new candlesticks, cups and other sacred vessels. While this work went on, Judas sent builders to repair the walls of Zion, the hill-fort at the heart of Jerusalem which David had conquered and occupied many centuries before (see page 93): it would be the Jews' best defence against another Syrian attack. Altogether, the work took five months, and when it was finished Judas decread an eight-day thanksgiving festival. The streets of Jerusalem filled with holiday crowds, and the Temple rang with trumpets, prayers and the sound of choirs singing hymns to God.

POWER POLITICS (page 174)

The Books of Maccabees in the Bible deal only with the first twenty years of Maccabee rule, the time of Judas and his brothers Jonathan and Simon. Other sources, including Roman historians, tell the story of the following century. The power-struggle in Jerusalem spanned four Maccabee generations, and very few leaders died peacefully in their beds. Judas' brother Jonathan (ruled 160–142 BC) was executed by the Syrians; Jonathan's brother Simon (ruled 142–134 BC) was poisoned at a banquet; the reign of Simon's son John Hyrcanus (ruled 134–104 BC) was marked by riots between the Pharisees (who believed in exact obedience to the ancient

Law of Moses) and the Sadducees (who thought that laws could be adapted to suit modern conditions, so long as a council of leaders, state and religious, all agreed). John's eldest son Aristobulus murdered his own mother and imprisoned his brothers to prevent them challenging his rule, and tried to make the Jews accept Greek ways. His reign lasted for only a few months, and then his brother Alexander (ruled 103–76 BC) took power. Alexander executed hundreds of political opponents, and fought bitter wars against the Pharisees, who declared his reign against God's law. He was succeeded first by his wife Alexandra (ruled 76–67 BC) and then by his son Hyrcanus (II). Hyrcanus' rule was challenged by his brother Aristobulus (II), and there was a four-year civil war, ended only when the brothers appealed to Rome to settle it. Pompey, general of Rome, led his legions to Jerusalem in 63 BC, made Hyrcanus high priest, took Aristobulus and thousands of other Jews to Rome as prisoners-of-war, and declared the Promised Land a subject state.

MARY'S SONG (page 175)

St Luke gives the words of a song he says Mary sang when she realised the true meaning of what the angel had promised her. The song has become known as the Magnificat, and is used in many Christian church services. The Authorised Version of the Bible gives its words as these:

> My soul doth magnify the Lord, and my spirit hath rejoiced in God my Saviour. For he hath regarded the low estate of his handmaiden: for behold, from henceforth all generations shall call me blessed. For he that is mighty hath done to me great things; and holy is his name. And his mercy is on them that fear him, from generation to generation. He hath showed strength with his arm; he hath scattered the proud in the imagination of their hearts. He hath put down the mighty from their seats, and exalted them of low degree. He hath filled the hungry with good things, and the rich he hath sent empty away. He hath holpen his servant Israel, in remembrance of his mercy, as he spake to our fathers, to Abraham and to his seed forever.

THE MESSIAH (page 176)

Messiah is the Hebrew word for "anointed one". In the time of King David any anointed person, king or high priest, could be so-called. But later, during the years of Jewish suffering and exile, the word came to mean one special person: a priest-king, descended from David, who would one day come to end his people's sorrows and lead them to everlasting happiness. When Jesus was born, many people believed that the ancient prophecies had been exactly fulfilled: he was the Messiah, the son of God sent into the world to save the human race. When people preached about Jesus in Greek-speaking countries, they called him by the Greek form of the word Messiah, "Christos" or Christ, "the anointed one". Although people of non-Christian religions (for example Jews and Muslims) disagree with the claim that Jesus was the Messiah, all Christians believe it: it is one of the foundations of Christianity.

SIMEON'S PRAYER (page 177)

St Luke gives the words of Simeon's prayer in the Temple, and (under the Latin name Nunc dimittis) they are still one of the best-loved prayers of the Christian church:

> Lord, now lettest thou thy servant depart in peace, according to thy word. For mine eyes have seen thy salvation, which thou hast prepared before the face of all people: a light to lighten the Gentiles, and the glory of thy people Israel.

THE STAR (page 177)

There are many different accounts of the star which guided the wise men to Bethlehem. Some people say that the Bible story is literally true: God sent a miraculous star, never seen before or since, to light the wise men's steps. Others say that the story is a myth. It appears only in St Matthew's Gospel, and St Luke mentions neither the wise men nor the massacre of the babies, simply saying that Joseph took his family home to Nazareth as soon as Mary and Jesus were able to travel. Modern astronomers give a third explanation. They say that Halley's Comet, whose orbit takes it round the Earth once every 76 years, would have been visible in the skies over Bethlehem some time towards the end of Herod's reign. The wise men (often called magi or "wizards") were skilled in "Chaldean science" (astronomy and astrology: see page 136), and would have been able to predict the comet's appearance months in advance, leaving plenty of time for them to travel to Judaea and make close observations when it actually arrived.

THE WISE MEN AND THEIR GIFTS (page 177)

Later legend has filled out the Bible story of the three wise men. Their names were Melchior ("king of light"), Caspar (or Gaspar, "the white") and Balthazar ("lord of treasures"), and each of them gave Jesus a gift. Melchior gave him gold, the gift suitable for a king. Caspar gave incense ("frankincense"), the gift mortals give to God. Balthazar gave him myrrh, the bitter herb used to scent the bodies of the dead: this was a sign of the bitter death he would one day suffer on the cross (see page 213).

JESUS' CHILDHOOD (page 178)

The Bible says little directly about Jesus between the ages of four and about thirty. Many people have made reconstructions of his childhood, based on hints and ideas from his later teaching. He knew the Books of Moses and the writings of the Old Testament prophets as thoroughly as any priest or teacher. He was knowledgeable about many of the crafts and skills of ordinary life: farming, fishing, shepherding, running a house, bringing up children. (Perhaps surprisingly, he never once mentions carpentry.) The picture is of a clever boy who divided his time between ordinary village life and the study of religion, of a young man his neighbours thought so much like everyone else that they were greatly surprised when he started preaching (see page 182).

Only one actual incident is mentioned in the gospels, and it fits the picture of Jesus given above. Every year, he and his parents went to Jerusalem for the Passover celebrations (remembering the time in Egypt, when God killed the first-born of every unbeliever, but passed over each Israelite house: see page 42). In the year when Jesus was twelve, his parents lost him in the Passover crowds. They thought that he must have gone to one of their friends or relations, but spent three days looking for him, without success. Then they found him: in an inner courtyard of the Temple, discussing God's law with priests and scholars as an equal, asking and answering questions as if he were a professor himself. Everyone was open-mouthed at his learning – except for his mother, who scolded him for disappearing without letting her or Joseph know. According to St Luke, Jesus replied, "Why did you look for me? Didn't you realise that I'd be about my father's business?" – an answer which no one (not even Mary and Joseph, who knew that he was the Son of God) could understand.

THE BIRTH OF JOHN THE BAPTIST
(page 178)

St Luke tells the miraculous story of John the Baptist's birth. Both Zachariah and his wife Elisabeth were in their eighties, and had long since given up hope of children. But one day, when Zachariah was burning incense in the Temple, God's angel appeared and told him that Elizabeth would conceive and bear a son, John – and that as proof that the news was true, Zachariah himself would be struck dumb until the child was named. Many Temple visitors that day witnessed Zachariah's dumbness, and realised that he must have seen a vision.

Nine months later, Elizabeth gave birth to a son, and her neighbours and relatives were delighted that God had ended her barrenness at last. They took the child to the Temple for the naming-ceremony, and asked Zachariah what name he was to be given. At first Zachariah could still not speak, and wrote on a wax tablet "His name is John". But as soon as the name was written Zachariah's tongue was freed of dumbness, and he poured out his gratitude and praise of God in words which have since become part of the morning worship of the Christian church. The prayer begins:

> Blessed be the Lord God of Israel, for he hath visited and redeemed his people, and hath raised up a horn of salvation for us in the house of his servant David, as he spake by the mouth of his holy prophets, which have been since the world began . . .

It continues, speaking directly to the child John:

> And thou, child, shalt be called the prophet of the Highest: for thou shalt go before the face of the Lord, to prepare his ways, to give knowledge of salvation unto his people by the remission of their sins, . . . to give light to them that sit in darkness and the shadow of death, to guide our feet in the way of peace . . .

SIMON AND JESUS *(page 185)*

This version of the story comes from Luke's gospel. In Matthew's and Mark's gospels, Jesus simply found Simon and his brother Andrew fishing, and called them to join him. John's gospel says that Andrew was one of the followers of John the Baptist, and he was among the crowd at the river Jordan when Jesus was baptised (see page 179). He recognised Jesus at once as the Lamb of God, the Messiah John the Baptist had said was coming to save the world. He hurried home, told Simon that he was going to follow Jesus, and asked Simon to go with him.

Simon and Andrew were natives of the town of Bethsaida, on the other side of the Sea of Galilee from Capernaum. But Simon had married a girl from Capernaum some time before, and gone to set up a fishing-business there with James and John. He lived with his wife and her mother, in the mother's house. On the day Jesus healed the madman in the synagogue (see page 183), Simon's mother fell ill with sudden fever, and Jesus cured her.

THE SERMON ON THE MOUNT *(page 185)*

The Gospels give several of Jesus' sermons, in some cases word for word as people later remembered them. The longest is known as the Sermon on the Mount, because Jesus preached it (as his custom was) on a mountainside, standing downhill from the crowd so that everyone could see and hear him clearly. In the Elizabethan English of the Authorized Version, Matthew's account of the sermon includes these verses:

Blessed are the poor in spirit, for theirs is the kingdom of heaven. Blessed are they that mourn, for they shall be comforted. Blessed are the meek, for they shall inherit the earth. Blessed are they which do hunger and thirst after righteousness, for they shall be filled. Blessed are the merciful, for they shall obtain mercy. Blessed are the pure in heart, for they shall see God. Blessed are the peacemakers, for they shall be called the children of God. Blessed are they which are persecuted for righteousness' sake, for theirs is the kingdom of heaven. Blessed are ye, when men shall revile you and persecute you, and shall say all manner of evil against you falsely for my sake. Rejoice, and be exceeding glad: for great is your reward in heaven. . .

Ye are the salt of the earth . . . Ye are the light of the world . . . Let your light so shine before men, that they may see your good works and glorify your father which is in heaven . . .

Love your enemies, bless them that curse you, do good to them that hate you, and pray for them which . . . persecute you, that you may be children of your Father which is in heaven: for he maketh his sun to rise on the evil and on the good, and sendeth rain on the just and on the unjust . . .

Lay not up for yourselves treasures upon earth, where moth and rust doth corrupt, and where thieves break through and steal. But lay up for yourselves treasures in heaven, where neither moth nor rust doth corrupt, and where thieves do not break through and steal: for where your treasure is, there will your heart be also . . .

Take no thought for . . . what ye shall eat or what ye shall drink, nor yet for your body, what ye shall put on . . . Behold the fowls of the air: for they sow not, neither do they reap . . . yet your heavenly Father feedeth them. Are ye not much better than they? . . . Consider the lilies of the field, how they grow: they toil not, neither do they spin – and yet I say unto you, that even Solomon in all his glory was not arrayed like one of these. Wherefore, if God so clothe the grass of the field, which today is and tomorrow is cast into the oven, shall he not much more clothe ye, O ye of little faith? . . .

Judge not, that ye be not judged . . . Why beholdest thou the mote that is in thy brother's eye, but considerest not the beam that is in thine own eye? . . . Thou hypocrite, first cast out the beam out of thine own eye, and then shalt thou see clearly to cast out the mote out of thy brother's eye . . .

Whosoever heareth these sayings of mine, and doeth them, I will liken him unto a wise man, which built his house upon a rock. And the rain descended and the floods came, and the winds blew and beat upon that house, and it fell not: for it was founded upon a rock. And everyone that heareth these sayings of mine, and doeth them not, shall be likened unto a foolish man, which built his house upon the sand. And the rain descended, and the floods came, and the winds blew and beat upon that house; and it fell, and great was the fall of it.

OLD WINE IN NEW SKINS *(page 186)*

Jesus followed this answer to the Pharisees with two comments meant to help the crowd to understand. As often he put a difficult idea in simple words, easy to follow. He was teaching that his message was new, for people who had not known it before: strict older beliefs (like those of the Pharisees) could be a hindrance and not a help. To make this easier to understand, he compared ideas to cloth and to wine. He said, "No one patches an old garment with new cloth, in case the old cloth tears even worse than before. No one puts new wine into an old wineskin, in case the skin splits and both it and the wine are wasted."

THE DEAD BOY *(page 187)*

Soon after healing the centurion's slave, Jesus went to preach
in the village of Nain, near Nazareth. At the gate he met a
funeral procession coming out of the village. A poor widow's
only son had died, and she and her neighbours followed the
procession, weeping. Jesus told her gently to dry her tears;
then he put his hand on the bier to stop the procession,
touched the boy on the shoulder and said, "Wake up." At
once the child sat up, swung himself from the bier and walked
through the crowd, still wrapped in grave-clothes, to take his
mother in his arms.

DEVILS INTO PIGS *(page 190)*

This account follows the version told by Mark and Luke.
Matthew says that two men, not one, were possessed by
devils, and that after Jesus drove the devils into the pigs and
the pigs ran into the sea, the people of Gadara were so
frightened that they asked Jesus to leave their town and not
go back. (It was not till much later, Mark says, after the
feeding of the 5000: see page 193, that they accepted him.)
Jairus (who in Luke's version was head of the synagogue in
Gadara: see page 190) is not mentioned in Matthew; Mark
says that he lived in an unnamed town on the opposite coast
of the Sea of Galilee from Gadara.

THE BLIND MEN *(page 191)*

All Gadara buzzed with news of the healing of Jairus' daughter, and when Jesus left the town next morning two blind men
ran after him shouting, "Son of David, have mercy on us!"
    Jesus said, "Do you truly believe that I can cure you?"
    "Lord, we believe."
    "So be it," said Jesus. At once their eyes were opened and
they could see. Their faith had cured them.

FEEDING THE HUNGRY (page 193)

Matthew and Mark tell of a similar, later miracle. Jesus had been preaching for three days in the hills, and had healed a huge crowd of sick people: lame, dumb, blind, maimed, paralysed and possessed with demons. He asked his disciples what food they had, and there was nothing but seven loaves and a few small fish. Jesus blessed the food, broke it in pieces and gave it to the disciples to distribute. There was enough to feed four thousand men, plus women and children, and to fill seven baskets with scraps.

PETER THE ROCK (page 194)

No one really knows the true meaning of Simon's nickname Peter. Several disciples took new names – "Christian" names – when they went to follow Jesus: Levi changed his name to Matthew, for example. Jesus' words here are a pun, made in Greek (which he and the disciples, like most people in Galilee, probably spoke as well as their native language, Aramaic). The Greek form of the name Peter is Petros, very close to the word petra, "rock". Later Christians believed that Jesus was foretelling the beginnings of the Christian church after his death and resurrection: Peter was one of its founders, and its first "bishop" or "supervisor" in Rome.

THE LORD'S PRAYER (page 195)

This prayer, known as "the Lord's Prayer", is the best-known of all Christian prayers. Many people know it, and say it every day, in the Elizabethan form of the words: "Our father, which art in heaven, hallowed be thy name. Thy kingdom come, on earth as it is in heaven. Give us this day our daily bread. Forgive us our trespasses, as we forgive them that trespass against us. Lead us not into temptation, but deliver us from evil." Some people always add the words (taken from Matthew's version, in the Sermon on the Mount: see page

284), "For thine is the kingdom, the power and the glory, for ever and ever, Amen."

THE RICH MAN AND THE BEGGAR
(page 198)

Jesus told another parable, to show that God did not always see goodness and badness in the same way as human beings. There were once two men (he said), rich and poor. The rich man dressed in expensive clothes and ate sumptuous food. The beggar lay in rags at his gate, begging for scraps, and the rich man ignored him. Both men died on the same day, and angels carried the beggar to heaven to feast with Abraham, while devils carried the rich man down to hell. As the rich man writhed in the flames of hell, he looked up and saw Abraham and the beggar, feasting. "Abraham," he groaned, "have mercy. Send the beggar: let him dip his finger in water to cool my tongue."

"No," said Abraham. "When you were both alive, he had misery and you had wealth. How did you help him? Between heaven and hell an unbridgeable gulf is fixed."

"Then please," begged the rich man, "send a messenger to my five brothers on the earth. Tell them to help the poor, or they, too, will end up in hell."

Abraham said, "They have the prophets – let them learn from them."

"If someone went from heaven, they would listen to him."

"No. If they won't learn from the prophets, why should they listen to anyone else? Even if someone rose from the dead, they'd still shut their ears."

SIMON THE LEPER; MARTHA AND MARY
(page 200)

As well as Lazarus, Martha and Mary, an older man lived in the house. His name was Simon, and he may have been Martha's husband or father. Nothing is known of him except that he was nicknamed "Simon the leper". Some people think that Jesus cured him, but this is not mentioned in any of the Gospels.

The Gospels say that when Jesus arrived in the house, Lazarus and Mary sat down excitedly with the disciples to hear him talk. But Martha, overjoyed to be entertaining her Saviour, began to cook the most delicious, mouth-watering meal she could think of. Preparing food for sixteen people was no easy task, and after a while she asked Jesus to send Mary in to help her. Jesus, however, said that she should have planned a simpler meal, and made time to listen to him. "You're busy doing many things," he said, "but Mary has chosen the single most important thing of all, to listen to God's word."

ZACCHAEUS; THE TALENTS (page 200)

On their way back from the river Jordan, Jesus and the disciples passed through Jericho. A huge crowd filled the streets to hear Jesus preach. A rich man, Zacchaeus, had heard of Jesus and often longed to see him. But Zacchaeus was a small man, and the crowd was too dense for him to push to the front. Instead, he climbed a sycamore tree and listened to Jesus from there. Jesus called him down and said that that day he and his disciples would eat in Zacchaeus' house. The crowd muttered crossly, "Zacchaeus is a money-lender, a sinner. Why do you eat with him?" Zacchaeus at once announced that he would give half his wealth to the poor, and if he'd ever cheated anyone, he'd pay them back four times over. Jesus joyfully told him that he'd proved himself a true believer, and that his sins were forgiven.

Later, to explain more clearly to the crowd, he told a story to show that it doesn't matter how much we own: what matters is what we do with it. "A rich man once had to travel to a distant country. Before he left he gave each of his servants some money to look after. He gave five talents (silver coins) to one man, two talents to another and one talent to a third. When he came back, he asked each man what he had done with the money. The first man said, 'Sir, I used your five talents for trading, and made five more.' 'Well done, good and faithful servant,' said the rich man. 'You've been faithful over a few things: your reward is to be given charge of many.' The second man said, 'Sir, I used your two talents for trading, and made two more.' To him, too, the rich man said, 'Well done, good and faithful servant. You've been faithful over a few things: your reward is to be given charge over many.' The third man said, 'Sir, I knew you were a hard man, reaping where you never sowed, gathering where you never scattered. I was afraid to lose my talent, and I dug a hole and buried it. Here it is, exactly as you gave it me.' 'You wicked, lazy servant,' said the rich man. 'You knew I was a hard man, who reaped where I never sowed, gathered where I never scattered – why didn't you give that coin to a money-lender to earn interest? Talents are for using, not burying. Take it away from him, and give it to the man with ten.' Just so, on the Day of Judgement when the Messiah comes in glory, surrounded by angels, he'll ask each of you what you did with the talents he gave you – and what will you answer then?"

BARTIMAEUS (page 200)

As Jesus and his disciples were leaving Jericho, they passed a blind man, Bartimaeus, who made his living begging at the side of the road. Bartimaeus held out his hands to Jesus and cried, "Son of David, have mercy on me!"

"Hush!" people told him. "The Master has no time for you." But Jesus stopped and called Bartimaeus over to him.

"What shall I do for you?" he asked.

"Lord, give me back my sight," said Bartimaeus.

Jesus said, "As you ask, so be it. Your faith has cured you." From that moment on Bartimaeus could see again, and he eagerly joined the crowd and went with Jesus back to Bethany.

ANOINTING JESUS *(page 201)*

This story echoes an earlier one, from Jesus' time in Capernaum. A Pharisee, Simon, had invited Jesus to dinner, and while they were eating a prostitute ran in with an alabaster perfume-jar. She washed Jesus' feet with her tears, wiped them with her hair and anointed them with perfume. Simon was furious because she was a sinner. But Jesus said, "Simon, two people once owed the same man money; one of them owed ten times more than the other. The creditor told them both to forget the debts. Which of them would you say would be most grateful?"

"The one who owed most."

"Exactly. So it is with you and this woman. You're sinless; she's a sinner. She needs my forgiveness more than you do."

Simon was embarrassed by this answer. He was even less pleased when Jesus turned to the woman and told her that her sins were forgiven and she could go in peace. "Who does he think he is, forgiving sins?" he muttered. Some of the other dinner-guests agreed with him, but others, impressed by all they'd heard and seen, believed in Jesus from that time on.

THE KING AND THE WEDDING-GUESTS
(page 204)

Jesus told a story to show the people that they should be ready, and willing, to celebrate the kingdom of heaven, whenever it came. "A king once made a wedding-feast for his son, and sent servants to invite his friends. But however many messages he sent, the friends always answered that they were too busy to come. In the end, they even beat and killed the messengers. The king said angrily, 'Forget them: they don't deserve to come. Go out into the highways and byways, and ask everyone you meet to come to the wedding.' The servants did as they were told, and the palace was soon crowded with wedding-guests. Most people were overjoyed to be invited, and dressed in their best clothes. But one man seemed hardly to care whether he feasted or not. He arrived in ordinary working-clothes, and said nothing to congratulate the prince on his wedding or to thank the king for inviting him. 'Throw him out!' said the king to his servants. 'He no more deserves this wedding-feast than those wicked people who refused to come.'"

THE TEN LAMPGIRLS (page 204)

When he was teaching people that they should be ready for the coming of God's kingdom, Jesus told a story about ten lampgirls. They went excitedly to meet a bridegroom, to light him home from his wedding-feast. But when they set out it was still daylight, and five of them were so thoughtless that they forgot to fill their lamps with oil. The bridegroom was late, and the girls all fell asleep. Then suddenly servants woke them, crying, "He's coming! He's coming!", and they rushed to light their lamps. The foolish girls asked the sensible girls to lend them some oil, but there was none to spare. Then the bridegroom arrived, the five sensible girls lit his way home, and the door was locked and bolted. The five foolish girls, who had been only half prepared, were left outside in darkness.

When Jesus told this story, he was thinking of the people's trust in God's Law and in the age-old beliefs and practices of the Jewish religion. He was telling the crowd that these things were not enough in themselves. They were like oil-less lamps, and without the fuel of belief in him, God's son, they would be no help in welcoming God's kingdom when it came.

THE PHARISEE AND THE TAX-COLLECTOR; THE RICH MAN AND THE WIDOW (page 205)

Jesus told a story to show that however poor or sinful we are, if we repent with all our hearts we will be given God's forgiveness. A show of goodness, by contrast, if our hearts are not in it, will not be enough. "Two people, a Pharisee and a tax-collector, went to pray in the Temple," he said. "The Pharisee stood and prayed in a loud voice, 'Thank you, God, for making me not like other people, greedy, wicked, sinful, like that tax-collector there. I fast twice a week, I give money to charity, I obey the Law in everything I do.' The tax-collector was too embarrassed by his own unworthiness even to look up at Heaven. He beat his breast with his hand and whispered, 'I'm a sinner. God have mercy on me.' Which of these people pleased God best?"

On another occasion, Jesus and his followers watched people making offerings in the Temple. Rich people were throwing sacks of silver into the treasure-chests. Then a poor woman, a widow, went up and dropped in two small copper coins. Jesus said, "She has given far more than they have: for they'll hardly notice what they've spent, whereas she has paid all she owns." The crowd realised that he was also talking of the kingdom of heaven. Only people who believed whole-heartedly in Jesus, who filled their minds and souls with him, would be given eternal life.

JESUS AND THE CRIPPLE (page 205)

Near the Sheep Market in Jerusalem there was a pool of clear, never-failing water. People believed that the water had healing properties. They said that every day an angel stirred it into waves, and the first people who stepped down into it would be cured of all disease. The Jews called the pool Bethesda, "House of Grace", and the Romans surrounded it with a five-arched, stone-built bathhouse.

Once, when Jesus visited the pool, a cripple clutched his coat and said, "Master, please help me. I've been coming here for thirty-eight years, hoping for a cure. But every time the waves appear, I'm so slow on my feet that other people get into the water before me. If someone would only lift me down, I'd be cured."

Jesus answered simply, "Get up, pick up your bed, and walk."

The man leapt up joyfully, picked up his mattress and hurried to the Temple to give thanks to God. Some Pharisees stopped him and said, "Don't you know it's the Sabbath? Carrying that mattress counts as work. You're breaking Moses' Law."

The former cripple answered, "All I know is, the man who cured me told me to pick up my bed and walk."

"Who was that? Who told you that?"

"Jesus Christ, the son of God," said the man, thinking that they would share his pleasure at being cured. But the Pharisees said to each other, "Not only does Jesus encourage other people to break the Sabbath laws, but he claims to be the son of God. Blasphemy after blasphemy! He deserves to die."

JESUS AND HIS DISCIPLES *(page 205)*

The disciples were deeply troubled by Jesus' preaching about such matters as the destruction of the Temple and his own forthcoming death. Sitting with them one day on the Mount of Olives, he tried to explain. The present world, the one they were used to, would pass away. The Messiah would come again in glory, to judge all human beings. He would say to some people, "Come and sit beside me. I was hungry, and you fed me, thirsty and you gave me drink; I was a stranger and you welcomed me, naked and you clothed me; I was sick and in prison, and you visited me." When the people asked, bewildered, "Lord, when did we do these things?" the Messiah would answer, "When you did them to the poorest, most insignificant person in the world, you did them to me." He would then turn to others and banish them forever, saying, "I was hungry and you gave me no food, thirsty and you gave me no drink; I was a stranger and you did not welcome me, naked and you gave me no clothes; I was sick and in prison, and you did not visit me." When they asked, "Lord, when did we none of these things?" he would answer, "When you neglected the poorest, most insignificant person in the world, you neglected me."

WASHING THE DISCIPLES' FEET (page 206)

The disciples were embarrassed when Jesus washed their feet because they thought of him as their master, and felt that it was wrong for him to behave like a slave towards them. But he explained that in God's kingdom there were no masters and no slaves: God's love made everyone equal. On Earth, therefore, all those who believed in God's son Jesus should treat each other as equals, as happy to be ruled as they were to rule. In later times, this teaching was one of the main reasons why the Romans persecuted Christians. They thought that Jesus had been preaching political revolution, the freeing of the slaves on whose hard work Roman wealth depended.

THIRTY PIECES OF SILVER (page 207)

Thirty pieces of silver, in the Roman empire, was the price of a low-quality slave. By taking this money from Caiaphas, Judas was technically selling Jesus to him. Later, Matthew says, when Judas saw Jesus' trial (see page 208) and realised that it would end in crucifixion, he took the thirty pieces of silver to Caiaphas and asked to buy Jesus back. Caiaphas refused – and Judas was so full of self-hatred at betraying his saviour that he hanged himself. Caiaphas used the thirty pieces of silver to buy the place where Judas killed himself, "Potters' Field", and buried him there.

JUDAS (page 207)

No one knows why Judas betrayed Jesus. John's Gospel bluntly says that "Satan entered into him". Medieval legend makes him a distant descendant of Cain, the first murderer (see page 5), and says that he was tainted with Cain's sin from birth. Modern Christian thinkers have suggested a third, subtler reason. They say that Judas was not really a traitor at all, but was in fact obeying Jesus' own orders. Jesus knew that he would be arrested and killed and would rise again, and that one of his disciples had to be the man to betray him. When he handed Judas the sop of wine-soaked bread, he was directly choosing him to be that man.

There are three different stories of what happened to Judas after Jesus' crucifixion. In one, he was so overcome by guilt that he hanged himself (see page 295). In another, he spent the thirty pieces of silver (the price for betraying Jesus) on a piece of land, but when he went to inspect it he fell headlong, "burst asunder in the midst and all his bowels gushed out". In the third, he was forgiven by Jesus and told that he could live like any other mortal until the Day of Judgement – and from that day to this he has grown older and more shrivelled, unable to die and tormented by his own mortality.

MARK IN THE GARDEN OF GETHSEMANE
(page 208)

Some accounts suggest that there were far more people in the Garden of Gethsemane than just Jesus, his disciples and Caiaphas' servants. A large crowd milled about in the darkness, including many of the people who had listened earlier to Jesus' teaching in the Temple and who loyally believed in him. But although no Romans were present, Caiaphas' servants were Temple guards, well-armed, and there was no way for Jesus' unarmed followers to resist them. The crowd scattered in panic – and one young man was so eager to get away that when Caiaphas' soldiers held him by the tunic, he wriggled out of it and ran off stark naked. The only Gospel-writer to include this story is Mark, and this has led people to suggest that the young man was Mark himself, and that his is an eye-witness' account of Jesus' arrest.

PILATE'S WIFE (page 211)

Matthew says that Pilate's wife tried to persuade him not to condemn Jesus, saying that she had "suffered many things . . . in a dream because of him". Pilate would have agreed with her, but he was reluctant to antagonise the crowd, which was clamouring for Jesus' death.

In later times, this story – together with Pilate's question to Jesus "Are you the king of the Jews?" – led to the idea that both Pilate and his wife were converted to Christianity, soon after Jesus' crucifixion and resurrection. There is, however, no hint of this either in the Gospels or in Roman accounts of the spread of early Christianity.

CRUCIFIXION (page 212)

Crucifixion was the standard Roman method of executing male criminals who were not citizens. (Citizens had the right to commit suicide, or to be executed by the sword.) A cross was made of wood, and the victim's hands were nailed to the cross-bars and his feet to the upright. As he hung there, the weight of his body gradually compressed his lungs until he choked to death. Sometimes it took minutes; sometimes it took hours or days.

In early Christian times, during persecutions such as those ordered by the mad Roman emperor Nero, Christian martyrs (people tortured or executed for their faith) were proud to be executed on the cross, to die in the same way as their saviour. The cross became one of the main symbols of Christianity – a long way from its earlier, Roman, associations with the deaths of worthless, low-class criminals.

MARY MAGDALENE (page 213)

There is more confusion about Mary Magdalene than about almost any other person in the Bible. Magdalene means "from Magdala", a village on the shores of the Sea of Galilee. Luke says that Jesus healed her of "evil spirits and infirmities" by driving seven devils out of her, and that she was one of several women who followed him and the disciples everywhere in Galilee, cooking, washing clothes and otherwise looking after them. She is not mentioned again by name until she stands with Jesus' mother and the other Mary at the crucifixion. But later Christian writers, long after the Gospels, claimed that she was the same person either as the woman who anointed Jesus with oil in the Pharisee's house (see page 291), or as Mary of Bethany, the sister of Martha and Lazarus, who also anointed him (see page 201). There is no proof of this: apart from the place she came from, her healing by Jesus and her friendship with Jesus' mother, nothing else is known.

THE MOMENT OF JESUS' DEATH (page 214)

Scientists have explained the events which accompanied Jesus' death as an eclipse of the sun and a particularly violent earthquake. (Jerusalem still suffers regular minor earth-tremors.) But Christians, beginning with the Gospel-writers, believed that the events were signs from God, and added other details which have no simple scientific explanation. In the Temple, the Holy of Holies was separated from public gaze by a curtain which hung from ceiling to floor. Only the High Priest was allowed into the sanctuary behind it, and then only once a year. At the instant of Jesus' death, the Gospels say, this curtain was ripped from top to bottom. Not only that, but the dead whose graves split open stood up like people wakened from sleep, walked through the Jerusalem streets in their grave-clothes, and were seen by many people – a foreshadowing of Judgement Day, when Jesus had prophesied that the graves would gape and the dead would gather with the living before God's throne.

NICODEMUS (page 215)

Nicodemus was a Pharisee and, like Joseph, a member of the Jewish council. He was impressed by Jesus' miracles, but his official position made him reluctant to declare openly that he was a believer. He went to Jesus secretly at night, and Jesus told him that to be truly saved a person must be "born again", that is baptised in Christian belief. John's account gives Jesus' actual words to Nicodemus, including some which have since become part of Christian worship:

> God so loved the world that he gave his only begotten Son, that whosoever believeth in him should not perish, but have everlasting life . . . God sent not his son into the world to condemn the world, but that the world through him might be saved.

GUARDS AT JESUS' TOMB (page 215)

Alone of the four Gospel-writers, Matthew says that Caiaphas and the Pharisees persuaded Pilate to set guards on the tomb, in case Jesus' disciples stole the body to back up their claims that Jesus had risen from the dead. When an angel appeared and rolled away the boulder from the tomb-entrance, the guards first shook with fear, Matthew says, and then "became as dead men" (that is, fainted). Later, to hide the news of Jesus' resurrection, Caiaphas' councillors bribed the guards to say that the disciples had stolen the body, exactly as predicted.

JOSEPH OF ARIMATHEA (page 215)

The Bible says no more of Joseph after he buried Jesus. But medieval legend tells how he was given charge of two relics, the Holy Grail (either the cup from which Jesus drank at the Passover Supper: see page 206, or the basin in which his blood was collected on the cross: see page 214) and the Holy Lance (the spear which stabbed Jesus on the cross: see page 214). Joseph took them from country to country, healing and converting people in Jesus' name. Finally, in Britain, he built Glastonbury Abbey to house the Grail and Lance. The story goes on to say that after Joseph's death the Grail and Lance stayed in the world only so long as human beings were honest and peaceable. As soon as violence and oppression began to flourish, the Grail and Lance disappeared from human sight, and despite a quest to find them by King Arthur's knights (led by Sir Galahad) they have been lost to mortals ever since.

THE EMPTY TOMB (page 216)

This version of the resurrection-story comes from John's Gospel. The other Gospel-writers give slightly different accounts of who found Jesus' tomb empty, and what they saw. Matthew and Mark say that an angel came down from heaven and rolled away the boulder from the tomb-entrance; then, when Mary Magdalene and Mary of Bethany went to the tomb to anoint Jesus' body, the angel told them that he was risen from the dead and had gone to Galilee, where the disciples were to follow him. Luke says that Joanna was with the two Maries, and that they saw not one angel but two; they ran to fetch Peter, and he was the first disciple actually to enter the empty tomb.

JESUS APPEARS TO HIS DISCIPLES (page 217)

The Gospel-writers describe several occasions after the resurrection when Jesus appeared to his disciples. At first the appearances were in or near Jerusalem. (For example, two of the disciples were walking on the hill-road from Jerusalem to Emmaus when a man joined them and began asking them about Jesus of Nazareth. It was not until he broke bread and gave it to them in the inn at Emmaus that they realised that he was Jesus himself.) It was not long, however, before the disciples went back to Galilee – and Jesus appeared to them there, on one occasion filling their nets with a huge catch of fish, exactly as he had on the day when he first called them to follow him (see page 184). Matthew says that Jesus' last appearance was to the eleven surviving disciples on a mountain in Galilee. He told them to go out into the world and teach, and ended with the promise "Lo, I am with you alway, even unto the end of the world." (This was a similar occasion to the one, described by Luke in the book Acts of the Apostles, on the Mount of Olives when Jesus ascended into Heaven: see page 219.)

SPEAKING IN TONGUES *(page 220)*

No one has ever explained exactly what "speaking in tongues" consisted of. The story told here (the origin of the Christian festival of Whitsuntide) is from the book Acts of the Apostles in the Bible New Testament, written by Luke, a Greek doctor. The Greek word for "speaking in tongues" is glossolalia, and means waggling the tongue and babbling simultaneously. Greek doctors recognised it as a common symptom of trances, fits and even of drunkenness – which is why some of the crowd on this occasion asked if the disciples had been drinking. But Luke also carefully says that every person there heard the disciples speaking in his or her own language, as if "speaking with tongues" meant talking a kind of universal language which everyone immediately understood. Some Christians explain this by saying that whatever sounds the disciples made, they were expressing joy in Christ, and that this was the "language" common to everyone. Others say that what happened was a straightforward miracle, needing no explanation: God wanted everyone to understand the disciples' words, and so it happened. Since the time of the early Christians (when speaking with tongues became a part of the services in several churches – Paul had to warn some congregations not to let it get out of hand) it has featured in many people's worship.

PHILIP AND THE AFRICAN *(page 226)*

Philip, one of the seven stewards appointed by the disciples, left Jerusalem during the persecution and made his way across the Samaritan Plain, to teach in the villages and towns along the Mediterranean Coast. He was walking one day along the desert road to Gaza (the Philistine town where Samson had once been imprisoned: see page 66), when the Holy Ghost brought him alongside two men in a chariot. One man was the chariot-driver, and the other was an African, a courtier of Queen Candace of Ethiopia. He was a Jewish convert, and had been visiting Jerusalem to worship in the Temple; now he was returning home. As the chariot dawdled along, he was resting against the side, reading – and Philip suddenly recognised words from the prophet Isaiah: "He was led like a lamb to slaughter". Philip asked him, "Do you understand what you're reading?"

"No," said the African. "Who was led like a lamb to slaughter? Did Isaiah mean himself?"

Philip began telling him about Jesus, the lamb of God, and how he was led to death to save the human race. He talked about Judgement Day and how all who believed in Jesus and were baptised would have everlasting life. The African stopped the chariot and said, "There's a pool of water over there. What must I do to be baptised?"

"Believe in Jesus with all your heart."

"I believe that Jesus Christ is the Son of God."

Philip took the African down to the water, and baptised him. They stood or a moment beside the pool and prayed. Then God's angels carried Philip out of sight, and the African climbed into his chariot and went on his way, rejoicing.

This African aristocrat was the first person from outside the Promised Land to be baptised a Christian. Later legends say that he took Christianity back to Ethiopia, and made many converts there.

SAUL IN JERUSALEM (page 228)

This version of the story follows the account in Luke's book Acts of the Apostles. Paul himself, remembering the events several years later in his Letter to the Galatians, says that after his conversion on the Damascus road and baptism by Ananias, he spent three years in self-imposed exile, coming to terms with his guilt at persecuting the Jerusalem Christians. It was only after that that he went to Jerusalem at last to face the hostility both of the Christians and the Jewish authorities. Although the Christians were terrified of him at first, they gradually accepted him. But the high priest's officials put a price on his head and forced him to escape to Tarsus for his own safety.

PETER'S MIRACLES *(page 229)*

When Peter left Jerusalem, he travelled west towards the coast, preaching in Christian communities on the way. His reputation as a healer made sick people flock to him – and in one village, Lydda, a paralysed man was carried to him, rather as the cripple had been let down from the roof before Jesus years before (see page 185). The man had a Roman name, Aeneas, and was perhaps a slave (Romans liked to nickname their slaves after such myth-heroes as Ajax, Hector and Aeneas). Peter said to him, "Aeneas, Jesus Christ makes you whole. Get up and make your bed." At once Aeneas leapt to his feet, cured, and everyone who saw the miracle "turned to the Lord" (as Luke describes conversion) and was baptised.

News of Aeneas' cure reached Joppa, and the family of a woman called Dorcas asked Peter to hurry there and help them. Dorcas, a devout Christian believer, was sick and near to death. Although Peter rode to Joppa as fast as he could, he was greeted with news that Dorcas had died. Her family took him to the room where her body lay, and Peter asked them to leave him alone with her. He knelt for a while and prayed, then turned to Dorcas and said simply, "Woman, wake up."

At once Dorcas sat up, yawning, and Peter led her by the hand back to her family.

CLEAN AND UNCLEAN *(page 229)*

Like every Jewish person of his time, Peter had never questioned the laws about diet in the book of Leviticus, thought to be part of the Law handed down by God to Moses at the time of the Ten Commandments (see page 47). The diet-laws said clearly that some creatures (such as sheep and cattle) were fit to eat while others (such as pigs and camels) were not. Jewish people had kept the law for centuries, until they had a horror of eating the meat of "unclean" creatures.

PETER AND HEROD AGRIPPA (page 231)

During the year Paul and Barnabas spent in Antioch, there was savage persecution of the Christians in Jerusalem. It was ordered by King Herod Agrippa, grandson of the Herod who had commanded the slaughter of children just after Jesus' birth (see page 178). His soldiers drove hundreds of Christians into exile, killed many of their leaders (including the disciple James) and imprisoned Peter. Herod intended to try Peter publicly at the time of the Jewish Passover and the Christian festival of Easter (the anniversary of Jesus' crucifixion and resurrection). To prevent Peter escaping, Herod kept him chained to two soldiers night and day, and set double guards on the dungeon door. In the middle of the night God's angel appeared to Peter, filling the dungeon with radiance, and said, "Get up, quickly!" Peter's chains fell from his legs and arms, and the angel led him out of the dungeon, past the sleeping guards into the streets, and left him.

Peter hurried to the house of Mary, the mother of Mark (the young man who escaped naked from the Garden of Gethsemane at the time of Jesus' arrest: see page 296). The Christians there gave him food and money for the journey, then smuggled him out of Jerusalem to Caesarea and safety. Next morning, when Herod found Peter gone, he ordered the crucifixion of the guards who had been watching him. He would have started a hue and cry after Peter, but he had more urgent business: a speech before a delegation from Tyre and Sidon. He stood in the palace hall, surrounded by his officials and dressed in glittering royal robes. At the end of his speech everyone began clapping, cheering and shouting, "We've been listening to a god, not to a man!" Herod bowed delightedly – and God's angel punished him by blasting him with a lightning-bolt from Heaven. Before the terrified people Herod's body crumbled in a moment from living flesh to a mass of writhing maggots, and he died without speaking another word.

MAGIC BOOKS *(page 232)*

This story impressed Luke (who tells it in Acts of the Apostles) partly because of the value of the books. In the ancient world, books were rare and expensive, and books of magic were among the highest-priced of all. The combined value of the soothsayers' books, Luke says, was 50,000 silver pieces – enough to buy ten thousand slaves or 100,000 sheep. If nothing else proved how sincerely the Greek fortune-tellers had been converted, the book-bonfire surely did.

EUTYCHUS *(page 233)*

Paul stayed in Troas for a week, and on the day before he left preached to a large gathering of Christians in an upstairs room. The meeting began as soon as people finished work in the afternoon, and went on through the evening. The room was small and crowded, and the heat from dozens of oil-lamps soon made it stuffy and stifling. A young man called Eutychus ("lucky") was sitting on the ledge of the open window, and the combination of tiredness from his day's work, the hot room and Paul's sermon worked on him like a lullaby. He fell into a deep sleep, slumped backwards out of the window and was killed on the cobblestones below. The room was so packed with people that it was some minutes before Paul realised what had happened. But then he shouted, "Don't worry! There's life in him still!", ran downstairs and gathered Eutychus into his arms. Helped by some of the Christians, he carried the young man back upstairs – and to everyone's joy Eutychus sat up, perfectly restored to life, and said, "I'm hungry." People fetched him food and drink, and Paul went back to his sermon, leaving everyone marvelling at the miracle he had worked so matter-of-factly in Jesus' name.

PAUL'S ESCORT *(page 233)*

At this time (the 50s AD), the Romans were terrified of revolt in Judea, which was one of their most troublesome provinces.

Before the guard commander realised who Paul was, he had taken him for a notorious Egyptian revolutionary, stirring up trouble in Jerusalem. Even when Paul's identity was known, the Romans could not risk him being assassinated on the way from Jerusalem to Caesarea, with the fighting that would follow between Christians and Jews. Their panic – and also something of Paul's importance – is shown by the fact that they took him to Caesarea by night, in darkness, and by the size of the escort they sent with him: two hundred heavily-armed footsoldiers, two hundred spearmen and seventy cavalry.

SHIPWRECK (page 233)

Because of storms, ships tried to avoid open sea and to hug the coast wherever possible. Paul and the Romans sailed north round Cyprus, then east along the coast of Asia Minor before striking south to Crete. From the Cretan harbour (hopefully called "Fair Havens") they expected to sail directly to Sicily. But storms blew the ship off-course,till it was lost in heaving, angry sea.The crew wept and prayed in panic, and the Romans wanted to throw all the prisoners into the sea to lighten the ship. But Paul said, "Stay calm. Eat and drink: no one will drown." His words gave everyone courage, and they sat quietly all night and let the storm blow itself out. Next morning they realised that they were not far from the island of Malta, and grounded the ship on a quiet part of the coast (it is still called "St Paul's Bay"). Those who could swim made their way to shore, and the others clung to barrels and planks from the cargo. Thanks to Paul, the entire crew and passengers, 376 people altogether, were saved. They spent the rest of the winter on Malta, and as soon as spring weather made the sea calm enough to sail, chartered a second ship and sailed for Italy.

PAUL'S LETTERS (page 233)

Only one of Paul's letters (to Philemon, asking him to forgive a runaway slave) is a private document. He sent most of the others to groups of people – the Christians at Corinth, Philippi, Thessalonica or Jerusalem, for example – and meant them to be read aloud and publicly discussed. They deal mainly with matters of belief. Paul explains Jesus' teaching, corrects wrong ideas (for example that only people who accept Moses' Law should be be converted) and talks about such matters as "how to pray" or "which is the greatest quality we can have, faith, hope or love?". If he had been able to go to the churches in person, he might have given talks or preached sermons on these matters; letters were the next best thing.

THE DISCIPLES' FATE (page 233)

The Bible says nothing of Paul's trial, or about the fate of the other preachers and disciples. Later books and myths give further information. Paul was never properly tried in Rome, because the Jerusalem authorities failed to send prosecution evidence in time. He went to preach in Spain, and returned to Rome in about 63 AD. When the mad emperor Nero blamed the Christians for the Great Fire of Rome in 64 AD, Paul was one of those arrested and executed. Peter also died in that persecution. Tradition says that he thanked the Romans for sentencing him to crucifixion, the same death as his saviour – and the Romans cruelly added to his punishment by crucifying him upside-down. Of Jesus' other disciples, only Philip and John died natural deaths. Philip died while visiting the Christians at Hierapolis. Legend said that the Romans exiled John to the Greek island of Patmos, where he founded a monastery (parts of which still stand) and wrote the book Revelation, forecasting the Day of Judgement. When he died, or rather "fell asleep in Jesus", as Christians of the time put it, legend says that people could see the dust-specks on his coffin rising and falling gently in the sunlight, as if the saint inside were breathing.

INDEX

Index

Index

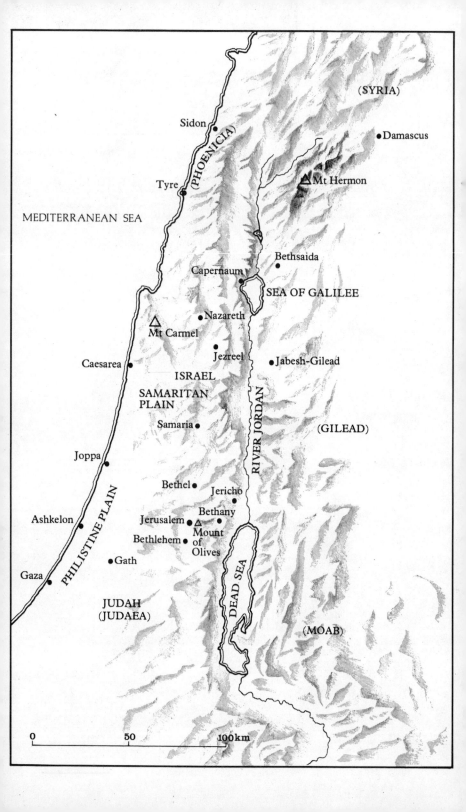

(SYRIA)

Sidon

• Damascus

△ Mt Hermon

PHOENICIA)

Tyre

MEDITERRANEAN SEA

• Bethsaida

Capernaum

SEA OF GALILEE

• Nazareth

△
Mt Carmel

• Jezreel

• Jabesh-Gilead

Caesarea

ISRAEL

SAMARITAN
PLAIN

RIVER JORDAN

(GILEAD)

• Samaria

Joppa

Bethel •

• Jericho

PHILISTINE PLAIN

Bethany

Jerusalem •
△
Mount
of
Olives

Ashkelon

Bethlehem •

• Gath

DEAD SEA

Gaza

JUDAH
(JUDAEA)

(MOAB)

0   50   100km